VALUING
FIXED INCOME
FUTURES

Other Titles in the McGraw-Hill Library of Investment and Finance

VALUING FIXED INCOME FUTURES

DAVID BOBERSKI

McGraw-Hill
New York   Chicago   San Francisco   Lisbon   London   Madrid
Mexico City   Milan   New Delhi   San Juan   Seoul
Singapore   Sydney   Toronto

2 3 4 5 6 7 8 9 0   DOC/DOC   0 9 8 7 6

ISBN-13: 978-0-07-147541-9
ISBN-10:   0-07-147541-9

This publication is designed to provide accurate and authoritative information in regard to the subject matter covered. It is sold with the understanding that the publisher is not engaged in rendering legal, accounting, or other professional service. If legal advice or other expert assistance is required, the services of a competent professional person should be sought.

> —*From a Declaration of Principles Jointly Adopted by a Committee*
> *of the American Bar Association and a Committee of Publishers*
> *and Associations*

McGraw-Hill books are available at special discounts to use as premiums and sales promotions, or for use in corporate training programs. For more information, please write to the Director of Special Sales, Professional Publishing, McGraw-Hill, Two Penn Plaza, New York, NY 10121-2298. Or contact your local bookstore.

Library of Congress Cataloging-in-Publication Data

Boberski, David.
  Valuing fixed income futures / by David Boberski.
    p. cm.
  ISBN 0-07-147541-9 (hardcover : alk. paper)   1. Futures.   2. Futures market.   I. Title.
  HG6024.A3B62 2006
  332.64′52—dc22

                                                    2006006600

For Anne,
the light of all lights

C O N T E N T S

LIST OF FIGURES

Figure 1–12

Figure 1–13

Figure 1–14

Figure 1–15

Figure 1–16

Figure 1–17a

Figure 1–17b

Figure 1–18

Figure 1–19

Figure 1–20

Figure 1–21

Figure 1–22

Figure 1–23a

Figure 2–3

Figure 2–4

Figure 2–5

Figure 2–6

Figure 2–7

Figure 2–8

Figure 2–9

Figure 2–10

Figure 2–11

Figure 2–12

Figure 2–13

Figure 2–14a

Figure 2–14b

Figure 2–15

Figure 2–16

Figure 2–17

Figure 2–18

Figure 2–19

Figure 2–20

Figure 2–21

Figure 2–22

Figure 2–23

Figure 3–1

Figure 3–2

Figure 3–3

Figure 3–4

Figure 3–5

L I S T   O F   T A B L E S

PREFACE

Futures are important to America. Treasury futures facilitate the government's fiscal policy by aiding in the digestion of new Treasury bonds. Eurodollar futures help promote home ownership by effectively hedging mortgage-backed securities, making them less expensive to originate and to own. There have been missteps along the way, but students of the market should never forget that the big picture is overwhelmingly positive and touches the lives of every American. In spite of their importance, these instruments remain relatively poorly understood by the people that can least afford the deficit: traders and risk managers. In fact, the fourth largest bankruptcy in American history was triggered in 2005, when Refco, a brokerage that specialized in futures trading, revealed losses from customers who had underestimated the risk they were assuming in the market. The problem isn't a lack of research devoted to the subject; in fact, forests have been felled to produce tomes on futures. The problem is a failure to grasp that their behavior changes along with the technology available to evaluate them.

Consider how you end up chasing your tail when studying a financial instrument; whenever you gain a deeper understanding, this impacts on how you trade it. Changes in transaction patterns have an impact on the price, and the cycle repeats itself. The contradiction that has spawned an entire industry of fixed income traders is that the more an instrument is studied, the more it changes! Every day two things happen: computers become more capable, and there is a longer history available to analyze. Incorporating new information into our analysis of financial products changes how they behave. To some extent, traders are victims of their own success, since price adjustments are speeding up along with our enhanced capability to interpret the changes. Faster responses mean faster price action, and there is no end to our struggle to precisely define how the latest technological and academic advances will be reflected in market prices.

The importance of futures to the fixed income market has been vividly illustrated in recent years, as the struggle to price them in an extremely low interest rate environment has literally shut down parts of the multi-trillion dollar Treasury market. In terms of the number of failed trades, where institutions were not able to take possession of Treasury notes sold to them, the effect was comparable to a terrorist attack or natural disaster. Every day there is enough potential energy in the Treasury futures market to either wreak havoc on the scale of a national catastrophe, or facilitate meaningful change in people's lives. Futures are important, and so is understanding them.

VALUING
FIXED INCOME
FUTURES

INTRODUCTION

Traders who relegate futures fair value analysis to the trash heap are likely to find themselves on it one day, because futures are the ultimate source of liquidity in fixed income markets and are the linchpin that allows every other market to function.

WHERE DO FUTURES FIT INTO THE LANDSCAPE?

Historically, futures markets have been the most efficient and inexpensive of all because of their transparency, negotiated prices, and relative lack of counterparty credit concerns. No one worries about whether the buyer or seller on the other side of a trade will perform because of the elaborate system of checks and balances that makes sure everyone who has access to the market is well capitalized enough to meet his or her commitments. Unlike any other market, transactions are guaranteed by a clearing corporation, which acts like an insurance fund for the industry making sure that no one loses money on a trade because of the default of another trader. This is not to say that money is never lost!

Trading is a zero-sum game, and in order for someone to make money, someone else has to lose it. Unique to futures markets is the fact that there is a great portion of the users who don't mind losing money. By and large, people and institutions buy stocks, municipal and corporate bonds, and mortgage-backed securities and seldom sell them short, but this not so for interest rate commodities like futures. These instruments are different because there are just as many people who short futures, hoping the price will fall, as there are people who long them, who profit from the price going up. What's more, many traders don't mind losing money, regardless of the move in prices, because they are hedging other securities. If $100 is lost on a futures hedge but $100 is gained on the increased value of a thrift's loan, then the hedger has done his job. In this example the thrift is happy to have lost the $100 since it eliminated this price risk for a loan, and the thrift could have just as easily have lost $100 if the loan value had fallen. Now imagine this story playing out to the tune of $6 billion a day changing hands between hedgers and speculators, and you can begin to understand the enormity of the futures markets.

Wall Street as we know it today owes its existence to the futures markets. Dealers can't make markets in someone else's inventory, which is why New York firms remain significant investors in the bonds they bring to market. Since brokerage is their business, not investing, dealers need to offset the interest rate exposure they accrue in the normal course of their business of making markets. Every time an investor sells a bond to a dealer that dealer ends up with interest rate risk it doesn't want. What's worse is that every dealer is levered to some extent, which means that its gains or losses are amplified. It would be convenient if dealers could find a seller every time they needed to, but sometimes the process takes time, and in the interim the market could hand them an unwelcome surprise. The problem is worse than it may appear. Consider this: no investor is ever trying to lose money on his or her trade, but doesn't that mean that the dealer taking the opposite position is always put into the money-losing trades? An infamous trader once likened dealers to the cow catchers on the front of steam trains to catch all the debris so a train could move forward, and there's a lot of truth to the idea that dealers are forced to take the other side of every good trade.

Investors rely on Wall Street to be ready buyers or sellers of the bonds they hold. What happens when dealers can't be dealers and are unable to find a seller at the same moment a buyer emerges? They rely on the futures markets as their source of liquidity. Futures are the linchpin of fixed income markets since they offer the dealers, who themselves facilitate transactions, an outlet for their risk. Eurodollars most often serve as a vehicle to hedge interest rate swap risk from dealers; anecdotally they account for as much as three-quarters of market volume. Treasury futures, of course, serve as an offset for Treasury notes and bonds in the cash market, but also for long-term fixed-rate corporate bonds and mortgages as well. The diagram below illustrates where futures fit into the commodity interest rate market.

Market		Fair Value Model
Eurodollar Futures	|	Convexity Bias
↓		
Interest Rate Swaps	|	
↕	|	TED Spreads
Treasury Notes	|	
↑		
Treasury Futures	|	Delivery Option

Traders are always moving to incrementally more liquid markets for their hedges, and futures are the foundation of the Treasury and swap markets. Issues that impact futures fair values impact every other market in the bond world.

This book addresses futures fair value, which highlights the differences of futures prices compared to their underlying risk, and the thrust of the effort goes into determining relative price movements between futures and cash securities, ignoring the general price trends in the market. The question we're trying to answer more often is, "What should the futures price be, given that we know the cash price?" rather than, "Are prices going up or down?" When yields rise in the fixed income market, all prices will fall, including futures and cash prices. Our concern is exactly how the futures price will fall in relation to the cash price, rather than predicting when the price will fall. In this book we largely ignore the broader economic environment. However, we would be remiss if we didn't provide at least some framework for price movements in the fixed income markets, and it's possible to boil down all of the possible types of curve changes into just three: level, slope, and curvature effects.

Changes in the level of rates move the yield curve in parallel, and a 5-basis-point increase in yields in the 2-year note would also lead to a 5-basis-point change in the 30-year bond. Over very long periods of time interest rates have been stable, as illustrated by Figure 0–1, which shows a history of long-term U.S. Treasury bond yields since the late 1700s. Perhaps 200 years is too long a history for bond traders, who may be interested in what happens to yields in the next 2 seconds, but it does present as complete a picture as is available for the level of rates in the United States. It also highlights an interesting fact. Interest rates were never extremely volatile until the 1970s, when inflation concerns and a stagnant economy caused a crisis of confidence in America and capitalism in general. For someone who has lived through "comparative systems" classes, where capitalism is taught alongside socialism and communism as valid alternative choices of economic systems, the spike in rates will come as no surprise. Of course, no such classes are taught today after the crumbling of communism and stagnation of socialist economies, but bond yield volatility, though much dampened, remains.

FIGURE 0–1

History of long-term U.S. Treasury yields

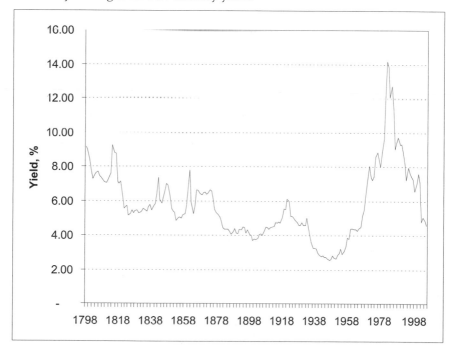

Part of the credit for getting yield volatility under control goes to advances in economic theory. The traditional theory explaining the level of rates is the Fisher hypothesis, which states that expected real interest rates are constant, and changes in bond yields come entirely from changes in inflation expectations. The so-called real yield, which is the bond yield that's left after subtracting for any erosion in purchasing power, can only be priced in expectation of future inflation levels. A reasonable rule of thumb is to add 3% real return to expected inflation to determine a long-term bond yield. Exactly how this should be implemented is another matter. Should headline or core values for the consumer price index be used? What about the employment cost index? As with many theories, Fisher's work sheds a great deal of light on the situation and provides a rough framework for predicting interest rates, but it is too imprecise for trading purposes.

The inherent problem is that traders need to price bonds today for economic conditions that are uncertain in the future. These expectations quite often turn out to be wrong. Ben Bernanke, who assumed chairmanship of the Federal Reserve in 2006, made comments in 2003 that are now notorious, warning the market about a deflation that never materialized. Unfortunately, the market did take note of his comments and drove down 10-year Treasury yields to just 3.5%, and there were people willing to buy notes at that level with the expectation that there would be dwindling inflation over the next 10 years. At the time Bernanke was one of the leading contenders to head the Federal Reserve, and since he said there might be deflation, traders figured that there had to be some truth to it; but they and the future chairman were wrong. Nothing even close to deflation ever materialized in the United States, and everyone who bought on the dip in yields was faced with higher than expected inflation eating away at their fixed returns. As one might expect, the level of rates is the most volatile type of yield curve movement, and there are relatively few "macro" traders—those who specialize in predicting the level of rates—who are able to make money consistently.

A more tractable series is the slope of the yield curve. If the level of long-term rates has held more or less steady over the years, then one might guess that this has been true for the entire yield curve, including short and long ends of the curve. As it turns out, this is generally true, but there has been an interplay in recent years as policymakers have changed short-term rates in order to affect the economy. Although there isn't quite as long a history of short-term rates as those for the long-term rates shown in Figure 0–1, data are available from the Federal Reserve going back to 1985. Figure 0–2 illustrates the 2-year versus 10-year yield in basis points, and it's clear that neither drifts too far away from the other. Of course, everything is relative and traders have adjusted their thinking about the slope of the curve to anticipate typical changes. The steepest the curve has ever been has been 266 basis points in July 2003, and the flattest is actually an inverted curve in April 2000 at around –45 basis points. Just from these numbers one might guess there is an asymmetry at work, where the curve normally has a positive slope and it's more common to see an upward rather than a downward slope to it. In fact, the curve has been upward sloping, where short-term yields are

FIGURE 0-2

Slope of the 2-year/10-year Treasury curve

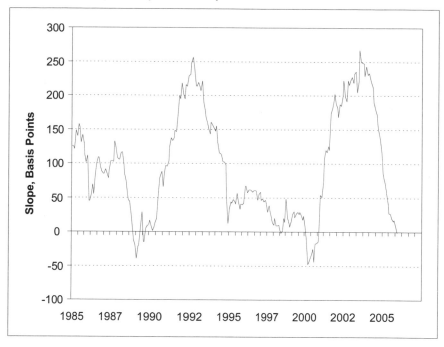

below long-term yields 92% of the time in Figure 0–2. In the 2-year versus 10-year parts of the curve, the 2-year yield has been within 10 basis points or less of the 10-year rate for 14% of the time, which includes the time the curve is inverted. If there is a "normal" shape to the curve, just how might one measure it?

One way is to reorganize the slopes in Figure 0–2 according to business cycles. There is a regular periodicity to changes in the slope of the curve, and policymaker actions only help to make the process more regular, as Figure 0–3 illustrates. Business cycles in the United States have lasted around 5 years on average from the trough, indicating the point of slowest or negative growth to the peak increase in GDP. The National Bureau of Economic Research (NBER) has published "official" start and end dates for every business cycle since 1854. Since WW II—the usual start date for traders interested in characterizing "modern" times—it's been typical for the 2s/10s curve to start its steepest slope near the trough of the business cycle. At the end of year 2 and heading into year 3, there has often been a sharp flattening, lasting until year 4. By the end of year 4 the curve has often lost all momentum and drifts sideways for several months or quarters with very little or inverted slope until the peak of the business cycle. Directly after the peak in the business cycle, the whole process reverses itself, and, although this period is not shown in the graph, there has often been a sharp steepening during recessions.

FIGURE   0–3

2-year/10-year Treasury curve slope by business cycle

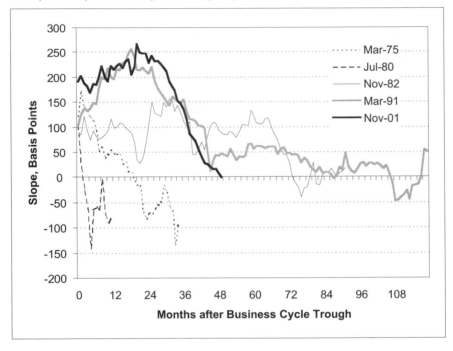

The link between GDP and the yield curve isn't perfect, and there have been a number of times when it hasn't held, but the most recent cycles are the most telling. There were oil shortages in the 1970s and a slowdown in GDP growth in 1973 that caused inflation to spiral while the economy slumped. The yield curve movements that resulted from the Federal Reserve rebuilding credibility were somewhat uncharacteristic of later cycles since they exhibited strong inversions, where 2-year yields were substantially above 10-year yields. The past three cycles, starting in 1982, 1991, and 2001 show remarkably similar patterns, likely due to the fact that they all occurred under two Fed chairmen who shared similar philosophies about how the institution should operate.

While it may be no surprise that an increasingly predictable Federal Reserve may push around the front end of the yield curve in the same way, this same pattern is evident further out the curve as well. Figure 0–4 illustrates the changes in the 10-year versus 30-year part of the curve by business cycle, and although the movements aren't as dramatic, the general pattern is the same. This is an interesting result since it confirms that there is a fundamental economic reason for the pattern, rather than simply being the product of manipulation by a monetary authority. The peak of the steepness between the 10-year and 30-year parts of the curve occurs just after the trough in the business cycle, and, just as

FIGURE   0-4

10-year/30-year Treasury curve slope by business cycle

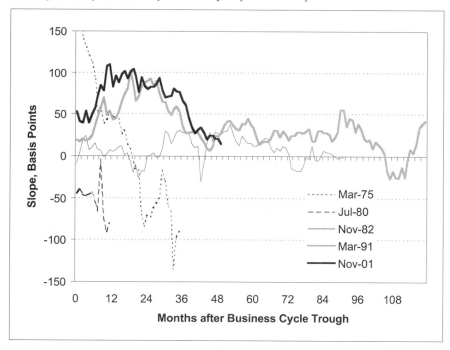

with the front end of the curve, the bulk of the flattening takes place in year 3, tapering off in the fourth year of an expansion. In the U.S. government market there is no default risk and one issue is just as good as another, but one factor that distinguishes maturities is their sensitivity to the inflation.

Since the average business cycle has been around 5 years in the United States, in all likelihood a 2-year note will live its life in the same inflation environment, increasing, decreasing, or remaining stable. A 10-year note, on the other hand, is likely to be outstanding during two complete business cycles, and of course 30-year bonds are initially priced with half a dozen or more cycles in mind. Since the real return on shorter-maturity bonds is more susceptible to changes in inflation, their yield should be heavily influenced by the business cycle, which also heavily influences changes in the price level. It's this imperative to deliver a positive real return that keeps short-term yields linked to the business cycle, since it is economic activity that drives changes in the price level. As it turns out, no matter what two parts of the curve we depict, similar patterns emerge, whether it's between 5- and 10-year maturities or 3- and 5-year maturities. Understanding the economic activity that's driving changes in inflation is an inescapable part of understanding the bond market.

Finally, there is a more subtle implication in the graphs of the two types of yield curve movements we've examined so far. The scale of the y axis in Figure 0–1, detailing changes in the level of rates, is in percentage points, whereas the scale in Figure 0–2 is in basis points, just 1/100th the size. Changes in the level of rates have been much more dramatic than changes in the slope of the yield curve, which leads to an important conclusion: parallel moves dominate the market. Even though there have been changes to the slope of the curve, an assumption of parallel yield curve movements is quite good! Parallel moves explain the vast majority of yield movements, and this assumption is so ingrained in the fixed income market that many aren't even aware that they are making it. For example, duration calculations, the most common measurement of risk in the fixed income landscape, assume parallel changes in yield. Since changes to the slope of the curve are less volatile than outright long or short positions, they're a favorite among traders seeking trades with relatively contained risk profiles.

The least volatile type of curve movement is a change in the curvature of the curve. While classifying them as convergence trades might be a stretch, it's possible to find quite consistent patterns. In order to measure the curvature of the curve, it's necessary to measure three points, and traders often refer to them as the anatomy of a butterfly with the body and two wings. To stretch the analogy further, the resulting yield history actually acts like a butterfly, where the yield of the securities making up the wings flaps up and down compared to the body, hopefully returning to the center position. The wings and body always have opposite signs, either long or short, and the sign of both wings is always the same. The structure in a butterfly position is deliberate, because if the signs of any of the legs don't follow either a long-short-long or short-long-short pattern, the position will be subject to changes in the slope of the curve. Of course, the purpose of trading butterfly spreads is to capture changes in the curvature of the term structure of rates; if a trader wishes to capture changes in either the level of rates or slope of the curve, the trader could do so in a simpler trade with fewer pieces and less effort. The objective in trading butterfly spreads is to be level and slope "neutral," meaning that changes can happen to either of these first two types of curve movements without creating profit or loss in the position.

Consider what would happen to a butterfly trade with 2-, 5-, and 10-year maturity legs, if the 5-year acted as a pivot point for changes in the yield curve, as it often has in the past. If the 2-year rose in yield by a basis point, while the 10-year fell in yield by a basis point, then the position would have no change in profit or loss, assuming that the 2- and 10-year legs were duration dollar-weighted. If rates rose in parallel, and the duration dollars of the body were equal and opposite to the duration dollars of the wings, then again there would be no change in profit or loss. If the profit or loss from movements in the 2- and 10-year legs didn't perfectly offset each other, there would be a change in the curvature of the curve, defined by our three points, and it's this risk that the trade is attempting to capture. There are a handful of imperatives when trading butterfly spreads, and the first is weighting the trade, while the second is the choice of maturities.

Even if our expectations about a curve reshaping are correct, a mistake in either of these two choices can curtail profits, or worse still, produce a loss.

One popular approach to butterfly weightings is where one-half the risk of the body is put into each of the wings. A single basis-point change in the opposing direction for the wings will produce no profit or loss in the position, which tends to work for trades over short time horizons. What many traders don't realize is that equal risk-weighted trades end up not quite as neutral as they might have anticipated. Over long periods of time, perhaps several months to several quarters, an equal risk-weighted trade will have a trend, either higher or lower, depending on what happens to the overall direction of the market. The reason for this is that there is a hidden variable at work, which has only recently been understood and compensated for. It turns out that the yield volatility of each part of the curve is different, and the general pattern is that shorter rates have higher yield volatilities than longer rates, creating a volatility curve that is downward sloping by maturity. Part of the reason for this parallels our earlier discussion about inflation expectations, where shorter bonds have less leeway to misjudge economic conditions and have to react more sharply to changes in the environment.

Figure 0–5 illustrates the differences between a butterfly spread that is equal risk-weighted and one that is truly level and slope neutral. The equal risk-weighted

FIGURE 0–5

2/5/10-year Treasury butterfly spreads

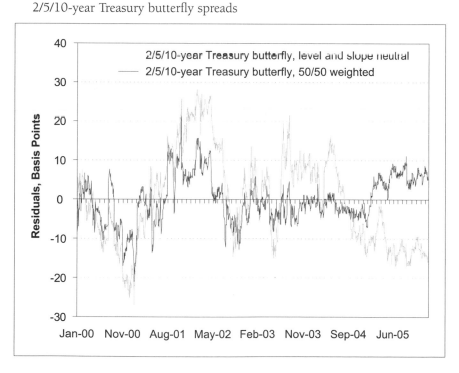

spread has been generally richening for the past 3 years, and if a trader were using zero as his expected mean reversion signal, he might be in for a long wait! Eventually this spread would return to the mean, because we know that rates in the United States have been stable and relatively well-behaved over long horizons, but the risk is that a trader's choice of weightings might depend on such a long horizon for mean reversion as to be irrelevant for trading. Short horizons tend to be the hallmark of reversion trades, and Figure 0–5 is evidence that not every attempt at representing the intended risk is successful. What happened in this series is that some of the risks of the other two types of curve movements, level and slope, leaked into our trade. The second series in Figure 0–5 is level and slope neutral, and if we regressed the series against changes in the level of rates, as represented by the body, and the slope of the curve, as represented by the wings, the resulting regression lines would be perfectly horizontal.

However, this brings us to the second point regarding choice of maturities. Notice that the series without a trend only meets our criteria for level and slope neutrality within the boundaries of the position. This means that if you measured the level of rates as anything other than the 5-year yield, which is the body of the position, or slope as anything other than the 2-year versus the 10-year spread, this particular trade with these particular weightings fails to be level and slope neutral. These terms have meanings that are sometimes cruelly specific. Unless the trader includes the pivot point for changes in slope of the curve within the maturity points of the wings, the trade would behave in unexpected ways. Why not just include every single point with as wide a spread between the wings as possible, perhaps from 6 months to 30 years? If the trade is too broad, it can't hope to represent a specific phenomenon. The broader the maturities between the wings, the more chance there is for a great number of factors to counteract the intended effect.

The market provided a clear example in late 2005. This was a period where the size of off-the-run 10-year Treasury issues was falling, and there had been a number of squeezes that bid up the price of issues that could be used to offset futures contracts in the delivery process (we detail the anatomy of a squeeze in subsequent chapters). Will a squeeze happen in the next few weeks? One way to create a butterfly trade that represents this unique effect as cleanly as possible is to buy the 7-year note, and sell 5- and 10-year issues against it. If the yield of a 7-year note falls because of a squeeze, the trade is profitable. What's the down side? If the squeeze doesn't happen, the bond could be cheaper than before the threat of a squeeze, or it may just lie at fair value in the middle of the 5-year and 10-year yields. In this way, the butterfly trade may present a payoff that is something close to digital. If the 7-year issue starts at fair value and there is a squeeze, the butterfly posts a positive return. If the squeeze fails to materialize, nothing happens, and the 7-year note may stay at fair value compared to the 5- and 10-year notes. There is no profit or loss. Consider that the butterfly position allows us to trade a specific phenomenon, whereas an outright long position leaves the position vulnerable to a change in the level of rates and a two-legged trade profits from changes in the slope of the curve. Of course, a trade that is too narrow guarantees that exactly nothing will happen, or it at least reduces the volatility to such a low level that it's unlikely to outweigh the bid/ask spread.

Given that yield curve movements can be organized into recognizable pieces, where do futures fit into the equation? By design their performance will be close to that of their underlying risk, meaning that a 5-year Treasury futures contract will perform closely to that of a 5-year note in the cash market, but it won't be exactly the same. This book studies how close that performance will be. When traders have access to credit, then even small differences can be exploited with leverage into large dollar figures so it's worth studying every difference, no matter the size. Multi-billion-dollar trades may be put on using leverage up to 100:1 in order to earn a fraction of 1 thirty-second. While the levered trader must thoroughly understand the performance of the futures contract, there is much to be gained by a broader audience of nonlevered investors seeking to add excess return to their portfolios. A single thirty-second in price equals 3 basis points in annual return. If a portfolio manager can earn a few thirty-seconds a quarter from judicious use of futures contracts, the addition to the bottom line can mean the difference between over- or underperforming a benchmark, or between managing a fund with average or above-average performance.

THE FUTURES MARKET

The common characteristics of all futures contracts, no matter the underlying risk, include quarterly expiration and a centralized clearing house to stand behind every trade. However, the landscape for exchange-traded derivates has changed dramatically in recent years as the Chicago Board of Trade (CBOT) and the Chicago Mercantile Exchange (CME) have expanded their product offerings to better suit the needs of mortgage hedgers, which are driving the expansion of the fixed income and derivatives markets. In recognition of this fact, the two in-depth hedging examples in this book involve mortgage-backed securities, the first with traditional structures of 30-year fixed-rate pass-throughs and the second with hybrid adjustable-rate mortgages (ARMs).

Traditionally, the CBOT specialized in contracts based on long-dated Treasury rates, while the CME focused on hedging money market risk. This split between product offerings has its roots in the agricultural markets that spawned both enterprises. The CBOT had developed a niche in products that could be stored for long periods like grains, while the CME focused on perishables like eggs and butter. For many years, the exchanges found it difficult to break from their historical specialties until the advent of electronic trading. In the first few years of electronic trading there has been greater innovation and a deepening of product offerings than there had been during the first few decades of trading in financial futures. Although trading at each exchange remains most vigorous in their original areas of expertise, the CBOT with long-dated Treasuries and the CME with short-maturity LIBOR products, each has grown into areas that were not traditionally theirs. Recently, futures on short-maturity Treasuries at the CBOT have grown more liquid, while the CME has steadily expanded trading of Eurodollars farther out the yield curve. The two major categories of financial futures and options available at both exchanges are:

Treasury note and bond futures (CBOT): 2-, 5-, 10-, and 30-year underlying maturities

Eurodollar futures (CME): 40 quarterly expirations representing 10 years of risk

While the underlying risks in each contract are different, all futures share some common characteristics. Futures represent forward prices, and differ from spot prices because of carry. In general, financial futures are positive carry markets, which means the forward price is below the spot price. Additionally, there is no initial cash flow required to initiate a long or short position, except for margin. Margin accounts help to ensure that traders can withstand daily price fluctuations of the contracts they hold and that each position is marked to market at the end of every day. If the daily price movement has wiped out the equity in a margin account, traders must either deposit additional funds or see their positions liquidated. This mechanism of daily settlement ensures that each morning of trading begins with entities that are financially sound, which is important because of another characteristic of futures: all trading is done in a centralized market.

To promote confidence in the centralized market, the CME Clearing House guarantees every matched trade. The advantage of this system is that futures traders don't have to consider the individual financial health of other futures traders, because the financial integrity of the exchanges is centralized in the Clearing House. Since 2004 the CME Clearing House has cleared trades for both exchanges, with average payments between accounts at $1.4 billion per day, with an astonishing single day peak of $6.4 billion changing hands. To further promote integrity in the system, customers doing business through a clearing member not involved in a default are insulated from losses incurred by the failure of another clearing member. In the event of a default the Clearing House is able to draw on resources valued at more than $41 billion at the end of 2005.

In contrast to over-the-counter transactions, where trading occurs directly between two counterparties, all futures orders are made public in the market and recorded. Before electronic trading, every trade had to be announced via "open outcry," which literally meant that a filling broker would shout the transaction to all of the specialists for those particular types of orders. In the electronic trading arena every order is recorded in an order book showing price and quantity. In futures markets today, identity is the only thing that remains anonymous, while price and quantity are perfectly transparent. One consequence of transparency and diminished counterparty credit risk is the standardization of products. In order to concentrate liquidity, the exchanges must standardize quotations and specifications of each contract so that obligations with the same underlying risk and expiration are fungible. The disadvantage of commoditization is that individual risks may vary from the available futures products. Understanding the structure and the "look and feel" of each contract can help to bridge the gap between the hedging needs of an individual and the standardized contracts available.

Futures Mirror Mortgage Convexity

Transparency and liquidity aren't the only reasons futures remain a vital tool for mortgage interest rate risk, and in the case of Treasury and Eurodollar futures, their very structures lend themselves to hedging bonds with embedded options like mortgages. Treasury futures have an explicit option that allows the duration of the contracts to drift in response to changes in interest rates, which echoes the mortgage prepayment option. The implicit option in Eurodollar futures also gives these contracts an edge over fixed-coupon bonds in hedging credit and mortgage spreads. Over short periods of time, in a tranquil market, for relatively small sizes, the choice of an instrument may have little impact on hedge effectiveness. However, businesses that rely on their ability to effectively manage interest rate risk should exploit the unique characteristics of futures to better realize their goal.

Understanding the long-term benefits of finding the right hedge instrument is no more complicated than Figure 0–6, which shows the daily convexity advantage of a 5-year Treasury during 2004. Bullet bonds are positively convex, and when rates change, the Treasury gains in value by a little bit more than duration would predict or loses value by a little bit less. These values are small on a daily basis, around 0.11 thirty-seconds in this example. However, over time these values are quite substantial, and 0.11 thirty-seconds per day is around three-quarters of a point for a full year. The convexity value of a Treasury is relevant to mortgage hedgers because it may represent their worst nightmare: a long mortgage, short Treasury position must make up almost 28 ticks a year just to break even on this hedge, without addressing the basis risk between mortgages and Treasuries. Interest rate swaps tend to have higher coupons and slightly lower convexities than like-maturity Treasuries, but the results are similar.

Treasury futures, on the other hand, have embedded options in them, which lower their convexity. For example, on June 1, 2005, the 5-year Treasury futures contract had a convexity that was just 39% of the on-the-run issue, 0.09 compared to 0.23; and the story is more dramatic for the 10-year point. A 10-year futures contract had a convexity that was 26% of the value of the on-the-run issue, at 0.20 compared to 0.77. If the average daily change is 0.11 ticks, then 10 trading days of these changes could be worth more than a full thirty-second. It's interesting to consider how traders will balk at giving up a tick on a trade but won't think twice about holding and then hedging a bond with an instrument that has dramatically more convexity and eventually costs them that same tick on the hedge.

Convexity differences mean there is a consistent advantage to shorting Treasury futures rather than the on-the-run cash issue. Of course, the opposite is true as well. If a hedger were already short a negatively convex mortgage, it

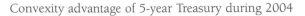

FIGURE 0–6

Convexity advantage of 5-year Treasury during 2004

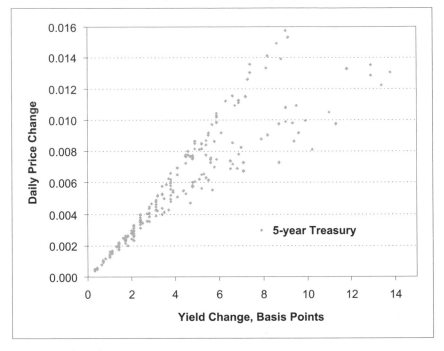

would make sense to hedge with a positively convex bullet. In this case, daily volatility helps the position. Switching between instruments, depending on whether one's net risk is positive or negative, may be too involved a process for most traders, but risks don't frequently flip-flop. Hedging a mortgage underwriting pipeline, for example, would consistently need an offsetting short position in either the futures or cash market, and futures offer a less convex and potentially less costly alternative.

Treasury and Eurodollar futures, though based on distinctly different underlying risks, share a link to volatility. There is no explicit option in Eurodollar futures, but their behavior is influenced by changes in volatility. For example, a 3-year strip of Eurodollar contracts had a dollar sensitivity to a 1% change in implied volatility of around 0.14 basis points, or 0.11 thirty-seconds at the end of 2005. As we detail later on, one basis point on a Eurodollar contract is worth $25, and one tick on a Treasury futures contract is worth $31.25. The sensitivity to volatility increases with maturity, and the dollar sensitivity in a 5-year strip is 0.40 basis points, or 0.32 thirty-seconds. Though a 5-year strip of Eurodollar contracts is less than twice as long in maturity, its sensitivity to changes in volatility is almost three times that of a 3-year strip of contracts. This sensitivity to changes in volatility is important when hedging mortgages with similar exposures. In late

2005, a 5/1 hybrid ARM had a dollar value per 1% change in volatility of about 2.1 thirty-seconds, which is partially offset by selling a Eurodollar strip. If this ARM were hedged with a cash Treasury or interest rate swap, the position would still be left with the full volatility exposure. In this example, the choice of a Eurodollar hedge offsets some of the interest rate and volatility risk of the mortgage.

In spite of the fact that Treasury and Eurodollar futures have different structures, the prices of each responds to volatility in ways that lend them to mortgage hedging. As Figure 0–6 illustrates, using positively convex Treasuries or interest rate swaps can be costly over long periods. While occasional hedgers may find little value in juggling their choice of hedge instruments, business that depends on managing interest rate risk should favor negatively convex futures for short positions. Similarly, mortgage hedgers that are concerned about their exposure to changes in volatility can begin to offset this risk with either Treasury or Eurodollar futures, potentially lessening the need to use naked options.

Calendar Spreads

One unique aspect of the futures market is that liquidity is concentrated in the shortest dated contracts, and positions need to be rolled from one quarter to another to retain the same interest rate exposure. In contrast, over-the-counter securities like Treasuries and interest rate swaps simply get closer to maturity as time goes on, which means that in order to retain the same risk profile, the original trade would have to be unwound and then reinitiated with a longer-dated bond. For example, selling a 10-year Treasury means that after one quarter it is only a 9-year, 9-month bond, and during this time the interest rate risk has fallen by about 4%. Unless the underlying risk has also shrunk by this amount, it's necessary to buy back the first bond and reinitiate the position with another sale of a 10-year Treasury. Futures traders have become so expert at this unwind and reinitiating trade that a separate market has evolved, called *calendar spreads*. As we'll see, consistent patterns emerge in the calendar spread market that may help futures users seamlessly manage this aspect of their hedge.

Figure 0–7 illustrates a familiar pattern where open interest and trading activity move from one quarterly contract to the next without affecting the total number of contracts outstanding. Each open contract has both a buyer and a seller, but the calculation of open interest is done using only one side of the market. Although it may look like open interest changes are sporadic when viewed across time in Figure 0–7a, this same information is better understood as a ratio, dividing the open interest in the nearby contract by the total number of contracts outstanding. Figure 0–7b does just that, and it's remarkable that over time the pattern of moving from one contract to the next is so similar.

Figure 0–7b compares open interest across each of the cycles in terms of the number of trading days left to expiration. With few exceptions, activity in the front contract can almost be anticipated to the day. This is important to traders looking for the "best" time to roll their positions from one month to another, and

F I G U R E   0–7a

10-year Treasury futures open interest over time

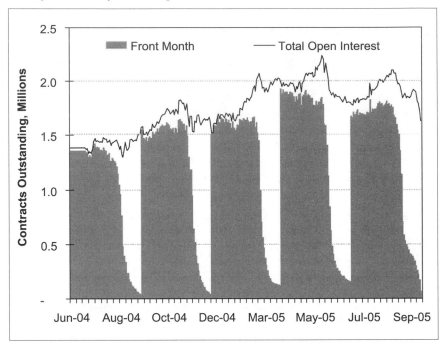

liquidity may be greatest during days when open interest is falling most rapidly in Figure 0–7b. However, there are an equal number of buyers and sellers, and moving from one calendar month to another doesn't necessarily have any implication on pricing, since there's always an offsetting transaction. The one possible exception to this rule of thumb may come from the fact that Treasury futures at the CBOT are settled by physical delivery. The window for these deliveries opens on the first day of the expiration month, and the holder of the short contract decides when to make delivery. Since many holders of long contracts do not want to accept the risk of taking delivery, they are required by their investment guidelines to roll out of the nearby contract prior to the delivery window opening.

The holder of a long contract runs the risk of taking delivery, and some believe this creates an inordinate amount of selling pressure in the nearby contract prior to the delivery window opening. However, this phenomenon is well known, and in most instances it won't be enough to drive pricing in the calendar spread. The important elements to consider when trading calendar spreads are the depth of the market and the proportion of contracts that have moved from one month to another. It's much easier to be selective about trading opportunities with 30 days left to expiration and only 25% of the roll completed than it is with 5 trading days left and 80% of the roll completed. The economics of calendar spreads

FIGURE 0–7b

10-year Treasury futures open interest displayed as a ratio

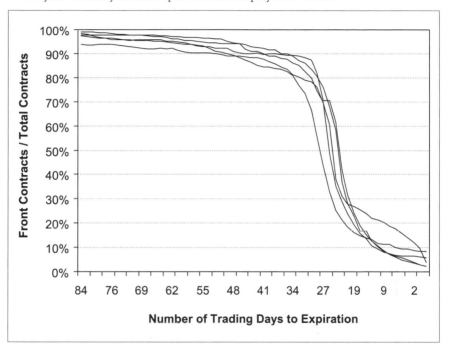

are no different from unwinding an old hedge and reinitiating a new one in the cash market, which happens with transparency and efficiency in futures.

Who Uses Futures?

Futures contract design has always been a balancing act between appealing to hedgers or speculators. If the contracts end up as literal representations of their underlying commodity, they will appeal to hedgers because of their straightforward design but have relatively little appeal to speculators, who live to parse out ambiguity. On the other hand, if the contracts stray too far away from representing their underlying risk, they will alienate hedgers, as purely speculative markets don't have much of a life span. In the case of agricultural futures, there are hedgers on both sides of the market, both buyers and sellers. Forward contracts began trading at the Chicago Board of Trade in 1851 to eliminate the farmer's risk that prices might fall after he had spent the money to sow his crop. Mill operators faced the risk of crop prices rising during the growing season, which meant the cost of their raw materials were rising faster than they could pass these costs along. Arbitrageurs would step in the middle of these natural users of the contracts, if either side didn't happen to come to the market at exactly the same time.

There is a natural rhythm to the trading year in agricultural commodities, and weather forecasters are often in more demand than quantitative analysts.

As mercurial as the weather may be, it's relatively simple compared to the contrivances of interest rate markets. No one is "naturally producing" the underlying commodity in financial futures markets, except perhaps the U.S. Treasury, and there are no distinct consumers of money (except everybody would like more, rather than less). In spite of this, the tension in financial futures parallels that of agricultural markets and is between hedgers and speculators. While it's sometimes the case that hedgers come to the market at exactly the same time with offsetting trades, it's more likely that a speculator provides the liquidity in the interim. In fact, financial futures markets sometimes resemble a Three Stooges episode, where the hedgers and speculators are paused at a door with one saying, "After you!" while the other says, "No, no, after you!" because each knows that the other's trade will influence the price in his or her favor. It's always more profitable to make the second trade after the first has forced prices to move your way. The problem is that neither side can wait for the other indefinitely.

There is a third type of trading that is unique to financial futures: long-term arbitrage. Very few people, if any, ever try to enforce the price of a bushel of soybeans with an arbitrage trade, which would involve taking delivery of the physical commodity from a farmer, loading it on a barge, and sailing it down the mighty Mississippi. This is not true in financial markets, where the threat of delivery always looms because transaction costs are so low and arbitrage trading is easier. If prices ever get too far out of line, the costs of making or taking delivery are miniscule, which means that the fluctuation of the contracts away from their "fair value" is normally similarly small.

This book is concerned with strategies for the third type of trader engaged in long-term arbitrage trades and is solely focused on fair value. The liquidity provided by these types of trades sometimes benefits other users of the contracts, but the trading tends to be infrequent and for large size and is never predictably buying or selling. Understanding the strategies of these traders, on the other hand, should be of tremendous interest to traditional hedgers and speculators. For example, if a hedger is adding duration with financial futures, the hedger has a range of alternatives including two that are discussed in this book: Treasury and Eurodollar futures. Which one is more expensive? Every hedger has been in the situation of buying contracts, only to see a long-term arbitrageur come into the market and cause a massive wave of selling. Could this activity have been anticipated? In some cases, yes.

Although the underlying risks in each market are different, both Treasury and Eurodollar futures share some broad similarities. Typically, both are positive carry markets, meaning the levered holder of the underlying risk accrues a coupon and pays financing costs on a daily basis, and the difference is the carry. In positive carry markets the forward price is below the current price (also called the spot price), and the farther in the future an obligation, the lower its price. Futures represent forward prices of their underlying commodity, and a futures

F I G U R E   0–8

Futures prices relative to spot prices

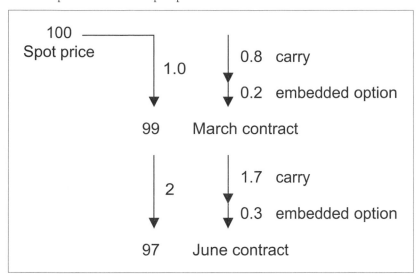

price in December should be lower than it is in September, all other things being equal. While there is a simple ordering in prices according to month in both types of financial futures, there is a subtler characteristic to these markets.

There are embedded options in Treasury and Eurodollar futures prices and their mispricing is the main source of interest for long-term arbitrage traders. In each case their price is lowered to account for this, as illustrated in Figure 0–8. Treasury futures have an explicit option allowing the holder of a short position to choose which issue to deliver into the contract to satisfy delivery standards. Eurodollars are slightly more complex because even though there is no explicit option, each is priced as if it is short a straddle. This implied option is referred to as the *convexity bias,* which serves to make their price lower than it would otherwise be. Understanding the behavior of these instruments means understanding each piece—one that is somewhat mechanical and one that is much more complex. This book is structured in four parts; the first chapter is on Treasury futures, the second on Eurodollars, and the third on TED spreads, which is the spread between the two. The final chapter details a method of anticipating market volatility to price options. This type of volatility mapping is relevant no matter the underlying contract, whether it's Treasury or Eurodollar futures.

TREASURY FUTURES: LANGUAGE OF THE BASIS

Simple rules govern the behavior or Treasury futures, but complex patterns can emerge when they interact. The rule of flowing water is a good analogy: Water always tries to move downhill. It's a simple rule, but one that also carved out something as elaborate as the Grand Canyon. What allows for the unique behavior of Treasury futures is that they are obligations on a basket of U.S. Treasury notes or bonds, rather than a single issue. The window for possible inclusion of an issue in the deliverable basket of a futures contract grows along with its maturity. For example, the window for 2-year futures is relatively narrow, from 1 year and 9 months to 2 years. The window for a 30-year contract is quite a bit wider, from 15 to 30 years. Figure 1–1 illustrates the notes and bonds that are deliverable into each of the contracts and how the maturity window widens with maturity. The size of the window matters since it allows for the issue represented by the contract to change: The wider the window, the greater the potential for change. Physical delivery is also unique to Treasury futures, and a contract held through expiration must be offset by delivering a cash Treasury issue.

The right of the holder of short contracts to choose which issue to deliver creates an implicit option. There are two basic rules of thumb to relating changes in the cheapest-to-deliver (CTD) issue to changes in interest rates:

- Maturity of the cheapest issue moves in the same direction as rates. As rates fall, so does the maturity of the CTD issue. As rates rise, so does the maturity of the CTD issue.

- Maturity of the cheapest issue follows the slope of the curve. A flattening curve shortens the maturity of the CTD, while a curve steepening extends the maturity.

These two rules hint at the criteria for a bond being considered the cheapest-to-deliver issue. As rates rise, the highest duration and longest maturity bond will fall in price more than the shorter maturity bonds with lower durations. Similarly, a steepening of the curve will cheapen longer maturity bonds with longer durations more than shorter maturity bonds with shorter durations. These rules imply that the dollar price of bonds in the basket helps to determine their status as being CTD, and this is in fact the case. The term *cheapest-to-deliver* literally means choosing the bond with the lowest dollar price, after accounting for

FIGURE 1–1

Deliverable bonds into Treasury note and bond futures

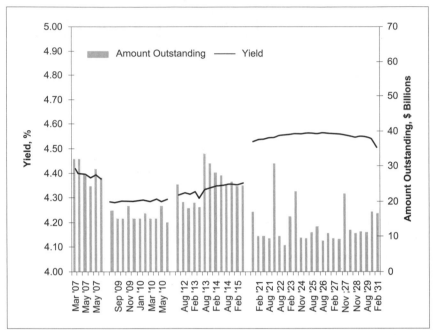

differences in coupon and for the fact that futures represent forward prices, including carry.

Differences in coupon and maturity are taken into account by a conversion factor. The conversion factor is the decimal price of the bond, as if its yield were 6%, after rounding the maturity down to the immediately previous first day of the delivery month. The conversion factors for bonds with coupons above 6% are above 1, representing a premium price, and bonds with coupons below 6% have conversion factors below 1. Though the same bond has different conversion factors for different contract expirations, the conversion factor remains the same throughout the life of each futures contract.

The duration of the futures contract drifts along with the maturity of the CTD issue. When interest rates are very low, the CTD issue tends to be the shortest in the basket, and the contract has a relatively short duration. Conversely, the interest rate sensitivity of the contract generally increases along with rising interest rates. This duration drift and the associated negative convexity that comes with it make Treasury futures a reasonable hedge for securities that face comparable duration drift, like mortgage collateral. However, the specific behavior of the embedded delivery option in Treasury futures is slightly different from the short call option in most mortgage collateral.

We can add one more rule to the two basic rules of thumb listed previously; this third rule is based on the right of the short to choose which issue to deliver into the contract:

- Futures underperform cash Treasury issues whenever there is a CTD switch. When there is a CTD switch, delivery option goes in-the-money.

Since the holder of short contracts must buy an issue in the cash market to make delivery, it would make sense that one would also look for the issue with the lowest price. However, the fact that the short is always substituting the cheapest bond means that futures underperform cash whenever there is a CTD switch. Suppose that the CTD issue is in the middle of the deliverable basket. In this case the CTD can switch to a shorter issue if rates fall or the curve flattens or to a longer issue if rates rise or the curve steepens. All behavior in these instruments is related to the original two rules. The first step to building a fair value model for these instruments is to review the well-worn vernacular of Treasury bond basis. In fact, Treasury futures are so often used to hedge that much of the language surrounding them was developed to describe differences between futures and the underlying notes used to price them.

Conversion factors normally garner attention because they are the singularly strangest aspect of Treasury futures. Treasury futures are not based on a single note but on one of a basket of potential deliverable notes. Each note has a different maturity and coupon, and conversion factors account for these differences. The conversion factor is literally the price per $1 of each note, as if its coupon were 6% and maturity were rounded down to the immediately previous first day of the delivery month.

For example, a note maturing in Aug '12 would round to June 1, 2012, for delivery into the June 10-year futures (which would have the ticker "TYH5," in which "TY" stands for a 10-year contract, "H" stands for the delivery month, and "5" for the delivery year). If the coupon of the note is above 6%, then the conversion factor would be above 1; if the coupon is below 6%, the conversion factor would be below 1. While many countries have adopted this style of contract with slightly varying details as to the specification of the conversion factor, at the Chicago Board of Trade (CBOT) conversion factors are four decimals. Since the coupon on Aug '12 is 4.375%, the conversion factor is 0.9136 in the September 2005 contract but 0.9108 in the December 2005 contract, to account for the fact that a slightly lower price is necessary to yield 6% with a note that has a 3-month shorter maturity.

Gross basis is the price difference in thirty-seconds between the Treasury note and futures price after it is multiplied by a conversion factor, and it is the sum of the net basis plus carry. Conceptually, this value is the price spread between today's price of the Treasury note and the forward price of the Treasury future. This difference is composed of embedded options and carry. The larger the gross basis, the lower the futures price relative to the price of the cash note. The gross basis is often the unit that traders quote markets in, and a quote of "30" means a price difference between the cash and futures price (multiplied by the relevant conversion factor) of 30 thirty-seconds.

For example, a basis of 5 ticks, with a contract price at 100 and a conversion factor of 0.9511 implies a cash price of 95 − 8+:

$$100 \bullet 0.9511 + 5/32 = 95 - 8+$$

Net basis is gross basis less carry. Traders have traditionally interpreted this value as the market price of delivery option. However, there are sometimes periods when the net basis is negative, which destroys the classical interpretation. This value may also reflect the market's expectation of receiving some proportion of the second-cheapest issue at delivery or of extraordinary costs to take possession of the bond in the repo (repurchase agreement) market. When the net basis increases, the futures price is lower relative to the price of the CTD note or bond in the cash market. This is also sometimes referred to as the *basis net of carry,* or *BNOC.*

Carry is the difference between what the note earns in coupon interest and what is paid in financing cost to borrow the money to buy the note, based on the full price of the bond. In an upward sloping yield curve, carry is positive because the yield of the note is above the short-term financing and costs are less than what the note accrues in interest. In this case forward prices will be below spot prices.

Cheapest-to-deliver is the single issue within the basket of eligible bonds that is least expensive for the short to purchase in order to satisfy delivery. If there were no delivery option, then the duration of the futures contract would equal the duration of the CTD bond divided by the conversion factor. Although the CTD bond does have the potential to change, the duration of the contract most closely approximates that of the CTD. There are three ways of identifying which bond in the eligible basket is CTD:

1. Highest implied repo rate

2. Lowest net basis

3. Lowest converted forward price

The third definition is the one most often used because it directly reflects the choice facing the holder of short contracts. Occasionally these definitions produce conflicting results and identify different bonds as being the cheapest, but the third choice is the most reliable.

Delivery option is the right of the holder of short positions to choose which issue is to be delivered into the contracts. Since each bond in the deliverable basket has a different price and duration, each will respond to changes in interest rates at a different speed from the others. At any one time there is a single issue that is least expensive to satisfy delivery, but changes in volatility or interest rates can change the potential for CTD switches, and in turn this also changes the value of the delivery option. Traditionally traders have viewed the net basis as the market price of delivery option, which holds as long as there isn't a squeeze on the deliverable issue.

Implied repo rate is the annualized rate of return from buying the Treasury note and earning the coupon on the face value, paying the repo rate on the full price of the bond, selling futures contracts, and then delivering the note into the contract during the last day of the delivery window. The lower the price of the contract, the lower the return will be when the note is delivered into it. A high value implies a high futures price relative to the cash note, but normally implied repo rates are below actual repo rates, indicating that the net basis is positive. This means that the market is pricing in accordance with some delivery option and contract prices are slightly cheaper than they would be based on carry alone.

Forward price is the spot price of the Treasury note less carry, from settlement to a date in the future. Sometimes traders will talk about a *forward yield*, which is simply the yield-to-maturity recalculated with the forward price. The difference between the forward and spot price of the note is also sometimes referred to as *the drop,* in reference to the fact that in positive carry markets the forward price is lower than the spot price. A forward price is not the market's expectation of the future price of the bond, but merely reflects carry.

Converted forward price is the forward price of the note or bond divided by the conversion factor. These values are most often used to determine which issue is the least expensive to deliver into the contracts.

Long/short basis refers to the Treasury note position, not the futures contract. A quotation of a *long basis* position means that the trader is long cash, earning the coupon on the face value while paying the repo rate on the full market value, and is also short the futures contract. A quote of *short basis* indicates a sale of the cash note, paying the coupon while earning repo, and simultaneously long futures contracts.

Individually, the pieces are simple, and a sample basis trade puts the puzzle together. Although we will spend time later developing fair value methodologies, let's suppose for this exercise that we decide futures are rich to 5.375% Feb '31, which is the cheapest-to-deliver bond at the time. Incidentally, this issue occupies a special place in the pantheon of Treasury bonds; it has served as the on-the-run bond for the longest of any other because the 30-year bond program was suspended in 2001, only to be revived in 2006. Although other programs, like the 3-year note, have also been suspended, these shorter issues subsequently matured. Feb '31 held the on-the-run torch for so long it may go down in history as the most traded bond ever. In practice though, on-the-run bonds are rarely the cheapest in the deliverable basket since they normally command a substantial premium for their liquidity.

Quotes on basis trades, as with other derivative markets, refer to the purchase or sale of the cash Treasury note, rather than to the derivative, which is the futures contract in this case. Since we assume that the futures contract is rich, we need to sell 30-year contracts and buy Feb '31 to create a long basis position. Since we are buying the cash issue, we need an offer on Feb '31 basis (rather than a bid, which would indicate the price a dealer would be willing to pay to buy Feb '31 from a customer). The quote on such a trade might be "8 offer and spot the contracts at

113-29." There is a lot of information in this verbal shorthand and, importantly, a few things that are missing. First of all, this quote is for a long Treasury note, short futures contract position, and is quoted in terms of the price difference between the two: 8 thirty-seconds. A quote that contains the phrase *spot the contracts* refers to the fact that the basis market is quoted as a price difference between the futures and cash markets, but it also implies the weighting between the two as well as the price of the cash issue. If the conversion factor is 0.9611, then a conversion factor–weighted basis trade uses 961 contracts per $100 million face of the Treasury issue.

The price where we will own Feb '31 is 109.73 (which is 109 and 23 thirty-seconds) in this example, and the price where we will be short the futures contract is 113.91 (113-29). Conversion factors are fixed, and it's presumed that everyone in the market knows what the conversion factors are, so the trader omits them in his quote, but we know that if the conversion factor is 0.9611, the calculation is:

$$\text{futures price} \bullet \text{conversion factor} + \text{gross basis} = \text{cash price}$$

$$113.91 \bullet 0.9611 + 8/32 = 109 - 23$$

The advantage of a conversion factor–weighted basis trade is that the profit and loss of the position can be easily calculated as a change in the net basis. Conversion factor–weighted basis trades are also the easiest to execute, since they're the convention of quotes among dealers. The disadvantage is that the position isn't normally duration neutral, which means that the profit and loss of the trade may be somewhat directional with changes in interest rates. The alternative to a conversion factor–weighted basis trade is a duration weight, where the DV01 (1-basis-point change in yield) of the futures contract and cash note are matched. Generally, duration-weighted trades are more common when market conditions mean that a switch is close, while factor-weighted trades tend to be more popular when there is a good chance that the current CTD bond will remain the cheapest at expiration of the contract.

The trade is far from complete, since we haven't found a way to pay for the long Feb '31 position! Arbitrage traders normally do not pay cash for their long positions, and it's hardly necessary given the depth of the financing market in Treasuries. In the repurchase market (the "repo" market, for short), we can borrow the funds used to purchase Feb '31 and pledge the issue as collateral against the loan. Since we are long the issue and accruing its interest, we need to pay some financing rate on the total dollars we had to borrow, which is the full price of the bond including accrued interest. The quotation in the repo market is in yield terms and might be something like "3.79 at 3.70," which indicates a bid of 3.79% and an offer at 3.70%. In this case, we're hitting the bid of 3.79% since we need to pay interest on the funds borrowed to purchase Feb '31. It's easy to get confused switching from a price quote in the basis to a yield quote in repo, but when asking the repo trader for a bid or offer, remember that you are going to get the least advantageous rate for your need. If you need to earn a rate, you get the lower one, which is the offer; if you are paying a rate, you get the higher yield, which is the bid. Furthermore, a "reverse repo" is the opposite sort of transaction. Rather than borrow money in a loan collateralized by a Treasury note, a reverse repo occurs when one has money to lend and accepts a note as collateral. This sometimes leads to the term "reversing in" a note or bond, indicating that the issue is being received in exchange for cash.

Switching between basis markets quoted in thirty-seconds and repo markets quoted on a money market basis has caused many an error on Wall Street trading desks. In addition to switching between price and yield, the yields in the repo market are quoted in a different basis than in the Treasury market. Repo trades have a relatively short horizon, and since repo is almost never traded in terms of longer than a year, it is normally quoted as a money market yield, with "actual/360" day count. Treasury bonds, on the other hand, have an "actual/actual" day count, and it's important to remember that a basis point in yield in repo does not precisely translate to a basis point in yield on a Treasury note, although they are close. It can also be cumbersome to have to call two desks to execute a multileg trade. For this reason, dealers are increasingly making markets in the net, rather than the gross, basis. A quote in the net basis implies not just the price difference between the cash and futures contract but also the rate at which a dealer would be willing to fund the Treasury note in the repo market.

After hitting the bid in the repo market, it's possible to determine how much carry will be paid from settlement to the end of the repo term, normally the last day of the delivery month (in a negative carry market, where repo rates are higher than the current yield of the Treasury, repo terms are to the first day of the delivery month). The difference between the gross and net basis is carry; and now that we have everything, we need to calculate carry. The gross basis can be dissected into two parts to determine the market price of delivery option, which is the interesting part of this trade. As we mentioned, it's most often this mispricing of the delivery option that attracts long-term arbitrage traders. The gross basis offer was originally 8 ticks. To figure out the net basis, we have to subtract carry, which is the difference between the current yield of Feb '31 with a coupon of 5.375 and an offer price of 111-13, and the bid in repo of 3.79%. This leads to a net carry rate of 103 basis points:

$$\text{coupon/price} = \text{current yield}$$

$$5.375 \, / \, 1.1142 = 4.82\%$$

$$\text{current yield} - \text{financing cost (repo rate)} = \text{net carry rate}$$

$$4.82\% - 3.79\% = 1.03\%$$

Now that we know the net carry rate, the difference in yield between what we're earning from the bond coupon we're long compared to the rate we have to pay for the money we borrow to purchase the bond in the repo market, we have to translate that rate into a dollar value. As a rule of thumb, 1 basis point of carry, on $1 million face, for 1 day is worth approximately $0.27. This $0.27 figure comes from dividing 1/360 and is only an approximation, because of the differences in day count we mentioned earlier. The reality is that everyone who trades basis has capable computer systems to calculate this value, but this rule of thumb is close enough for decision-making purposes. In this case, the horizon of the trade is 80 days, which means that the dollar value of the interest earned is:

$$103 \bullet 0.27 \bullet 80 = 2,224.80$$

Since we quoted the gross basis in thirty-seconds rather than dollars, we have to take the $2,224.80 and divide by $312.50, which is the dollar value of 1 thirty-second for $1 million face of a bond:

$$2,224.80 / 312.50 = 7.1$$

The value of carry, expressed in thirty-seconds, is 7.1. Since we know the gross basis of 8 thirty-seconds and the carry value of approximately 7.1 ticks, we also know the net basis, which is the difference between the two: 0.9 ticks. We're narrowing in on the essence of the trade with this net basis calculation. The reality is that many different gross basis values and carry rates can produce the same net basis. As one might guess, the net basis value is the most stable of any of the others. Even though basis traders execute in multiple markets, they are really trading changes in the net basis, which is the drop in price of the futures contract that's left after accounting for carry. There is no uncertainty in any of the pieces in a basis trade except for the fair price of the futures contract, since the Treasury note and repo are both fixed-rate bonds. On the other hand, the right of the short to choose which issue is delivered into the contract means that there is some uncertainty about how to price delivery option, and exactly what constitutes a "fair" futures contract price is a matter of some discussion.

Stepping back, it might seem like the authors of the Treasury futures contract did something strange by intentionally introducing uncertainty into the pricing of their product. When 30-year contracts were first unveiled in 1977, personal computers weren't available, and these calculations may seem impossibly cumbersome to traders today who are used to instant gratification. Remember though that the speed at which the market absorbs information depends on the tools that are available to analyze the securities. It may have been more difficult to perform the calculations in the early days of basis trading, but the flip side of the coin is that prices didn't move as often or as dramatically as they do today. In the early days of the bond market, brokers would literally carry paper certificates in their briefcases and "show" them to customers. A 4% coupon general obligation municipal bond might be issued at par, and years later it might still be priced at par. Technology is a double-edged sword, and traders are perpetually making life more difficult for themselves by getting better at their jobs.

While the majority of contracts are offset before delivery, and a trader may live his or her entire career without making or taking delivery, there are rare instances when it makes sense to do so. Recently, net basis values have been so low that there has been little room to pay transaction costs, and traders interested in squeezing every last nickel out of the contracts have held them through delivery. There is one wrinkle worth mentioning with holding contracts through delivery in a conversion factor–weighted basis trade, which is trading the "tail." Delivery is made with equal face value of the Treasury note or bond against the notional value of the contracts. However, a conversion factor–weighted basis trade using a factor of 0.9 would only have a notional face value of 90% of the face of the cash issue. For every $100 million of a note that one is short, there would only be 900 futures contracts that are held as long positions against it. Ideally, the long holder of contracts receives the cash note and is able to offset short positions seamlessly, but if the conversion factor isn't exactly 1, it will be necessary to do a small trade for the difference between 1 and the actual conversion factor, which constitutes the tail. In this case the trader who is long futures needs to buy back the $10 million face of the note he or she is short so that delivery can be made with equal face values.

Recently the CBOT switched settlement to a volume-weighted average price of trades in the electronic market, which makes it relatively simple to know what price the contracts will settle to and what the corresponding price in the cash market for the CTD note should be. Unless the profit or loss on the trade is very small, trading the tail is of little consequence, since the profit or loss on the tail is calculated as the difference between the volume-weighted price of the contracts multiplied by the conversion factor and the executed price in the cash market. Of course, this difference (if any) is multiplied by the difference between 1 and the conversion factor to translate the profit to the positions as a whole. For example, if one loses 10 ticks by falling asleep during the last minute of trading of the contracts and wakes up to find the price of the CTD note 10 ticks higher than the volume-weighted price of the futures contract, this loss would only account for 1 tick on the trade as a whole, since the tail in our theoretical example was 0.1. Conversion factors are rarely so far from 1 or markets so volatile that it would be unusual for a trade in the tail to substantially impact profit or loss on the trade as a whole. However, if one goes through delivery but doesn't trade the tail, one will be left with an outright long or short position.

Example: Hedging 30-Year Fixed-Rate Pass-Throughs

Before parsing out some of the vagaries of the contract, it's useful to consider an example of how Treasury futures are used to hedge mortgages, in this case 30-year fixed-rate pass-throughs. These types of mortgages are by far the largest part of the market, and although they have been around for about as long as Treasury futures, there are still debates on Wall Street about the best way to hedge them. In the late 1990s, as the supply of Treasury securities dwindled, the trend was to move away from hedging mortgages with Treasuries in favor of interest rate swaps. Deteriorating government finances have once again led to a dramatic growth of the Treasury market, and there are many indications that 30-year and 15-year pass-through mortgage hedgers are once again relying on the government market to offset their risk.

F I G U R E   1–2

Empirical duration for 30-year mortgage coupon stack

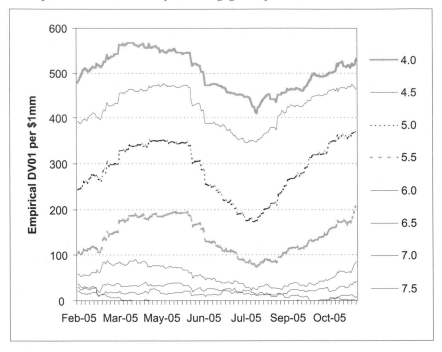

Figure 1–2 sidesteps a minefield by showing a rolling empirical duration for the 30-year fixed-rate to-be-announced (TBA) mortgage coupon stack compared to 10-year Treasury rates. The minefield we're referring to is the lack of consensus about how to model the duration of a mortgage. Just as there is some ambiguity about how to price the embedded options in Treasury futures, this same ambiguity exists in mortgages. No two Wall Street dealers model mortgage durations the same way. Evaluating mortgage models isn't the thrust of this book, and so we simply rely on historical mortgage and Treasury prices to calculate their sensitivity to one another. Ignoring questions like "Will history repeat itself?" let us move on to the next step in our hedging example, which is allocating the risk of each bond along the yield curve. Suppose the empirical DV01 for the 5.5% mortgage were $200. An easy solution is to just offset this risk in one instrument, like the 10-year Treasury futures. The face value of 10-year Treasury futures is $100,000. If we calculate the duration at 6.5 years, with a market price of 100, the DV01 of the futures contract is $65, and an appropriate hedge ratio is 3.08 contracts to the $1 million face of the mortgage ($200 divided by $65).

However, the cash flows for mortgage pass-throughs are well spread out along the yield curve, literally extending from 1 month to 30 years in the future.

Can we do better than matching 30 years of risk with just a single maturity point like the 10-year note? A more accurate method that can better track nonparallel rate changes in the curve is to use partial durations. If we know the cash flows for the mortgage, we can also calculate the duration and partial durations.

Figure 1–3 illustrates the projected cash flows for the 5.5% coupon 30-year pass-through we want to hedge as well as how those cash flows fall into the partial duration buckets. Since the 5.5% mortgage is the current coupon in this example, the bond with a price closest to par, it's representative of a portfolio of new-issue mortgages a bank would have to hedge. It's important to keep distinct the differences between Figures 1–2 and 1–3; the first graph shows the price sensitivity of a bond, while the second illustrates how that price sensitivity is spread out along the curve. If we were to sum up the percentage allocations from Figure 1–3, they would equal 100%.

Multiplying the price sensitivity from Figure 1–2 by the allocation in Figure 1–3 tells us the total risk of the position and where it's allocated along the curve. How we aggregated the partial duration buckets isn't an accident: they match up with the available maturities of Treasury futures. Now all we have to do is divide the risk in each bucket by the risk of the Treasury futures contract to construct a

F I G U R E   1–3

Cash flow for 30-year mortgage and partial durations

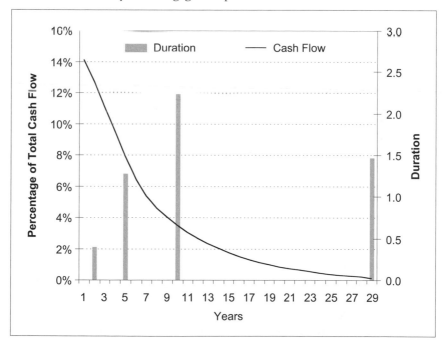

FIGURE 1–4

Futures hedges for fixed-rate mortgage collateral

Futures		2y	5y	10y	30y	2y	5y	10y	30y
		37	41	62	109				
						Treasury Futures			
FNCL	**DV01**	Risk Allocation, %				Contracts / $100 million			
4.5	532	5	16	29	50	69	206	251	245
5	477	5	18	31	46	70	210	236	200
5.5	373	7	22	32	39	72	199	192	133
6	194	10	24	32	35	51	111	99	62
6.5	71	7	24	42	27	14	41	48	18
7	34	8	25	41	25	7	21	23	8
7.5	1	9	28	41	22	0	1	1	0
8	7	13	31	41	16	3	6	5	1
FNCI									
4	454	19	41	40	0	235	451	292	0
4.5	380	25	52	23	0	259	476	140	0
5	317	21	38	37	4	178	294	188	12
5.5	183	24	41	33	2	120	180	97	4
6	69	28	43	29	0	53	72	32	0
6.5	42	33	50	17	0	38	51	12	0
7	9	30	40	27	2	7	9	4	0
7.5	3	29	41	28	2	3	3	1	0

hedge ratio, as illustrated in Figure 1–4. If all parts of the curve move in parallel, then using 10-year futures contracts alone as a hedge would be adequate; but if there is a flattening or steepening, then the cash flows in Figure 1–3 would be discounted at different rates, which would not be captured by using just the 10-year contract alone as a hedge. While a perfect hedge would slice our hedge maturities into as many cash flows as there are in the mortgage, using four points along the curve goes a long way toward improved accuracy. It brings up another point though, because greater accuracy also means greater complexity. Rather than trading just one 10-year contract we now have to use varying amounts of four different contracts, and the time it takes to implement such a trade has a cost of its own.

In addition to the advantages of the carry calculations in a futures trade as outlined previously, there is an economic reason to consider involving the carry calculations. There are times when the carry of on-the-run bonds is different from those of the cheapest-to-deliver bonds, even though they are normally close to one another and are close substitutes. In the 2-year and 5-year contracts, where the delivery window is very narrow, the two also move closely together in yield. In the 10-year and 30-year contracts, the gulf in maturity between the cheapest

TABLE 1–1

Net Carry Rate, Basis Points

Maturity	Cash	Futures	Spread
2 year	63	63	0
5 year	113	59	54
10 year	93	195	–102
30 year	166	82	85

and on-the-run issue is 3 years and 15 years, respectively, and there is less of a chance of their moving closely together in yield. Luckily, in a current-coupon 30-year pass-through more than two-thirds of the risk is on the front end of the curve, where the hedge effectiveness of futures and on-the-run bonds is quite close.

Of course, futures reflect the carry rates of the cheapest issues, and if they are different from the on-the-run issues, then we can choose between them depending on which offers the most advantageous financing. Wouldn't we rather be long a futures contract that is earning more in daily carry than an on-the-run cash bond, assuming it affords similar hedge effectiveness? For example, if we used all on-the-run instruments from Table 1–1 in hedging our 5.5% mortgage, then the net carry rate would be 124 basis points compared to 112 basis points if we used all futures. What if we alternated between cash and futures, depending on which offered the highest carry? In this case we would earn 156 basis points if we were long the hedge and short the 5.5% mortgage. Of course, we could just as easily be short the hedge and long the mortgage, so we would reverse the decisions to pay as little as possible, which was 79 basis points. A 77-basis-point gap between the hedge with the highest and lowest carry equates to about 24 ticks per year, which is certainly worth keeping track of.

WHAT IS THE NET BASIS?

Pricing the net basis in Treasury futures is among the most complex issues in financial economics. Decades of historical prices, advances in technology, and a mountain of cursory and often redundant examinations of these contracts have all contributed to some traders' cocksure insistence that they understand how to price the net basis. Without fail, these are the first people to cry foul when the contracts behave in ways that may be improbable, but are not unpredictable. Treasury futures are a victim of their own success, because the vast majority of the time their behavior supports the claim that the superficial analysis permeating Wall Street is sufficient to understand them. However, there are exceptions! As strange as it may seem, there are conditions in which buying the contracts lowers their price. What other financial instrument might boast such confounding behavior? This section serves as a road map to understand when the contracts provide solid ground on which to build hedges, and when this ground might turn into quicksand.

As a beginning we examine two competing implementations of the same principle: proof by contradiction. It seems that there are as many different ways of valuing delivery option as there are traders of the contracts. Rather than attacking the problem head-on, a reasonable place to start is to determine how the contracts would behave if there were no delivery option. After establishing this baseline, we can begin to describe the behavior of the contract more realistically and then measure the difference between the baseline and the modeled behavior to value the embedded option. The first approach we study relies on the market prices of naked options, while the second is a numerical solution based on a simple algorithm. We contrast these approaches to closed-form solutions and finish by studying those situations in which models break down. It's interesting to note that although we study competing implementations, each with good and bad aspects to them, the conceptual framework begins with a world where the phenomenon we're studying does not exist.

Establishing a Baseline

A delivery option grants the holder of short contracts the right to choose which issues out of a basket of eligible bonds are to be bought and subsequently delivered into the contract. Just as with any other purchase, it makes sense for the short to choose the least expensive bond available to satisfy an obligation to the CBOT, and this issue is labeled the *cheapest-to-deliver* issue. Understandably, the performance of the contract follows the price of the issue that is most likely to be used to satisfy delivery, even though 99% of all futures contracts are offset before delivery. However, what if this right didn't exist? In this case the bond that is cheapest today remains cheapest until expiration, no matter what happens to interest rates. The performance of the contract would mirror that of the cheapest issue without exception. This situation is illustrated in Figure 1–5a, which shows a simple price/yield relationship for an issue in the middle of the deliverable basket, which we'll assume is the cheapest issue into the bond contract. The x axis of this chart shows parallel yield changes in the on-the-run Treasury note. No matter how rates change, the contract performs just like the price/yield of the original issue. This graph represents the baseline performance against which we will subsequently measure the performance of the contracts. While Figure 1–5b is diagrammatic to clearly illustrate the phenomenon, Figure 1–6 shows just how close the performance of cash and futures contracts can be. Only on the bottom right of this chart does there begin to be some difference in performance, indicated by a widening gap in price as rates rise, but even here the values are quite small. This work highlights just how efficient the fixed income market is for traders to spend so much time analyzing small differences.

Our original two rules regarding futures performance were that (1) the cheapest issue moved in the same direction as the level of rates and (2) it followed

Treasury note versus Treasury futures performance

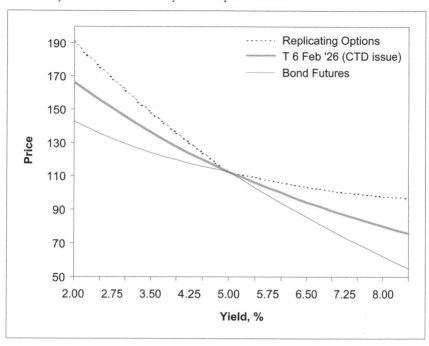

Same performance viewed as differences from the CTD note diagram

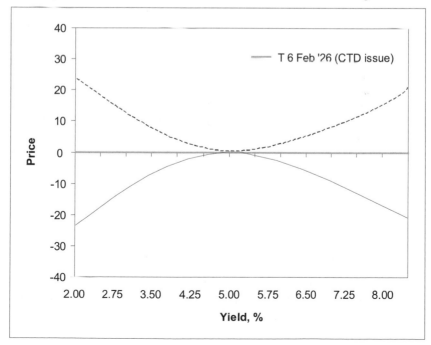

FIGURE 1–6

Actual price/yield performance of the futures versus CTD note

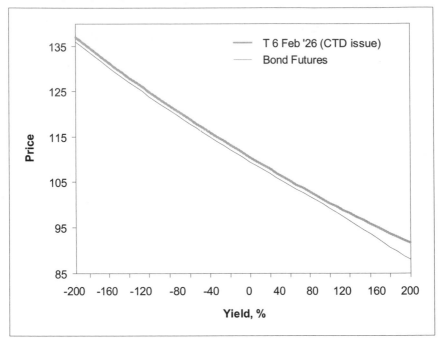

the slope of the curve. When rates increase or the curve steepens, longer issues are more likely to be cheapest. Suppose we reexamine the performance of the contracts, except this time we grant the short the right to choose which issue to deliver into the contract. When rates rise, moving to the right on the *x* axis in Figure 1–5a, there will eventually be a point in time when the note that was originally cheapest no longer has the lowest price in the basket. Intuitively, this makes sense because longer maturity issues probably have a longer duration, and these bonds fall in price faster than shorter maturity and duration bonds. The statement needs to be qualified with a "probably" since each bond may have a different coupon and it's at least theoretically possible that a very low coupon but shorter maturity bond would have a longer duration than some of the higher coupon but longer maturity issues. Practically speaking, though, interest rate movements have seldom been so dramatic as to cause adjacent issues to deviate from the simple pattern: longer issues have longer durations.

When interest rates rise, the longer duration issues are going to fall in price by more than the shorter issues. Although a note may be originally the cheapest issue today, there will be a point when the adjacent bond with a longer maturity is cheapest. Suppose that the new CTD issues change from Feb '21 to Nov '22, which is 1 year and 9 months longer in maturity than the original CTD. If we keep sliding to the right on the x axis, then we are continuing to cheapen longer duration bonds faster than shorter duration bonds, and eventually Nov '22 will no longer be the cheapest issue. The pattern goes on, but what's interesting about this approach is that we are building a complex picture of futures behavior by following one simple rule. In this illustration we can ignore our second rule since we are only examining parallel shifts along the x axis. In Figure 1–6 we originally slid to the right to find the performance of the contract when there was a CTD switch, but what happens when we slide to the left, in a lower rate scenario? If Feb '21 were the shortest issue in the deliverable basket, it would be impossible to switch to a shorter issue when rates fall. Moving to the left in this diagram means that the futures performance matches that of the original CTD and there is only a difference in performance between the cash and futures as rates rise.

The actual price difference between the futures and the original CTD issue can be as large as a point under a 200-basis-point increase in rates. It is remarkable that even though the cash and futures contracts in the preceding graphs have the same duration, differences in convexity between the two can lead to a dramatic difference in performance. What good is it to measure the shortcomings of the futures contract? Now that we know exactly what the difference is, we can match a naked options position so that the futures plus options portfolio performs identically to the original CTD issue. The beauty of this approach is that naked options on futures already trade at the CBOT and are priced by the market. If we are able to determine the correct proportions of naked options, we can rely on market prices to value the net basis, rather than some esoteric equation from a closed-form model that may or may not be consistent with the current market environment. See Figures 1–7a and 1–7b.

The first step in constructing a basket of options whose payoff mirrors that of the futures underperformance compared to the cheapest issue is to first identify the universe of possible choices. Options on 10-year Treasury futures are struck in 1-point increments. Since the DV01 of a 10-year instrument is usually around $80 per $100,000 face, and the dollar value of a thirty-second on a futures contract is $31.25, this means that every basis point in yield change on a 10-year instrument represents about 2.5 basis points in yield. This rule of thumb means that every point in price on a 10-year futures contract represents about 12.5 basis points in yield. This is a useful yardstick since we can estimate how far out-of-the-money the option strikes would have to be in order to mirror the futures underperformance relative to the CTD.

For example, suppose that the nearest switch from a shorter to a longer maturity issue were 25 basis points away in yield. Since we know that futures underperform cash whenever there is a CTD switch, we also know that we need an option to make up for this deficit. In this case we would need an option struck about 2 points out-of-the-money. Of course, it would be optimal to use an option with the exact same strike as the CTD switch point, but as we mentioned, futures options have fixed strikes, and with this approach we have to make do with the instruments that are available. It's entirely possible that a CTD switch might

Futures and option performance using a single strike to replicate futures underperformance

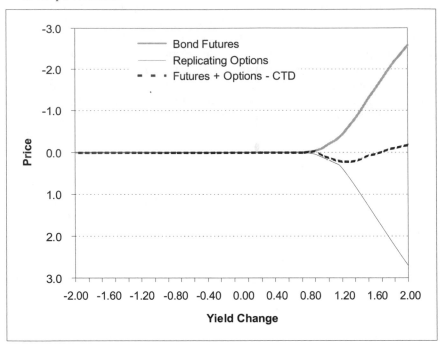

Hedges get better as we add more option strikes

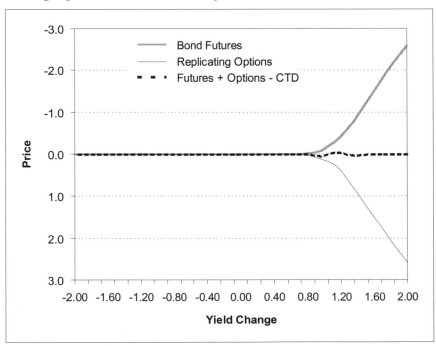

happen at a yield level that's in the middle of two available strikes, in which case there would be no perfect match of the futures underperformance with the naked options portfolio. How closely can naked options replicate the payoff of delivery option?

Figure 1–7a is an actual measurement of the futures and cash performance from the diagram in Figure 1–5a. This chart measures the futures underperformance relative to the CTD and adds the first out-of-the-money put, with a weighting of one options contract for every four futures contracts (we refer to options per one futures contract, in which case this 1:4 weighting would be written as 0.25 options per future). The solid line showing a "hockey stick" pattern illustrates the payoff of the naked option, while the jagged black line closer to the x axis illustrates the combined payoff from the futures and option position relative to the CTD. Not perfect? In fact, the resulting hedge is horrific, and the vertical gaps between the jagged line and the x axis represent a hedging error of up to 8 ticks, about one-quarter of a point. The general strategy is a good one, but the implementation needs to be refined before the tool is any use for trades. One way to do that is to borrow a tool from statistics and perform the equivalent of a linear regression.

What if we defined the vertical distance between the jagged line and the x axis as a squared value? The advantage of squaring the numbers is that they are all positive and small outliers stick out. Summing all of those squared deviations is one measure of the effectiveness of our hedge, and the process of minimizing that value is the same used in regression. If 0.25 isn't the right weighting of the first out-of-the-money put in Figure 1–7a, then maybe it should be 0.30. This change in the weighting moves the sum of squared errors from 11.7 to 12.2, which means that the hedge is less effective since the square of the vertical distance has grown. Knowing that an increase in the ratio hurts hedge effectiveness, we can go the other way and lower the ratio to 0.20, which changes the sum of squared deviations to 10.7. In this exercise we're searching for the smallest values possible, and this new weighting results in a value which is slightly better than the one resulting from our original guess. You can imagine the process going forward: iteratively searching for weightings in order to minimize the target value, which is the sum of the squared distances between the x axis and our futures plus options portfolio performance. When a weighting increases the target value, the rule could be to move the weighting in the other direction. Conceptually, we are setting the performance of these two portfolios so they are equal:

$$\text{futures} + \text{options} = \text{CTD Treasury note}$$

We said that this iterative search is borrowed from regression, because the process is similar to fitting a straight line through a cloud of values. In a simple linear regression the line always passes through the average of the x and y values, but the slope is changed so that the sum of the squared vertical distance between the regression line and the data points is minimized. One can imagine spinning a line about the average value of a cloud of data so that it's closer to some points but farther away from others. The final slope of the line is the single value to minimize the vertical difference of all the points, both above and below the line. The analogy fits in this case because all spreadsheet programs allow for a minimization routine, where values can be iteratively searched to achieve certain objectives. In the case of determining the fair value for the net basis using naked options, we are searching for option weightings so that the futures plus options portfolio best replicates the performance of the CTD.

With a single option in the available universe of hedge instruments, the best result that can be achieved is a sum of squared errors of 10.7 in the example depicted in Figure 1–7. It's impossible to determine if this value is good or bad since we have nothing to compare it to. The next step is to add in another option strike even further out-of-the-money and to search for two weightings based on the same error minimization approach. Using two options, with weightings of 0.07 and 0.17 for the first and second out-of-the-money options, the sum of squared errors falls from 10.7 to 0.008, which is near zero and an indication that we've made substantial progress in making the error as small as possible. There is an emerging tension: the more precise we make our hedge, the more moving parts are involved, and veteran traders appreciate that complexity can sometimes be a serious impediment to execution.

One way to get a handle on the basket of options that should comprise the universe of available convexity hedges is to look at history as a rough guide to future yield movements. The standard deviation of movements along the yield curve since 1990 is shown in Table 1–2.

The general pattern is that yield volatility increases as maturity falls. Since we know that 1 point in price in the 10-year futures contract equals approximately 12.5 basis points in yield, we might guess that option strikes a few points out-of-the-money would be sufficient to cover most rate movements. Table 1–2 also gives us an indication that the severity of rate movements away from current levels is necessary to study in order to calculate the futures underperformance compared to the CTD issue.

Figure 1–7b represents a convexity hedge with enough strikes to cover the most probable yield curve shifts. The drooping sold line indicates the futures

T A B L E   1–2

Volatility along the Treasury Yield Curve

2 year	314 basis points
5 year	224 basis points
10 year	150 basis points
30 year	100 basis points

TABLE 1–3

Naked Options Strikes and Weightings

Strike	Type	Ratio	Price (decimal, 'sixty-fourths)
104	Put	0.03%	0.4062, '26
100	Put	0.20%	0.0332, '2
		Total premium	0.0184, '1.2

underperformance relative to the CTD, and the upward sloping line is the payoff of the options basket that best mirrors this pattern. Finally, the wiggling thick line along the x axis is the performance of the futures and options portfolio. Table 1–3 shows the weightings on each option strike to create the upward sloping line in both charts a and b in Figure 1–7 (in this case the futures performance relative to the CTD doesn't change, only the resulting performance after we adjust for the convexity hedge using options). No deviation in this portfolio compared to the CTD is greater than 1.4 ticks, which is a relatively accurate hedge. Why go through all this trouble just to find a portfolio that breaks even across yield curve changes?

Notice that so far we've only been talking about the ratios of each option, not about their prices. It isn't an accident that we set up Table 1–3 the way we did because multiplying the ratio of each option by its market price gives us the total premium of the portfolio. The original objective was to use market prices of naked options to gauge the fair value of the delivery option, which could then be compared to the market price of the delivery option to search for discrepancies. If the total premium from the table is less than the net basis of the futures contract, then it makes sense to buy the naked options and sell the delivery option priced as the net basis for the futures contract. Since the holder of long contracts is short the option, this position would be short cash, long contracts, and long naked options, in a short basis position.

The opposite trade is always possible as well, where a trader sells the naked options and buys the delivery option by going long the basis position; but practically speaking most traders would rather sell the delivery option rather than buy it, since the traditional perception is that the delivery option is normally slightly rich to other options. Another problem is that the premium in the delivery option sale is not immediately collected, but money is spent right away on the naked options purchase. For many large accounts cash flow is not an issue, and profits or losses are the only concern. However, these same accounts definitely charge some interest rate for the debit balance caused by the mismatch in timing of the cash flows, which is a drag on the profitability of the trade. At the end of this section we examine squeezes and other periods of unusual behavior.

Positives and Negatives in Valuing Net Basis

Relying on the market price of naked options is the best and most easily defensible approach for valuing the net basis, since it involves the least modeling and manipulation of any available method. Ten years ago a search of possible weightings of naked options would have been an impractical waste of computer time, given the speed and expense of computers then in use. Potentially many thousands of different options portfolios have to be evaluated to find the one with the best fit, but computer power is becoming less expensive every day, so such extensive searches are becoming easier to implement. The only "model" involved is to determine the appropriate ratios of naked options with an empirical search based on the resulting accuracy of the hedge. Since the market prices the naked options, there's very little criticism that can be leveled at this approach: our fair value price for the net basis is based on market prices of naked options. However, there is one glaring problem with this method, which is that naked options trading at the CBOT expire approximately a month before trading stops on the Treasury contract and approximately 5 weeks before the last delivery day. What this means is that there will be some period of time when the naked options will not guard against yield curve changes. Theoretically this slight mismatch in expiration of delivery option versus naked options could lead to a small but persistent bias, in which the naked options appear slightly cheaper than delivery option, providing a false signal to sell the basis.

Practically speaking, this is rarely a problem; since so many traders use the naked options for these trades, the net basis tends to trade like a slightly shorter option than a formula like Black-Scholes (BS) might predict. One way to measure the difference is to take the BS formula and substitute the last trading day for the actual expiration, as in Table 1–4, thereby increasing the time value and perhaps compensating for the shortcomings of this approach.

It makes sense that in Table 1–4 the BS price is higher than the market price since any option is worth more if you extend its life. Because the payoff of each option remains the same, no matter its premium, we can use the original weightings to find a fair value for the net basis. In this case the fair value is 4.3 ticks, which is still below the net basis. If the net basis is above the fair value derived from either of these approaches, it's a reasonable indication that there is a mispricing and delivery option is too high. However, this "fix" by substituting a

TABLE 1–4

Black-Scholes Option Price with Longer Expiration

		Actual Expiration	Matching Contract Expiration
104	Puts	0.4062, '26	0.5758, '37
100	Puts	0.0332, '2	0.0971, '6

theoretical price for a market price abandons the most attractive part of the analysis, which is the reliance on market prices. Who knows how the market would price the naked options if their expiration actually were 5 weeks longer? There's no way to tell for sure, and as a practical matter, most traders acknowledge this shortcoming but still find value in this approach.

Another interesting question is: What time is it? This is not a trivial matter when dealing with options, because, as Table 1–4 illustrates, longer options always command higher prices than shorter options with otherwise identical characteristics. If there were some sort of mismatch between the timing of the payoffs in our minimization algorithm, it could distort the whole analysis. However, this isn't a problem if the original analysis is done with the intrinsic value of the options and the converted forward price of the deliverable basket. In both cases the instruments are evaluated at the end of the horizon, with no intrinsic value. Conversely, it's also possible to run the analysis with current prices and payoffs in the options, except it would be necessary to employ a model like Black-Scholes to determine the behavior of the option prior to expiration. The beauty of our original approach is that there is no ambiguity surrounding intrinsic value—just the difference between the current price and the strike price of each option.

It all comes down to shapes. Prior to expiration, the payoffs of a typical option across interest rate changes will look less like a hockey stick and more like a gradual arch, since the time value will smooth out the price change of the option around the threshold of moving from out-of-the-money to in-the-money. The answer to the question of timing is that it doesn't matter, as long as we capture the naked option and delivery option at the same point in time, either today or at some point in the future. Just as with the naked options, time value in the delivery option is going to create a payoff function that's somewhat curved across changes in rates, rather than simply a binary in- or out-of-the-money payoff. As long as they're captured at the same moment, the time values in the naked option and delivery option should cancel each other out.

Finally, there is a minor quirk that comes up when experimenting with different implementations to this approach, which also has to do with a timing issue. In order to search for CTD switch points, we take the Treasury notes and change their yield to search for the lowest converted forward price in the basket, recording the points where there is a switch. However, it's possible to find a slightly different set of switch points by ignoring carry and dividing the price of each deliverable Treasury by its conversion factor. The carry is the only difference between the two approaches, and the resulting differences in switch points are subtle, as reflected in Figure 1–8. Why use the converted forward price if we are trying to determine the behavior of the contract at expiration? At expiration there will be no carry and unless yields change from current levels; then the appropriate prices to use in the analysis are today's prices! By using the converted forward price we might be unintentionally introducing a yield curve reshaping that we don't intend to because one issue or another is special in the financing market and might have a very different converted forward price spread relative to the other bonds in the basket.

FIGURE 1-8

CTD switch points using alternative calculations

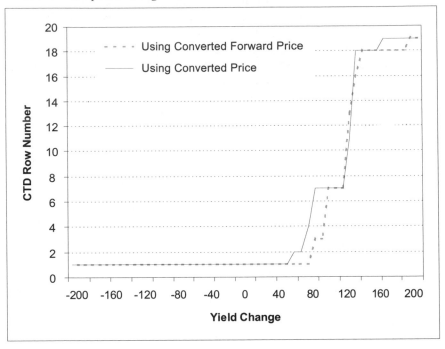

A subtle assumption is built into the convention of using converted forward prices. Typically, the yield spreads of bonds won't change significantly whether they're evaluated on a spot or forward basis, in spite of the fact that they each may have different financing rates. With different carry for each bond this could only be possible if the bonds that are special richen somewhat to account for their more advantageous carry. Traders will sometimes talk about bonds being "fair on a forward basis," which is an interesting way to describe the same phenomenon: bonds that are special in repo are also normally bid up in price. The important question is how we measure what this premium should be. One approach to estimate the yield change for a bond with a financing advantage is by the equation:

$$\text{Adjustment} = \frac{(\text{GCrate} - \text{Srate})\text{Time}}{\text{Duration}}$$

In this equation GCrate is the general collateral rate, Srate is the special rate, Time is the fraction of the year represented by the term repo rate, and Duration is the modified duration of the issue. This equation matches the dollar amount of the financing advantage to the price change of the bond. This makes sense since the holder of this bond should be willing to pay a slight premium to own a bond with a lower borrowing rate; but in order to prevent a free lunch, he or she would have to expect to give back those extra dollars earned by an increase in yield of the bond. Although it's not always the case, if a bond normally offers $100 in carry more than other similar bonds, the holder expects to give back $100 in price when the bond is no longer special. This raises an interesting question: Is it possible to go long on a bond that is special on term repo, but sell it before the financing advantage has evaporated and the price falls?

In practice, this is extremely difficult to do. It is worth mentioning in the context of futures valuation because the CTD issue sometimes behaves more predictably than most other bonds. Normally this bond will be special on term repo leading up to the delivery month, but will cheapen after the last trading day because there is less arbitrage activity. Although there is no way for a levered account using repo to take advantage of this, there are important implications for nonlevered accounts that also lend their bonds as a matter of course. Perhaps in this situation a trader could go long the bond and lend them out to a date just prior to the last trading day, swapping into a cheaper issue before trading in the futures stops. The goal, of course, is to capture the richening of the issue but not giving those dollars back up again when the trade is unwound. Although this is sometimes possible, predicting when an issue will cheapen is difficult because it doesn't depend on strictly economic factors. Over the years, the waxing and waning of perceived aggressiveness of regulators has emboldened or cowed various arbitrageurs from attempting squeezes, as we will examine in the final section of this chapter.

A Numerical Solution to the Value Delivery Option

An alternative to implementing the original concept of a proof by contradiction, where we measure the value of delivery option by studying a world where it doesn't exist, is with an interest rate tree. Rather than relying on the market price of options, which is by far the most desirable and easily defensible approach, it's possible to take some of the same information from the first example and construct an interest rate lattice to parse out the information we want. As we've mentioned before, both approaches have positive and negative characteristics, and the most important drawback with this approach is that it ignores some of the available information about naked options prices. Turning this statement on its head, though, illustrates why the lattice approach is worth considering: What if there aren't sufficient market prices of naked options available to use our first approach? In this case our replicating options model would be impossible to implement, and it would be necessary to find an alternative.

Much of the information in this second approach is based on the early stages of analysis in the replicating options model. Again, the first step is to build a price/yield table of the futures contract as if the short did not have the right to choose which issue to deliver and is stuck making delivery with the issue that is currently cheapest. In this case the price/yield of the futures contract would equal that of the cheapest issue. This is the baseline for our comparison, and once again we measure the performance of the futures contract by repricing the issues in the deliverable basket under parallel yield curve movements, taking the futures price as being equal to the lowest converted forward price in the basket. However, it's at this point that the two approaches diverge. Rather than finding a basket of options to mirror the futures underperformance relative to the CTD issue, we take the two columns of prices, one with the CTD issue fixed and one where it floats, and use them as the terminal values in an interest rate tree. Depending on how the trees are constructed, they boil the columns of prices down to a single value, and the difference between these two values constitutes the delivery option value. There are a few ambiguous steps here, and one is exactly how to construct an interest rate tree, since there are several theoretically sound approaches. We examine two simple examples from the most popular theoretical camps: equal jump sizes versus equal probabilities as illustrated in Figure 1–9.

As an aside, it's important to keep in mind that interest rate lattices and option models of this sort are popular on Wall Street, but not as popular as closed-form

FIGURE 1–9

Two binomial lattices with matching terminal values: equal probabilities and equal jump sizes

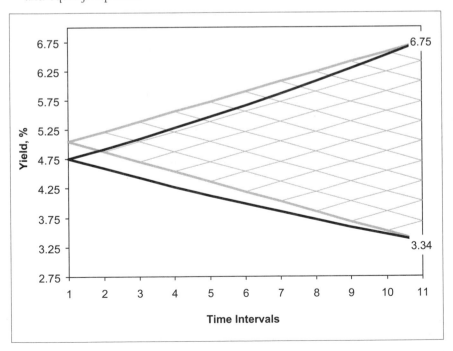

modeling, where the option is described with an equation that is computationally simple and can be described by a single formula. Taking a complicated phenomenon and making enough simplifying assumptions so that a mathematician can write a formula describing it is a cottage industry in New York. Functions can only have a limited number of degrees of freedom before they become impossibly complex and a numerical solution is necessary. Securities analysis has always been subject to a cruel reality: those with a financial interest in understanding securities are only interested in gaining enough expertise to make money. Everyone involved in conducting this research is being sponsored by a firm with an interest in the bottom line, and "good enough" is often where the work stops.

There are three major categories of valuation: replicating baskets from our first example, numerical solutions, such as we're working through now, or closed-form solutions, which we believe are largely irrelevant for trading. Unfortunately, it's the third choice that is the most popular. What few people realize is that there are many different closed-form models to price interest rate derivatives, like options on swaps, just as there are many competing methods of pricing mortgage options. In fact, if you took one model and tried to use it for another instrument, it would often yield results that are wildly different from market prices. As it turns out, each model needs to be "calibrated" to replicate market prices. The calibration process involves adding arbitrary factors to make up for the deficiencies introduced by all of the simplifying assumptions necessary to create an algebraically tractable equation. One basic question all consumers of these closed-form solutions should be asking themselves is: If the models are so good, why aren't they interchangeable between markets? If a model that prices options on swaps is "right," then why can't it be used to price options on mortgages or futures?

The answers to this question could occupy researchers for some time, but in the interim there are robust solutions that leverage technology, like the numerical solution we detail next. Research didn't go in this direction when futures were first introduced in the late 1970s because the computer power didn't exist and what was available was prohibitively expensive. Simple closed-form solutions were the only avenue open to researchers at the time. Considering that the first Apple Macintosh was only available in 1984, it's remarkable how recently significant computer power was available to evaluate these instruments. Anyone who used the first Macintosh can attest to the fact that although it was revolutionary in its implications, it was not a powerful analytical engine, and personal computers were largely irrelevant to securities analysis until the early 1990s. It took around a decade before computers became fast enough to make it possible to evaluate a horribly inefficient numerical solution, which would be somewhat realistic but extremely wasteful of computer calculations, in just a few seconds.

Once we have two columns representing the performance of the contract with and without delivery option, it's time to do something with that data. The simplest first step is to take the average of each of the series. The average of the series without delivery option, where the CTD is fixed, is 111.38. The second series, where the CTD was allowed to float as an indication of the actual performance of the contract with delivery option, is 111.16. Is 0.32 points, which is the difference between the two average values, the answer we're looking for? As it turns out, no; or only in limited situations. If the trade-off between price and yield were linear, then a simple average would be a much more palatable solution. In this case, each series is slightly curved, and price/yield doesn't move 1:1. A simple average may make sense if the yield change we're evaluating is very small, but the standard deviation work we did earlier indicated a likely yield change of 50 basis points about two-thirds of the time in the 30-year sector of the curve, and an average over these changes will be too heavily influenced by the convexity of each series. How do we get around this problem?

One way is with a binomial tree, which is an approximation of a continuous random process and helps us span the gap between the way the world looks today and how it will evolve in the future. It's not a stretch to suppose that under some situations prices will go up and that in others prices will go down. The way that we build the interest rate tree will define exactly how this is done. Suppose we break up the time period from now until the expiration of the futures contract into pieces, and at each interval we allow prices to either increase or decrease. The tension in building a tree comes from the fact that we need to either assume equal jump sizes or equal probabilities to prevent the tree from building in systematic biases over time.

Choosing equal jump sizes means that at each period we build in a chance of yields moving up or down by a fixed amount, say 5 basis points up or down. The alternative is to choose equal probability of yields moving up or down, but in this case 50% of a large yield will produce a greater basis point jump than 50% of a small yield. Figure 1–9 illustrates that the shapes of the resulting trees are difficult to convey any way other than graphically. The equal probability tree is asymmetrical in gray and ends with a value that is farther above the current level of the equal jump size tree. Both are theoretically defensible, and there's no scientific reason to choose one over the other, but, remembering that the ultimate goal of this work is to trade futures, it's useful to choose the one that best matches the market behavior.

Although it's certainly not always the case, when yields are high, volatility tends to be high, and normally the opposite is true as well. Statisticians call this phenomenon *heteroskedasticity*, meaning that the volatility changes along with the magnitude of the observations. Yield swings tend to be higher when yields are at 12% than they are when yields are at 4%. Figure 1–10 makes the story concrete. During the 1980s 10-year Treasury yields were relatively high, around 11% on average, and the average standard deviation of the series was 2.25%. From 1990 to 2000 yields were much lower, at around 6% on average. The measurement of standard deviation is consistent with our story, at just 1.06%. This pattern is clearly consistent with a constant percentage change approach than it is with an equal jump size model. The equal jump size model would have made the standard deviations equal in both periods, which probably would have underestimated the volatility in the 1980s and overestimated it in the 1990s.

FIGURE 1–10

Example of heteroskedasticity in 10-year Treasury yields

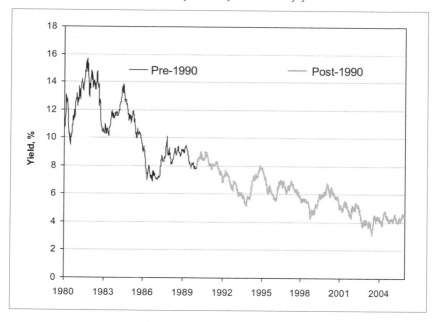

Figures 1–11 and 1–12 illustrate our implementation of two sets of interest rate tree approaches. Both sets of trees contain a matrix of values allowing the CTD issue to change and one where the CTD cannot change, which is the baseline for our analysis. Neither tree is "discounting" the prices, and it's a mistake to imply they do since the terminal values we're interested in are converted forward prices based on today's yield levels. It would be convenient if we could use the same baseline CTD performance in each case, but notice that the two columns of terminal values to the far right are not exactly equal, even though they are measuring the same process, which is the performance of the contract without delivery option. Although the process is the same, it's being evaluated at different yield levels. The equal probability and equal jump size trees produce different results even though they use the same volatility input. It's important to take a moment to illustrate the differences of futures performance without delivery option. The difference in values indicates just how important, and how arbitrary, the choice of a rate tree is.

One thing New Yorkers are not is self-conscious. The fact that so much finance is done in New York influences the entire industry, which certainly includes the style of analysis. Unfortunately, this philosophy has seeped its way into the work on Wall Street. Analysts may guarantee that there is a right and

FIGURE 1–11

Delivery option valuation using equal jump-size lattice

Rate Tree

0	1	2	3	4	5	6	7	8	9	10
4.75	4.92	5.10	5.28	5.47	5.66	5.86	6.07	6.29	6.51	6.75
	4.59	4.75	4.92	5.10	5.28	5.47	5.66	5.86	6.07	6.29
		4.43	4.59	4.75	4.92	5.10	5.28	5.47	5.66	5.86
			4.28	4.43	4.59	4.75	4.92	5.10	5.28	5.47
				4.13	4.28	4.43	4.59	4.75	4.92	5.10
					3.99	4.13	4.28	4.43	4.59	4.75
						3.85	3.99	4.13	4.28	4.43
							3.72	3.85	3.99	4.13
								3.59	3.72	3.85
									3.46	3.59
										3.34

CTD Fixed

113.02	111.0	109.0	107.0	105.0	103.0	100.9	98.7	96.5	94.3	92.4
	114.8	112.8	110.8	108.8	106.8	104.8	102.8	100.7	98.4	96.0
		116.5	114.5	112.5	110.5	108.5	106.5	104.6	102.7	100.5
			118.2	116.2	114.2	112.2	110.2	108.2	106.3	104.5
				119.8	117.9	116.0	114.0	111.9	109.8	107.9
					121.5	119.6	117.7	115.8	113.8	111.4
						123.1	121.2	119.4	117.5	116.0
							124.6	122.8	120.9	118.8
								126.2	124.5	122.8
									127.6	125.9
										129.1

0.17, 5.4 ticks

CTD Floating

112.85	110.7	108.5	106.1	103.3	100.2	96.3	91.3	85.1	77.8	70.4
	114.7	112.7	110.6	108.4	106.2	103.7	100.8	97.0	91.8	84.5
		116.5	114.5	112.5	110.4	108.4	106.3	104.2	101.7	98.6
			118.2	116.2	114.2	112.2	110.2	108.2	106.3	104.5
				119.8	117.9	116.0	114.0	111.9	109.8	107.9
					121.5	119.6	117.7	115.8	113.8	111.4
						123.1	121.2	119.4	117.5	116.0
							124.6	122.8	120.9	118.8
								126.2	124.5	122.8
									127.6	125.9
										129.1

wrong way to construct an interest rate tree, granted of course that they have to make a handful of choices when deciding on an approach. It's not often that anyone starts a meeting by saying, "I tossed a coin before I walked in here, and everything else I'm going to tell you hinges on the fact that it came up 'heads.'"

F I G U R E   1–12

Delivery option valuation using equal probability lattice

Rate Tree

0	1	2	3	4	5	6	7	8	9	10
5.05	5.22	5.39	5.56	5.73	5.90	6.07	6.24	6.41	6.58	6.75
	4.88	5.05	5.22	5.39	5.56	5.73	5.90	6.07	6.24	6.41
		4.71	4.88	5.05	5.22	5.39	5.56	5.73	5.90	6.07
			4.54	4.71	4.88	5.05	5.22	5.39	5.56	5.73
				4.36	4.54	4.71	4.88	5.05	5.22	5.39
					4.19	4.36	4.54	4.71	4.88	5.05
						4.02	4.19	4.36	4.54	4.71
							3.85	4.02	4.19	4.36
								3.68	3.85	4.02
									3.51	3.68
										3.34

CTD Fixed

108.84	107.0	105.2	103.4	101.7	100.0	98.3	96.8	95.3	93.8	92.4
	110.7	108.8	107.0	105.2	103.4	101.6	99.9	98.3	96.7	95.3
		112.5	110.6	108.8	107.0	105.2	103.4	101.5	99.8	98.2
			114.4	112.5	110.6	108.8	107.0	105.2	103.3	101.3
				116.4	114.4	112.4	110.5	108.8	107.0	105.4
					118.5	116.3	114.3	112.3	110.5	108.7
						120.6	118.4	116.2	114.1	112.3
							122.7	120.6	118.4	116.0
								124.9	122.8	120.8
									126.9	124.8
										129.1

↑
0.50, 16 ticks
↓

CTD Floating

108.34	106.2	103.9	101.4	98.5	95.2	91.3	86.8	81.6	76.0	70.4
	110.5	108.5	106.4	104.3	101.9	99.1	95.9	92.0	87.3	81.6
		112.5	110.5	108.6	106.7	104.6	102.4	99.8	96.7	93.0
			114.4	112.5	110.6	108.7	106.9	104.9	102.8	100.3
				116.4	114.4	112.4	110.5	108.8	107.0	105.4
					118.5	116.3	114.3	112.3	110.5	108.7
						120.6	118.4	116.2	114.1	112.3
							122.7	120.6	118.4	116.0
								124.9	122.8	120.8
									126.9	124.8
										129.1

U factor 0.17

Figure 1–10 proves the point that there are many different theoretically consistent approaches and mere judgment is often the only guide. In this case both binomial tree implementations are theoretically correct, but they produce major differences in price, as much as 10.6 ticks in this example, which is the difference between 16 and 5.4 ticks. In an environment where the bid/ask spread is normally just one-quarter tick, how could anyone sleep at night knowing that legitimate alternative models produce valuations 40 times what they would normally pay in the bid/ask spread? The construction of the tree is the Achilles heel of this approach, but it's not without merit in situations where a robust naked option market isn't available.

There is a small trick in the numbers listed in Figures 1–11 and 1–12, which underscores just how easy it can be to go awry with this type of valuation approach. We first listed the same terminal values on the right-hand side to feed into the trees and calculated that the difference between the two valuation approaches was 10.6. This value highlights the difference between the mathematics of the two, given the same input, but it ignores the fact that the equal probability tree should end with a higher yield than the equal jump size tree. Conceptually, the values in Figures 1–11 and 1–12 move from right to left, and the inputs are taken "backward" through time to arrive at a price today. The reality is that we need to begin with today's yield, go forward in time to determine at what yield levels we should be evaluating the futures contract, and then use the trees to go backward in time to arrive at a futures contract price.

Figure 1–13 does just that, and it's evident that the yield levels at the rightmost portion of the trees are different from those in Figure 1–9. Of course, these different

FIGURE   1–13

Two binomial lattices with different terminal values

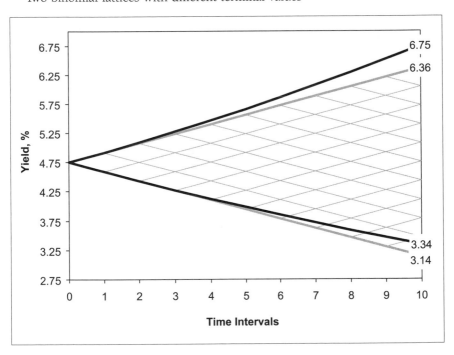

input values are going to result in different output values, and while the results of the lattice using equal jump size in Figure 1–12 don't change, the equal probability lattice results are even lower than they were the first time around in Figure 1–11. The calculated value in Figure 1–14 falls from 5.4 to just 3.8 ticks, and

F I G U R E   1–14

New delivery option valuation using equal jump-size lattice

Rate Tree

0	1	2	3	4	5	6	7	8	9	10
4.75	4.92	5.09	5.26	5.43	5.60	5.77	5.94	6.11	6.28	6.45
	4.58	4.75	4.92	5.09	5.26	5.43	5.60	5.77	5.94	6.11
		4.41	4.58	4.75	4.92	5.09	5.26	5.43	5.60	5.77
			4.24	4.41	4.58	4.75	4.92	5.09	5.26	5.43
				4.07	4.24	4.41	4.58	4.75	4.92	5.09
					3.90	4.07	4.24	4.41	4.58	4.75
						3.73	3.90	4.07	4.24	4.41
							3.56	3.73	3.90	4.07
								3.39	3.56	3.73
									3.22	3.39
										3.05

CTD Fixed

111.92	110.0	108.1	106.3	104.6	102.8	101.1	99.4	97.7	96.0	94.5
	113.8	111.9	109.9	108.1	106.3	104.5	102.9	101.2	99.4	97.5
		115.8	113.8	111.8	109.9	108.0	106.2	104.6	102.9	101.3
			117.9	115.8	113.7	111.7	109.8	107.9	106.2	104.5
				119.9	117.8	115.8	113.7	111.6	109.6	107.9
					122.1	119.9	117.8	115.8	113.7	111.4
						124.2	122.0	119.8	117.9	116.0
							126.5	124.1	121.8	119.8
								128.8	126.4	123.8
									131.3	129.1
										133.5

0.12, 3.8 ticks

CTD Floating

111.80	109.8	107.7	105.7	103.4	101.0	98.1	94.5	90.0	84.6	78.7
	113.8	111.8	109.8	107.9	105.9	103.9	101.6	98.9	95.5	90.6
		115.8	113.8	111.8	109.8	107.9	106.1	104.3	102.4	100.3
			117.9	115.8	113.7	111.7	109.8	107.9	106.2	104.5
				119.9	117.8	115.8	113.7	111.6	109.6	107.9
					122.1	119.9	117.8	115.8	113.7	111.4
						124.2	122.0	119.8	117.9	116.0
							126.5	124.1	121.8	119.8
								128.8	126.4	123.8
									131.3	129.1
										133.5

although the process generating the input values for the calculation doesn't change, the new lattice is capturing different prices from that process. In this case there happened to be fewer switch points when the series is measured along a rate spectrum from 3.05% to 6.45%, compared to the original spectrum from 3.34% to 6.75%. Twisting and turning through various approaches should illustrate that even though the work is analytical, it reflects the opinions and considerations of the modeler.

The wild card option is another aspect of the delivery option worth noting, although at practice traders routinely ignore it. Notes or bonds that are delivered at the beginning of an expiration month rather than the end in a positive carry market are noteworthy for a number of different reasons, none of which include the wild card option, chatter about which fills the market. First and foremost, early deliveries are significant because they signal that there is a limit on how rich a contract can become before basis sellers find some way to take advantage of it. Sometimes contracts have been so rich that it was possible to pay up to 10 ticks for the prompt delivery cost to take possession of a note in the financing market, fail to deliver the bonds back, forgo carry from now to the end of the month, and use those notes to deliver into contracts at the end of the month.

It is likely that some of the holders of long contracts never intend to go through delivery and are just trading the calendar spread, but their presence sometimes keeps open interest "artificially" high during the last few weeks of trading. Although there is always the theoretical risk of early delivery during the last 3 weeks of trading, it rarely happens in positive carry markets. Holders of long contracts routinely pay lip service to this risk, without taking it seriously. If any of these holders of long contracts didn't intend to take delivery, they would certainly not be interested in holding on to the notes or bonds, and may deliver them back out to the market as soon as they receive them, which can then be used to satisfy other deliveries, and so on. In this way it's possible that notes that are delivered early may end up satisfying many times their value in repo failures.

Why is the wild card option sometimes the talk of the town? To understand why, it's important to review the mechanics of the option. This option enables the holder of short contracts to wait until 8 p.m. Chicago time to decide whether or not he is going to make delivery using the 2 p.m. closing price. Suppose this holder of short contracts is also conversion factor weighting his trade, so that he is short less than 1,000 contracts for every $100 million face of the issue he is long. Since deliveries are made 1:1 with a face value that matches the notional value of contracts, the holder of a long basis position has more cash Treasury notes than he is going to make delivery with, and this "tail" must be sold. Suppose further that there is a significant rally in the market after the futures close, and the value of this tail increases enough to offset the carry that could be earned by holding onto the bonds. One can imagine a scenario where the conversion factor is low enough, and the rally after 2 p.m. is big enough, so that the tail is worth

FIGURE 1-15

Inter-day yield changes for CTD issue

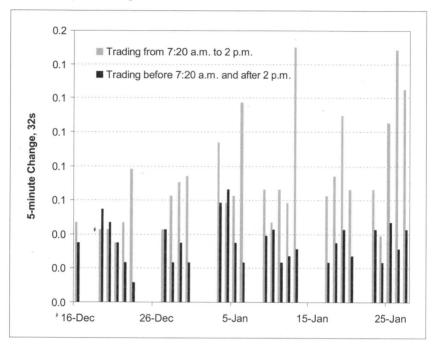

more than the carry that is given up by delivering early. Why discount this possibility?

Figure 1–15 illustrates the inter-day yield changes for the Aug '12, which was the cheapest-to-deliver note for two cycles in 2005 for the 10-year note contract. The dark-shaded bars highlight the price action between 2 p.m. Chicago time and the end of the trading day in New York, at 4 p.m. Visual inspection illustrates much less volatility in the cash market after the futures close, which makes sense. If futures are often the hedge against cash Treasury positions, why would anyone want to take the risk of assuming large positions without a way to offset that risk? The average trading day price volatility has been more than 2.6 times as volatile as during the "night" session, which begins after the 2 p.m. close in Chicago, and Table 1–5 shows that the chances of the wild card option being in-the-money is near zero. If carry from today to the end of the month is approximately equal to 1 tick, then it's necessary for the price to move by 11.2 ticks for gain on the tail to offset forgone carry because of early delivery. Given the price volatility we calculate, an 11.2 tick move would be approximately 7.5 standard deviations during the last two hours of the trading day, and the probability of this move is zero (to 10 decimal places). Why spend time worrying about something so unlikely to happen?

TABLE 1-5

Is a Wild Card Option Likely to Have Value?

Aug '12 Conversion Factor: 0.9108
Tail: $1 - 0.9108 = 0.0892$
5-minute standard deviation ticks: 0.304
2-hour standard deviation, ticks: 1.5

BASIS MATRIX

Fair value models are important to people who require consistent exposure to the market, and regardless of whether they're right or wrong about predicting the absolute price of the contract, it's the relative changes and sensitivities that traders are often looking for. These types of strategies necessitate rolling from one contract month to the next, never letting any single contract expire. However, a different style of analysis is necessary for arbitrage traders who use considerable leverage in their positions and might have to go through delivery to enforce fair value on the contract. Remember that in futures no initial cash flow is necessary to initiate a long or short position except for margin. In this case there are two values to consider before buying or selling the basis: the market value of delivery option and the intrinsic value of the option at expiration. What constitutes intrinsic value for delivery option? Answering this question requires a deeper understanding of delivery option, including nonparallel changes to the yield curve. Rather than twist the models we developed so that they work in a way that wasn't originally intended, we return to first principles and start from scratch.

The very first example in the book was to calculate a forward price from a cash price and then search for the cheapest issue within a basket of Treasury notes. How did we know it was the cheapest issue? Without evaluating the converted forward price for every bond eligible for delivery, it's impossible to know which one is the cheapest. It's all relative! As it turns out, even the prices of the issues that aren't cheapest tell us information about how to value the contract. Specifically, the differences in converted forward prices allow us to measure when a particular issue will become the cheapest issue and in what rate environment. Building a matrix of all these switch points allows us to visually interpret the payoff for various basis trades under a vast array of yield curve scenarios. A basis matrix measures changes in two dimensions, the level of rates and slope of the curve, but it ignores changes in curvature. It might appear as if this is a significant omission, but this third type of reshaping has accounted for only about 1% of all Treasury yield curve movements over the past decade.

What makes an issue the "cheapest" is that its converted forward price is lowest compared to all of the others in the basket. In fact, this is the most reliable way of identifying the issue, rather than calculating an implied repo rate or searching for

TABLE 1-6

Net Basis Values for Each Issue

Issue Maturity	BNOC	BNOC – CTD
5/15/2013	10.0	0.0
8/15/2013	12.2	2.2
11/15/2013	21.0	11.0
2/15/2014	29.4	19.4
5/15/2014	36.4	26.4
8/15/2014	45.7	35.7
11/15/2014	53.8	43.8
2/15/2015	64.7	54.7
5/15/2015	72.2	62.2
8/15/2015	79.8	69.8
11/15/2015	93.5	83.5

the lowest net basis, which sometimes gives contradictory results. While our initial analysis ignored the prices of the other bonds, once it is determined that they are not the cheapest issue, this is the starting point in building a basis matrix.

Consider Table 1–6, which illustrates the net basis for every issue in the 10-year futures contract. The net basis for May '13 is the lowest at 10; then there is a 2.2-tick jump to Aug '13, which is the next longest and second cheapest issue, then 8.8 ticks to the third cheapest. As we mentioned before, an increase in interest rates will cheapen the longer maturity issues faster than the shorter maturities, and as interest rates rise, the price spread between the net bases in Table 1–6 will fall. Obviously, there will be a point where interest rates could rise so much that one of the longer issues would have the lowest converted price and become CTD. Whenever there is a CTD switch, delivery option begins to have some intrinsic value, because the right of the holder of short contracts to substitute issues has value, and the holder can choose to deliver whichever issue she pleases besides the one that was initially cheapest under the old rate scenario. One might say that the strike price of delivery option is the point where there is a CTD switch point.

The fact that we can find the point where delivery option swings from expiring worthless to having some value doesn't tell us how to value the option, but it does hint at how we might do so. In this example, yields are rising so that the shortest issue isn't cheapest any more, and we have already said that the futures contract mirrors the performance of the cheapest issue as it moves farther out the curve in bear market moves. Of course, the net basis for the cheapest issue is always zero at expiration (by definition), but what about the net basis for other issues? Rather than tracking the futures performance as it mirrors the performance of longer issues, we can track the net basis for our original CTD issue and begin to measure differences between bonds as they gain or lose CTD status. If we sell delivery option in a short basis trade, we don't know what's going to happen to interest rates between now and expiration, but we can measure how much lower the net basis could have been if we had chosen a non-CTD issue but were fortunate enough to have that issue become CTD in the future.

For example, Figure 1–16 shows the same pattern of net bases as in Table 1–6, except that at each point we've subtracted the net basis of the cheapest issue. If interest rates didn't change, this is the incremental cost of delivering each issue. Put another way, suppose we sold delivery option today. The most we could hope to earn in this situation is 100% of the option premium, which is represented by the net basis in Table 1–6. However, if interest rates rise enough, another issue will become cheapest and the net basis for our original issue will rise, as shown in the dark lines of Figure 1–16. This is equivalent to the intrinsic value of the delivery option, which is the price we have to pay to buy back the option at expiration. If we sell delivery option for 5 ticks, of course we want it to expire worthless, in which case we could buy it back for 0 ticks.

There is another line in Figure 1–16 which shows that interest rates can rise to such an extent that we would have to buy back delivery option on the Aug '12

FIGURE 1–16

Net basis yields are low for short issues when values are low, and the opposite is true as well

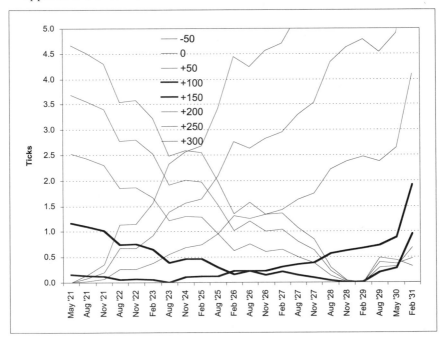

issue at 5 ticks, which is equal to the price we sold it at. This is the breakeven point on the trade where the intrinsic value of delivery option equals the premium we collected for selling the option. The only problem is that unlike other options, we don't collect any premium up front from selling delivery option! The net basis usually decays like any other option, but there are periods when the value of the net basis is only enforceable through delivery (we'll follow up on this point again at the end of the chapter). Imagine constructing a column of these net bases for the original cheapest issue at various yield increments, say every 5 basis points, and charting them. Remembering that if we are evaluating the basket of Treasuries under parallel yield changes, we might label this the "zero" column, denoting no change in the slope of rates, but only changes in the level.

What would happen if we twisted the yield curve, steepening it by 5 basis points and repeated the exercise? Returning to our original rules, we know that a steeper curve is going to cheapen the longer maturity bonds more than the shorter maturity issues, making them more likely to become the cheapest issue. These rules provide an intuitive understanding of the behavior of the contract, and knowing them lets us predict that a 5-basis-point steeper curve should move us closer to a switch of the cheapest issue. Of course, the opposite is true if we shock the curve and make it flatter in 5-basis-point increments. What we're left with is a two-dimensional representation of the payoff by selling delivery option when Aug '12 is the cheapest issue; these values are graphed in Figure 1–17a. Since it's the shortest issue in the basket, a rally in rates or flattening of the curve can't shift the CTD issue to any shorter maturities, and the values in the lower left-hand portion of the matrix are all zero, indicating that delivery option expires worthless at these points, and Aug '12 remains cheapest.

Toward the upper right-hand corner of the matrix it's a different story. In bear steepening scenarios the CTD switch points come one after another, and the maturity of the CTD issue (and duration of the contract) extends dramatically. In these scenarios, the option we're short ends up with quite a bit of intrinsic value, and the shading shows where the premium we collect in the form of the net basis is equal to or higher than the intrinsic value of the option. This shaded portion is like struggling in the surf at a beach where there's still hope of reaching shore, but it's clear the currents are dangerously close to carrying you out to sea! The worst thing that can happen to a short option position is for the market to race to a spot in the unshaded area, which is where the intrinsic value of delivery option is greater than the premium we collect via the net basis. Of course, these are the scenarios where a short delivery option position loses money.

To highlight the extension in duration and switch of the cheapest issue, we repeat the analysis in Figure 1–17b, but instead of recording the net basis for the CTD issue at each level of rates and slope of the curve, we record which issue is cheapest. Predictably, in bear-steepening moves the maturity of the cheapest issue increases, but this matrix shows just how bad the situation can get for a delivery-option seller caught in an unexpected rate move. In just a few dozen basis points the maturity of the cheapest issue in the 30-year basket can jump from a 15-year

FIGURE 1-17a

Net basis values at expiration using the 100% shortest issue

30y	Flatter					10s/30s Slope			Steeper					
	-10	-5	0	5	10	15	20	25	30	35	40	45	50	55
5.50	0	0	0	0	0	1	2	7	14	31	54	80	105	130
5.45	0	0	0	0	0	0	1	4	11	26	48	74	99	124
5.40	0	0	0	0	0	0	1	3	8	21	41	68	94	119
5.35	0	0	0	0	0	0	1	2	5	16	35	61	88	113
5.30	0	0	0	0	0	0	0	1	4	12	29	55	82	108
5.25	0	0	0	0	0	0	0	1	2	8	23	49	76	102
5.20	0	0	0	0	0	0	0	1	1	5	18	42	69	96
5.15	0	0	0	0	0	0	0	0	1	3	13	36	63	90
5.10	0	0	0	0	0	0	0	0	1	2	9	29	56	84
5.05	0	0	0	0	0	0	0	0	1	1	6	22	50	77
5.00	0	0	0	0	0	0	0	0	0	1	3	16	43	71
4.95	0	0	0	0	0	0	0	0	0	1	2	11	36	64
4.90	0	0	0	0	0	0	0	0	0	1	1	8	29	58
4.85	0	0	0	0	0	0	0	0	0	0	1	4	22	51
4.80	0	0	0	0	0	0	0	0	0	0	1	2	15	44
4.75	0	0	0	0	0	0	0	0	0	0	1	1	9	37
4.70	0	0	0	0	0	0	0	0	0	0	1	1	6	30
4.65	0	0	0	0	0	0	0	0	0	0	0	1	3	23
4.60	0	0	0	0	0	0	0	0	0	0	0	1	1	15
4.55	0	0	0	0	0	0	0	0	0	0	0	1	1	8
4.50	0	0	0	0	0	0	0	0	0	0	0	0	1	4
4.45	0	0	0	0	0	0	0	0	0	0	0	0	1	1
4.40	0	0	0	0	0	0	0	0	0	0	0	0	1	1
4.35	0	0	0	0	0	0	0	0	0	0	0	0	0	1
4.30	0	0	0	0	0	0	0	0	0	0	0	0	0	1

FIGURE 1-17b

Matrix indicating the CTD issue for each scenario

30y	Flatter					10s/30s Slope			Steeper						
	-10	-5	0	5	10	15	20	25	30	35	40	45	50	55	60
5.50	5/21	5/21	5/21	5/21	8/21	8/21	8/22	8/23	8/25	8/27	2/29	5/30	5/30	5/30	5/30
5.45	5/21	5/21	5/21	5/21	5/21	8/21	8/22	8/22	8/25	8/27	5/30	5/30	5/30	5/30	5/30
5.40	5/21	5/21	5/21	5/21	5/21	8/21	8/21	8/22	8/23	8/27	8/29	5/30	5/30	5/30	5/30
5.35	5/21	5/21	5/21	5/21	5/21	8/21	8/21	8/22	8/23	11/26	8/29	5/30	5/30	5/30	5/30
5.30	5/21	5/21	5/21	5/21	5/21	5/21	8/21	8/21	8/22	8/25	8/29	5/30	5/30	5/30	5/30
5.25	5/21	5/21	5/21	5/21	5/21	5/21	8/21	8/21	8/22	8/25	8/27	5/30	5/30	5/30	5/30
5.20	5/21	5/21	5/21	5/21	5/21	5/21	8/21	8/21	8/21	2/25	8/27	5/30	5/30	5/30	5/30
5.15	5/21	5/21	5/21	5/21	5/21	5/21	5/21	8/21	8/21	8/22	8/26	5/30	5/30	5/30	5/30
5.10	5/21	5/21	5/21	5/21	5/21	5/21	5/21	8/21	8/21	8/21	2/25	5/30	5/30	5/30	5/30
5.05	5/21	5/21	5/21	5/21	5/21	5/21	5/21	8/21	8/21	8/21	2/25	5/30	5/30	5/30	5/30
5.00	5/21	5/21	5/21	5/21	5/21	5/21	5/21	5/21	8/21	8/21	2/25	8/27	5/30	5/30	5/30
4.95	5/21	5/21	5/21	5/21	5/21	5/21	5/21	5/21	8/21	8/21	8/21	8/26	5/30	5/30	5/30
4.90	5/21	5/21	5/21	5/21	5/21	5/21	5/21	5/21	8/21	8/21	8/21	2/25	5/30	5/30	5/30
4.85	5/21	5/21	5/21	5/21	5/21	5/21	5/21	5/21	5/21	8/21	8/21	2/25	5/30	5/30	5/30
4.80	5/21	5/21	5/21	5/21	5/21	5/21	5/21	5/21	5/21	8/21	8/21	8/21	5/30	5/30	5/30
4.75	5/21	5/21	5/21	5/21	5/21	5/21	5/21	5/21	5/21	8/21	8/21	8/21	2/25	5/30	5/30
4.70	5/21	5/21	5/21	5/21	5/21	5/21	5/21	5/21	5/21	5/21	8/21	8/21	2/25	5/30	5/30
4.65	5/21	5/21	5/21	5/21	5/21	5/21	5/21	5/21	5/21	5/21	8/21	8/21	2/25	5/30	5/30
4.60	5/21	5/21	5/21	5/21	5/21	5/21	5/21	5/21	5/21	5/21	8/21	8/21	8/21	5/30	5/30
4.55	5/21	5/21	5/21	5/21	5/21	5/21	5/21	5/21	5/21	5/21	5/21	8/21	8/21	5/30	5/30
4.50	5/21	5/21	5/21	5/21	5/21	5/21	5/21	5/21	5/21	5/21	5/21	8/21	8/21	2/25	5/30
4.45	5/21	5/21	5/21	5/21	5/21	5/21	5/21	5/21	5/21	5/21	5/21	8/21	8/21	8/21	5/30
4.40	5/21	5/21	5/21	5/21	5/21	5/21	5/21	5/21	5/21	5/21	5/21	5/21	8/21	8/21	5/30
4.35	5/21	5/21	5/21	5/21	5/21	5/21	5/21	5/21	5/21	5/21	5/21	5/21	8/21	8/21	5/30
4.30	5/21	5/21	5/21	5/21	5/21	5/21	5/21	5/21	5/21	5/21	5/21	5/21	8/21	8/21	2/25

note to a 30-year note, representing a move from the very shortest to very longest issues in the 30-year basket. Of course, we can choose any issue to sell against the contracts in a short basis position, and we're not limited solely to trading the cheapest issue in the basket. As a practical consideration, liquidity is better for the CTD issue than any other off-the-run bond, and the two most active points of trading on the Treasury curve are the on-the-run issue and futures CTD points.

Figures 1–17a and 1–17b illustrate the net basis for the shortest issue in the basket, but what do the same calculations look like for the longest issue in the basket? Figure 1–18 illustrates the net basis at expiration for the second longest issue in the basket, the "old" on-the-run bond, which is the bond issued prior to the current on-the-run issue. As we've mentioned before, Feb '31 is the on-the-run bond at the time of this writing, but it is too rich to be cheapest under the rate scenarios shown. In this scenario it's clear that bear-steepening moves, in the upper right-hand corner of the matrix, help the position, while bull-flattening moves pull the cheapest issue farther down on the yield curve and hurt the basis trade using the on-the-run issue. This much we could have guessed based on first principles regarding the movement of the cheapest issue. What we couldn't have guessed is that there is no "cushion" for rates to move before there is a change in the basis and notice that there are no "flat" parts of this surface, where all of the values are the same until our chosen issue is CTD. In the matrix of values for the cheapest issue there was a large portion where the values were all the same, at zero, indicating that rates could move anywhere in this area without changing the ultimate payoff of the trade. It's a different story when we are dealing with selling a noncheapest basis. This is an important characteristic of the contract: when you use an issue that isn't cheapest, there is always a change in the basis until the bond itself becomes the cheapest issue. Figure 1–17 illustrates that rates could move anywhere in the bottom left-hand corner without changing the result; delivery option would expire worthless, and the short seller of basis would collect the entire net basis.

Using a bond that isn't cheapest to buy or sell against the contract means that the payoff is always changing, until that bond becomes the cheapest issue. Figure 1–18 illustrates this by showing that the net basis values are constantly changing everywhere in the matrix except for the upper right corner, when the on-the-run bond becomes cheapest. The fact that noncheapest bonds are constantly engaged in producing profit or loss makes them look a lot like outright long or short positions. This isn't necessarily a problem, and in fact it's a characteristic that can be exploited, as we'll see later on. Before learning how to exploit this characteristic, we consider the payoffs for the final case, when an issue is in the middle of the deliverable basket.

The matrix in Figure 1–19 illustrates the payoffs for selling an issue that's in the middle of the deliverable basket. Rather than the lower left-hand corner or the top right-hand being the comfortable places where a delivery option seller is able to collect the whole net basis, there is a relatively narrow diagonal channel where delivery option expires worthless and the seller is able to collect the whole

FIGURE 1–18

Net basis values at expiration using the second-to-longest issue

	Flatter					10s/30s Slope			Steeper						
30y	-10	-5	0	5	10	15	20	25	30	35	40	45	50	55	60
5.50	196	170	144	119	94	70	48	28	11	3	0	0	0	0	0
5.45	204	177	151	126	101	76	53	32	14	3	0	0	0	0	0
5.40	212	185	159	133	108	83	59	37	17	4	0	0	0	0	0
5.35	220	193	166	140	115	89	65	42	21	6	0	0	0	0	0
5.30	228	201	174	148	122	96	71	47	25	9	1	0	0	0	0
5.25	237	209	182	155	129	103	78	54	30	11	1	0	0	0	0
5.20	245	217	190	163	136	110	85	60	36	14	2	0	0	0	0
5.15	254	226	198	171	144	117	92	67	42	19	4	0	0	0	0
5.10	263	234	206	179	151	125	99	73	48	24	6	0	0	0	0
5.05	272	243	214	187	159	132	106	80	55	30	10	0	0	0	0
5.00	281	252	223	195	167	140	113	87	62	37	13	0	0	0	0
4.95	290	261	232	203	175	148	121	94	68	43	18	1	0	0	0
4.90	299	270	240	212	183	155	128	101	75	50	25	5	0	0	0
4.85	309	279	249	220	192	163	136	109	82	56	31	9	0	0	0
4.80	319	288	258	229	200	172	144	116	89	63	38	13	0	0	0
4.75	328	298	267	238	208	180	152	124	97	70	44	19	0	0	0
4.70	338	298	277	247	217	188	160	132	104	77	51	25	4	0	0
4.65	349	317	286	256	226	197	168	140	112	84	58	32	7	0	0
4.60	359	327	296	265	235	205	176	148	120	92	65	39	13	0	0
4.55	369	337	306	275	244	214	185	156	127	99	72	46	20	0	0
4.50	380	348	316	284	253	223	193	164	135	107	79	52	26	2	0
4.45	391	358	326	294	263	232	202	173	144	115	87	60	33	7	0
4.40	402	369	336	304	272	241	211	181	152	123	95	67	40	14	0
4.35	413	379	346	314	282	251	220	190	160	131	102	74	47	20	0
4.30	424	390	357	324	292	260	229	199	169	139	110	82	54	27	1

FIGURE 1–19

Net basis values using a bond with maturity in the middle of the basket

	Flatter					10s/30s Slope			Steeper						
30y	-10	-5	0	5	10	15	20	25	30	35	40	45	50	55	60
5.50	2	2	1	1	0	0	1	5	12	29	52	76	101	126	150
5.45	3	2	1	1	0	0	0	3	9	23	45	71	96	120	145
5.40	3	2	2	1	0	0	0	2	6	18	39	65	90	115	139
5.35	3	2	2	1	1	0	0	1	4	13	33	59	84	110	134
5.30	3	3	2	1	1	0	0	0	2	10	27	53	79	104	129
5.25	4	3	2	2	1	0	0	0	1	6	21	46	73	98	124
5.20	4	3	2	2	1	1	0	0	0	3	16	40	67	93	118
5.15	4	3	3	2	1	1	0	0	0	1	11	34	60	87	112
5.10	4	4	3	2	2	1	0	0	0	0	7	27	54	81	107
5.05	5	4	3	3	2	1	1	0	0	0	4	20	48	75	101
5.00	5	4	3	3	2	1	1	0	0	0	1	14	41	68	95
4.95	5	4	4	3	2	2	1	0	0	0	0	8	35	62	89
4.90	5	5	4	3	3	2	1	1	0	0	0	5	28	56	83
4.85	6	5	4	3	3	2	1	1	0	0	0	2	21	49	76
4.80	6	5	4	4	3	2	2	1	0	0	0	0	14	42	70
4.75	6	5	5	4	3	3	2	1	1	0	0	0	7	35	63
4.70	6	6	5	4	4	3	2	1	1	0	0	0	4	28	57
4.65	7	6	5	4	4	3	2	2	1	0	0	0	1	21	50
4.60	7	6	5	5	4	3	3	2	1	1	0	0	0	14	43
4.55	7	6	6	5	4	4	3	2	2	1	0	0	0	7	36
4.50	7	7	6	5	5	4	3	2	2	1	0	0	0	2	29
4.45	8	7	6	6	5	4	3	3	2	1	1	0	0	0	22
4.40	8	7	7	6	5	4	4	3	2	2	1	0	0	0	14
4.35	8	8	7	6	5	5	4	3	2	2	1	0	0	0	7
4.30	9	8	7	6	6	5	4	3	3	2	1	1	0	0	0

FIGURE 1–20

Net basis values using a mix of issues, 75% CTD, and 25% longest issue

| | Flatter | | | | | 10s/30s Slope | | | Steeper | | | | | | |
30y	-10	-5	0	5	10	15	20	25	30	35	40	45	50	55	60
5.50	49	42	36	30	23	18	14	12	14	24	41	60	79	97	116
5.45	51	44	38	31	25	19	14	11	12	20	36	55	74	93	112
5.40	53	46	40	33	27	21	15	11	10	17	31	51	70	89	108
5.35	55	48	42	35	29	22	17	12	9	13	26	46	66	85	104
5.30	57	50	44	37	30	24	18	13	9	11	22	41	61	81	100
5.25	59	52	45	39	32	26	20	14	9	9	18	37	57	76	96
5.20	61	54	47	41	34	28	21	16	10	7	14	32	52	72	91
5.15	63	56	49	43	36	29	23	17	11	7	11	27	47	67	87
5.10	66	59	52	45	38	31	25	18	13	7	8	22	42	63	83
5.05	68	61	54	47	40	33	26	20	14	9	7	16	37	58	78
5.00	70	63	56	49	42	35	28	22	16	10	6	12	32	53	74
4.95	73	65	58	51	44	37	30	24	17	11	6	8	27	48	69
4.90	75	67	60	53	46	39	32	25	19	13	7	7	22	43	64
4.85	77	70	62	55	48	41	34	27	21	14	9	6	17	38	59
4.80	80	72	65	57	50	43	36	29	22	16	10	4	11	33	54
4.75	82	74	67	59	52	45	38	31	24	18	12	6	7	28	49
4.70	85	74	69	62	54	47	40	33	26	19	13	7	5	22	44
4.65	87	79	72	64	57	49	42	35	28	21	15	9	4	17	39
4.60	90	82	74	66	59	51	44	37	30	23	16	10	4	11	34
4.55	92	84	76	69	61	54	46	39	32	25	18	12	6	6	28
4.50	95	87	79	71	63	56	48	41	34	27	20	13	7	4	23
4.45	98	89	81	73	66	58	51	43	36	29	22	15	9	3	17
4.40	100	92	84	76	68	60	53	45	38	31	24	17	10	4	11
4.35	103	95	87	78	71	63	55	47	40	33	26	19	12	6	5
4.30	106	98	89	81	73	65	57	50	42	35	28	20	14	7	2

net basis. In this case, both bull and bear steepening moves hurt the position, but there is little tolerance for these types of moves. The net basis values represented in Figure 1–20 are like ocean depths on a navigation chart. If we're trying to stay in shallow water we want as low a value as possible, but if the currents of the market pull us out in a bear steepening or bull flattening move, then we literally find ourselves in deep water, with a strong chance of the trade ending up unprofitable.

Earlier we mentioned that there was a way to exploit the fact that when we use issues that aren't cheapest they always face changes in their payoff and they have different, and sometimes opposite, payoff patterns than the issue that's currently cheapest. What if we weren't sure whether rates would go up or down? Steeper or flatter? In such a case, what we would want to do is construct a payoff matrix with as gentle an increase in net basis values as possible in any direction. Rather than use 100% of the shortest issue and be killed in a bear steepening move, or use 100% of the longest issue and face the same pain in a bull flattening, why not combine the two? If the risks are polar opposite, then a combination of the two may create a more stable payoff matrix. The trick now is to determine exactly what proportion of each issue to use, and how to formalize the selection criteria.

Figure 1–20 illustrates a matrix using the longest and shortest bonds where half of the longest and half of the shortest bonds in the deliverable basket are used. Compared to Figure 1–17b, it's clear that the addition of the longest issue in the basket has moved the breakeven boundary toward the upper right-hand corner, affording more bear-steepening protection than using 100% of just the shortest issue. What's the trade-off for this protection? If you look at the lower left-hand corner, you can see that the values there are no longer zero; they're less than the values of the original matrix that used 100% of the longest issue. In order to gain bear-steepening protection it's necessary to give up some bull-flattening protection. Just how might we juggle these competing interests?

It is necessary to formalize criteria for how much of which issues we include in our basis trade. Figure 1–20 includes 75% and 25% of the shortest and longest issues in the delivery window just as an easy illustration, but it's easy to imagine how the payoffs in the matrix can be manipulated in order to provide more protection in one direction, at the cost of increased exposure in the opposing direction.

Before we formalize one possible criterion, let's make another observation about the shape of the payoff matrix: if the slope of the curve moves 1:1 with the level of rates, then there is no change in the payoff. If the level of rates rises by 1 basis point and the slope of the curve flattens enough so that the yield on the cheapest issue falls by 1 basis point, then there is no change in the basis. So far, we've just been discussing bear-steepening and bull-flattening moves, but we have ignored the much more common types of curve reshapings, which are bear flattening and bull steepening. Rather than moving toward the bottom left- and top right-hand corners, these two types of movements would move toward the top left and bottom right corners. For now, let's suppose that we ignore what's likely to happen and proceed as if we know nothing about historical curve movements or what might happen in the future (many seasoned bond traders might agree that this is the appropriate course of action, since market moves may be essentially random in the short run).

If it's true that we are completely agnostic about future rate moves and believe that rate changes are truly a random process in the short run, then we want to construct as stable a payoff matrix as possible centered around the current level of rates. The center of the matrix should be at current values of the level and slope of the curve, and we should choose weightings of the longest and shortest issue to create as gradual an increase as possible in the value of the net basis. We're guessing that a bear move is just as likely as a bull move and our payoffs shouldn't be biased whether rates move one way or the other. What this literally means is that the value of the net basis should be as stable as possible in opposing directions: bull/bear moves or steeper/flatter moves. Luckily, we can use many of the same tools we developed for calculating the optimal options basket to attack this problem.

Suppose that we treat the problem of determining the optimal basket of issues as a minimization problem, so it can be solved in a spreadsheet framework.

FIGURE 1–21

Optimal issue mix, 90% CTD, and 10% longest issue

	Flatter					10s/30s Slope			Steeper					
30y	-10	-5	0	5	10	15	20	25	30	35	40	45	50	55
5.50	20	17	14	12	9	8	7	9	14	28	49	72	94	117
5.45	20	18	15	13	10	8	6	7	11	23	43	66	89	112
5.40	21	19	16	13	11	8	7	6	9	19	37	61	84	107
5.35	22	19	17	14	11	9	7	6	7	15	32	55	79	102
5.30	23	20	17	15	12	10	8	6	6	12	26	50	73	97
5.25	24	21	18	16	13	10	8	6	5	9	21	44	68	92
5.20	25	22	19	16	14	11	9	7	5	6	17	38	62	86
5.15	25	23	20	17	14	12	9	7	5	4	12	32	57	81
5.10	26	23	21	18	15	12	10	8	6	4	9	26	51	75
5.05	27	24	21	19	16	13	11	8	6	4	7	20	45	70
5.00	28	25	22	19	17	14	11	9	7	5	4	14	39	64
4.95	29	26	23	20	18	15	12	9	7	5	3	10	33	58
4.90	30	27	24	21	18	16	13	10	8	6	4	7	26	52
4.85	31	28	25	22	19	16	14	11	8	6	4	5	20	46
4.80	32	29	26	23	20	17	14	12	9	7	5	3	14	40
4.75	33	30	27	24	21	18	15	12	10	7	5	3	8	33
4.70	34	30	28	25	22	19	16	13	10	8	6	4	6	27
4.65	35	32	29	26	23	20	17	14	11	8	6	4	3	20
4.60	36	33	30	27	24	21	18	15	12	9	7	5	3	14
4.55	37	34	31	27	24	21	18	16	13	10	7	5	3	7
4.50	38	35	32	28	25	22	19	16	14	11	8	6	4	4
4.45	39	36	33	29	26	23	20	17	14	12	9	6	4	2
4.40	40	37	34	30	27	24	21	18	15	12	9	7	4	2
4.35	41	38	35	31	28	25	22	19	16	13	10	7	5	3
4.30	42	39	36	32	29	26	23	20	17	14	11	8	5	3

The minimization is the difference between the net basis in opposing moves; bear steepening and bull flattening. It's possible to build on the work we've already done finding the appropriate weightings for various baskets of naked options and apply the same technique to a different problem. If we set up an equation whose value is the sum of the squared differences between opposing cells in the matrix, then it should be possible to have the computer search for weightings between issues to minimize those differences. It's interesting how the same tools can be applied to different, but related, problems; the results are shown in Figure 1–21. This matrix shows the results of combining payoffs from Figures 1–17a and 1–18 of the shortest and longest issues in the basket in a very specific way. One of the constraints we placed on our optimization is that the allocation of face weights between the two issues had to sum to 100%, meaning we didn't want any more or less risk exposure than we would otherwise have with a factor-weighted basis trade. The opposing "corners" of the matrix are the same. There is no bias built into this basis trade; it performs equally well in all opposing rate moves. Having said that, it's impossible to make a judgment about whether we should base a trade on this weighting until we know what the maximum profit can be for the trade. As in any option sale, the maximum profit possible is to keep the entire option premium as measured by the net basis.

The higher the net basis, the greater the area covered in the breakeven analysis. It's true that the market tends to price the net basis higher when there is a CTD switch within just a few basis points in level or slope change, but our analysis illustrates that this is irrational given our method of taking advantage of the increase in option premiums. Instead of shying away from basis trading when there is an imminent CTD switch, when the market may be significantly discounting the contract price and assuming high net basis values, these are the best times to be a basis trader. While everyone else is wondering which deliverable issue he or she should be using, the key to gaining an advantage over the competition is to structure a trade so that you're largely indifferent about which way rates move. In order to do this, we have to use a basket of deliverable issues rather than just one. Although it's impossible to be completely neutral in all aspects of the trade, especially changes in repo rates, this analysis makes it clear what risks the position entails.

Before moving on, it's important to understand how to use this matrix in practice since the allocation between issues can get quite complex, especially in futures with wide deliverable baskets like the 30-year contract. No model can be a substitute for good judgment, but tools like the basis matrix can help make clear exactly what risks a position entails, which assists in the decision-making process. The clearer the facts can be presented, the easier it is to decide what trade makes sense. Should we be long or short the basis? So far we've focused on selling delivery option, which means selling the cash Treasury note and buying the futures contract. Selling options for a living might not be clinically proven to shorten your lifespan, but sometimes it sure feels like that. Every news story is a potential reason for the market to race away from you, and it can be quite nerve-racking. Option buyers, on the other hand, pray for chaos!

There's been a perception over the years that delivery option was consistently overpriced and the contracts were cheap for long periods of time. As we can see, delivery option is a basket option, which is more complicated to analyze than straight American or Bermudan options, and this difficulty sometimes commands a premium in the market. Replacing holdings of Treasury notes with Treasury futures has been the hallmark of many of the largest fixed income money managers, but questions about the future of the contract parallel questions about the market as a whole. Since 1977, when 30-year Treasury futures were first introduced, interest rates have been generally falling, as the Federal Reserve regained credibility under Paul Volcker; his legacy was continued with Alan Greenspan. Both of these Fed chairmen pursued policies of opportunistic deflation, lowering rates slightly less frequently than was probably needed to keep prices stable, and hiking rates slightly more than was strictly necessary to get inflation under control.

The result was that in 2003 inflation had fallen to such an extent that deflation became a concern, which no one would have guessed would be a topic of conversation in the late 1970s or early 1980s. As inflation fell, so did long-term bond yields and delivery option values. Many traders who relied on being long Treasury futures as a cheap source of duration floundered because they were no longer available. Knowing the mechanics of the contract, we can understand that interest rates had fallen to such an extent that there was little chance of a CTD switch or anything other than the shortest issue being CTD. Will the next 10 years continue to bring falling interest rates, where the United States ends up mired in a deflation scenario like Japan? Japanese government bond futures contracts have similar mechanics to Treasury futures at the CBOT, but the market rarely prices in any chance of the CTD switching, and the net basis is normally quite low or zero. If the next decade does bring a return to higher interest rates, it's clear that the Bernanke era in fixed income markets must be slightly inflationary, bringing with it higher interest rates and probably higher delivery option values. In fact, there is little alternative, since policymakers can see how difficult it has been to reenter an inflationary track in Japan once the price level and interest rates fall beyond a certain point. This is a long way of explaining that futures contracts may no longer be a cheap source of duration in a rising rate environment but may initially underprice delivery option values in the beginning of the Bernanke era.

The basis matrix can be easily adapted to serve the needs of long basis trades. All that needs to be changed is to invert the shading from Figure 1–22. Rather than interpreting the shaded areas of Figure 1–22 as the regions where a trade is doomed, it represents the objective for a long delivery option trade, and where the market must move to in order for the position to turn a profit. Of course, in this situation the option buyer wants to buy the option for as little as possible, minimizing the white space. Rather than breaking into a cold sweat at every article coming across the news wires, option buyers pray for chaos and for news that can push the market to a spot in the rate matrix where there is a substantial enough CTD switch to overcome the premium they spent to get long the option. Basis is a unique trade though, because as we mentioned, unlike naked options where the premium is exchanged at the inception of the trade, there is no initial transfer of money for assuming a long or short delivery option position; the premium that is represented by the value of the net basis is paid over time through the profit and loss of the position.

Yield Betas

So far in our explanation of the net basis we've dealt with parallel changes in the level of rates in the replicating options basket and with changes to the level of rates or slope of the curve with the basis matrix. What if both the level and slope of the curve move at the same time? In this case we would need to find a way to describe the links between the two in a reasonable way, and one such approach is with yield betas. Models are supposed to be abstractions of reality, but in making simplifying assumptions, the risk is that we cut away so many relevant details that

F I G U R E   1–22

Inverse of "optimal" matrix requires yields to move to the shaded area

30y	Flatter					10s/30s Slope			Steeper					
	-10	-5	0	5	10	15	20	25	30	35	40	45	50	55
5.50	20	17	14	12	9	8	7	9	14	28	49	72	94	117
5.45	20	18	15	13	10	8	6	7	11	23	43	66	89	112
5.40	21	19	16	13	11	8	7	6	9	19	37	61	84	107
5.35	22	19	17	14	11	9	7	6	7	15	32	55	79	102
5.30	23	20	17	15	12	10	8	6	6	12	26	50	73	97
5.25	24	21	18	16	13	10	8	6	5	9	21	44	68	92
5.20	25	22	19	16	14	11	9	7	5	6	17	38	62	86
5.15	25	23	20	17	14	12	9	7	5	4	12	32	57	81
5.10	26	23	21	18	15	12	10	8	6	4	9	26	51	75
5.05	27	24	21	19	16	13	11	8	6	4	7	20	45	70
5.00	28	25	22	19	17	14	11	9	7	5	4	14	39	64
4.95	29	26	23	20	18	15	12	9	7	5	3	10	33	58
4.90	30	27	24	21	18	16	13	10	8	6	4	7	26	52
4.85	31	28	25	22	19	16	14	11	8	6	4	5	20	46
4.80	32	29	26	23	20	17	14	12	9	7	5	3	14	40
4.75	33	30	27	24	21	18	15	12	10	7	5	3	8	33
4.70	34	30	28	25	22	19	16	13	10	8	6	4	6	27
4.65	35	32	29	26	23	20	17	14	11	8	6	4	3	20
4.60	36	33	30	27	24	21	18	15	12	9	7	5	3	14
4.55	37	34	31	27	24	21	18	16	13	10	7	5	3	7
4.50	38	35	32	28	25	22	19	16	14	11	8	6	4	4
4.45	**39**	36	33	29	26	23	20	17	14	12	9	6	4	2
4.40	40	37	34	30	27	24	21	18	15	12	9	7	4	2
4.35	41	38	35	31	28	25	22	19	16	13	10	7	5	3
4.30	42	39	36	32	29	26	23	20	17	14	11	8	5	3

nothing of value is left. In dealing with level or slope changes individually, we ignore the reality that the two often move together.

Figure 1–23a compares the slope of the 2-year/10-year spread in basis points against the level of 10-year rates. It's not readily apparent from a time series of the two just how they move together because the level of rates has been generally falling over the time period. Since the early Volcker years and throughout the Greenspan era, the Federal Reserve has followed a conscious policy of opportunistic deflation, dragging down 10-year rates from as high as 7.57% in 1995 to a low of just 3.37%. The scatter plot in Figure 1–23b gives a better idea of the relationship between the two. Although the spread between the two has certainly been variable, these data make a few things clear. The most important is the sign of the relationship, which is negative, indicating that, as one variable increases, the other decreases. As 10-year rates rose, the slope of the curve fell. Second, the level of rates explains a little over 40% of the variation in the slope of the curve, as measured by the R-squared, which is substantial for a model with a single variable. Measuring the history of both series gives an indication of how they've moved in the past, but it doesn't say anything about why the two have behaved as they have.

FIGURE 1–23a

10-year Treasury yield and 2-year/10-year spread

FIGURE 1–23b

Slope and yield have moved in opposite directions in the past

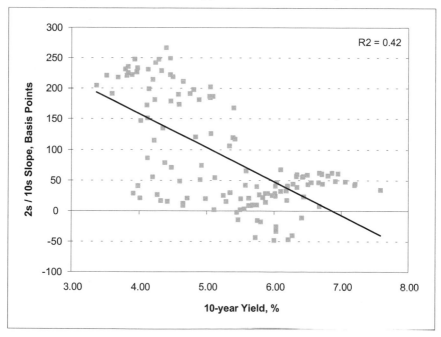

   This exercise indicates that our simplifying assumptions regarding parallel yield curve movements may have made our model too simple! Volumes have been written about yield curve movements, but a quick overview must begin by segregating yield curve movements by economic business cycle. The National Bureau of Economic Research (NBER) maintains the official start and stop dates for each business cycle in the United States since before the Civil War. Knowing that British blockades on American ports during the War of 1812 have little bearing on today's business cycle, we focus only on business cycles since 1970, when the 2-year note was introduced. Business cycles have been an ever-present characteristic of U.S. economic growth, and although the specifics of each cycle change because of technology and population, there are similarities which can be drawn across time. Anyone who believes that today is the end of history, and there is nothing to be learned from the past, should keep in mind that global shipping tonnage was as high during the height of the British Empire in the 1870s as it was a hundred years later in 1970 after two world wars and the protectionist policies that followed. Imagine how different the technology of a clipper ship is to a modern container ship! In spite of ever-improving technology, it took the world a century for global shipping to equal levels achieved with far simpler technology. Conceit over technological marvels probably isn't new—all business cycles contain common elements: people for labor, money for capital, and technology to combine the two.

   In the United States, business cycles have lasted an average of about 5 years from the worst trough of a recession to the peak of an expansion. Although there has been some variability, a 5-year cycle is a reasonable rule of thumb, and we plot GDP with recessions highlighted in Figure 1–24. In the introduction to this book, we looked at how the yield curve responded to changes in the business cycle, but neither Figures 0–3 nor 0–4 match the deliverable windows for note or bond futures. In Figure 1–25 we plot the slope of the 7-year/10-year Treasuries, which corresponds to the window for eligible deliverables for 10-year note futures, according to business cycles, and some general patterns emerge. First, the slope of the curve begins near its steepest point and then falls as the business cycle progresses. After about 3 years, the curve tends to lose its flattening momentum and spends the remainder of the expansion with very little slope. Prior to the very end of the expansion, the curve has inverted slightly and remains inverted during the initial stages of the recession, before the cycle repeats itself. The reason for this pattern has to do with changes in inflation and policymakers' response to it.

   Without getting too deeply into the dynamics, the one critical piece of information needed to unravel this pattern is that it takes between 18 months and 2 years for a change in the Fed Funds rate to impact GDP. This time lag for monetary policy is why the Fed has to preemptively change the funds rate in anticipation of where the economy is going to be several months or years down the road. It also explains why the flattening in the yield curve has generally stopped 3 years into an expansion. If hikes in Fed Funds slow GDP 2 years into the future

FIGURE 1-24

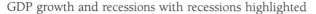

GDP growth and recessions with recessions highlighted

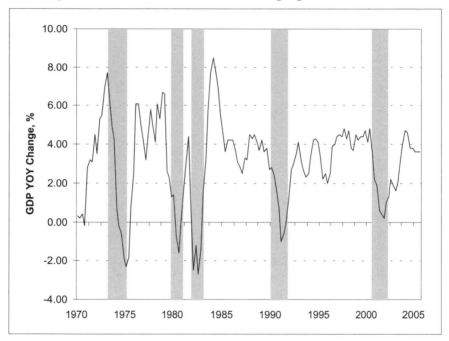

and business cycles are 5 years on average, then rate hikes in year 3 should hit GDP just at about the peak of the expansion. In fact, it's the mission of the Fed to cool the economy during expansions and provide a boost during recessions. If the Fed continued to hike rates right up until the end of an expansion, those hikes would hit GDP during a recession. Rather than acting countercyclically and dampening business cycles, the Fed risks amplifying them with poor decisions. Bringing this broad concept down to specific recommendations is a topic for a different book, but it all contributes toward the idea that there are patterns in yield curve reshaping: slope moves at the same time as the level of rates.

One way to describe the nonparallel rate movements is with a ratio of changes of the short end to the long end of the curve. For example, in this scenario a parallel movement between the 5-year and 10-year points would be measured as a yield beta of 1:1, or 1 for shorthand, since the second value is always equal to 1 in this ratio. If the 5-year yield rose by more than the 10-year yield, then the ratio would be something like 1.2:1, or a yield beta of 1.2. The one assumption in a ratio is that we've identified the two points. A yield beta of 1.2 for 2s/10s implies a very different yield change for the 7-year than if the yield beta described movements for 5s/10s. In fact, we've already measured the yield

FIGURE   1–25

7-year/10-year Treasury slope by business cycle

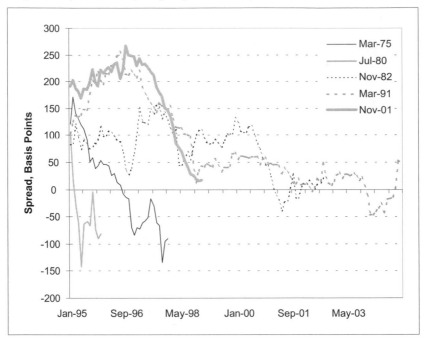

beta for the 2s/10s curve in the lower part of Figure 1–23. The slope of this line is –56 basis points, indicating that the 2s/10s slope fell by 56 basis points for every 100-basis point rise in 10-year yields.

Figures 1–23a and 1–23b highlight another aspect of yield beta analysis: they are statistical measurements that change over time. Even the most stable statistical relationships are subject to small variations over time, and it's this slight drift that interests us when using yield beta analysis. Figure 1–26 illustrates a rolling 90-day history of regression slopes for the scatter plot in Figure 1–23a. It's evident that the slopes have been relatively stable over long periods of time, but there has also been some short-term variability. Visually interpreting the yield betas in this diagram is straightforward, and it's relatively easy to get a handle on where the latest 90 days of history are compared to the extremes. As we'll see later on, this visual interpretation can be carried over to the basis matrix, where the impact of a nonparallel shift can be quickly evaluated. How would the two valuation methods that we've presented so far be changed if we used a yield beta approach to pricing the deliverable basket?

Before turning to the numbers, we can guess the direction of the impact on valuations, if not the magnitude. Remember the two original rules of Treasury

F I G U R E   1–26

Rolling regression showing how yield beta changes

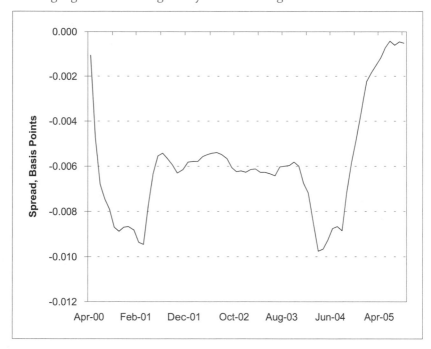

futures behavior: the maturity of the cheapest bond moves in the same direction as changes in the level of rates, and it follows the slope of the curve. If we have a yield beta that is greater than 1, we know that for every 1 basis point move in the back end of the curve, front-end yields will increase by more than 1 basis point, flattening the curve. If both movements influenced the maturity of the cheapest issue in the same direction, it would be clear exactly what was going to happen. In this case, the two rules of behavior are in conflict; higher rates mean there's pressure to move to a longer maturity, but a flatter curve should be moving the cheapest issue to a shorter maturity. In this case, any movement of the cheapest issue would depend on the magnitude of these effects. Which one dominates the other?

Our work calculating how the slope of the curve moved with the level of rates is more useful than it may have at first seemed. Based on the yield beta we calculated from Figure 1–23a of –55.7:100 for the 2s/10s slope, we can infer what the yield beta would be for the 7s/10s slope by simply scaling the value based on maturity. Since there is a 3-year gap between the 7- and 10-year points and our original estimation was for a 5-year gap between the 2-year and 10-year points, we can scale our yield beta by three-eighths, which is –21:100. Although no one knows what's going to happen in the future, if the past repeats itself, then the 7-year will move by 1.21 times the movement in the 10-year yield. If you guess that a scalar changing the 7-year yield by just over 1.21 basis points for every basis point change in 10-year rates means that the level effect dominates the slope effect in terms of moving the CTD maturity, you'd be right! It turns out that empirically the front-end yield movements are usually not large enough to outweigh the effect from a change in the level of rates.

Yield betas do have the effect of dampening the impact of changes in the level of rates. If there is some flattening to counterbalance rate increases, then we might guess that the CTD switch points would be farther away from the ones we determined with strictly parallel curve shifts. From rule three of our first principles governing the behavior of the contracts, stating that contracts underperform cash whenever there is a CTD switch, we can guess that the more distant the CTD switches, the less often the contracts underperform the cash issue. This also means that the convexity of the contract is higher under nonparallel yield beta shifts than it would otherwise be with parallel moves and that delivery option would be modeled to be less valuable, since the convexity of the contracts is often less negative than under nonparallel moves. The cascade of consequences that follows from understanding a handful of basic rules and empirical evidence is extremely useful. In this case, we've been able to anticipate the behavior of a complex option without having to put pen to paper and do any calculations. What began as a series of cause and effects for the novice will grow into an expert's intuition if one remains focused on first principles.

Figure 1–27 contains the original futures performance relative the cheapest issue, but it also reworks the analysis using yield beta values. The effect of the yield beta calculation on the performance of the contracts would have been obvious if we had started from this graph, but running through the exercise without the numbers helps develop an intuition about why the results are what they are. In this case, it's clear that the CTD switch points are farther away than under parallel yield shifts and that the contract performance more closely resembles that of the cheapest issue. This is illustrated in the basket of replicating options as well. Rather than buying a basket worth 1.2 sixty-fourths, as we did in our original analysis for Figure 1–7a, the options basket that corresponds to the performance of the yield beta line only costs a little under 1.0 sixty-fourth. It might be tempting to use a ratio between yield betas and option premium, but this is one situation where a simple trade-off will be misleading.

We find similar conclusions with our second valuation method employing two different interest rate trees. Using a lattice with equal jump sizes and parallel shifts in rates for 10-year futures, the resulting price of the contract was 113-21+; but when we used the prices that resulted from the yield beta, the price was just 113-23+, which is a difference of 2 thirty-seconds. If the 10-year basket moves in nonparallel ways, where the shortest issue moves more than 1 basis point for every basis point move in the on-the-run issue, then the CTD switch points move farther away. Instead of a switch happening when rates might rise by 25 basis

FIGURE 1–27

Futures performance, with and without yield beta calculation

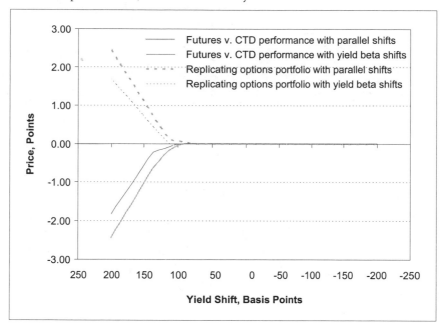

points, the switch might be delayed until rates move up 30 basis points. We know that futures underperform the cash issue whenever there is a CTD switch, and of course, fewer switches mean less optionality and higher futures prices. Delaying the switches means that futures perform more closely to the cash issue, and the price should rise, as it did in this example.

The basis matrix is perhaps the easiest valuation tool to evaluate yield betas with because they can simply be represented by a straight line tilted off the y axis. In this context we might represent a yield beta of 1:1 as a parallel move in yields, since the short rate is moving in lock step with the long rate. In the matrix such a line would be vertical and doesn't stray between columns containing values for different slopes. Conversely, a yield beta of 0:1 indicates that the short rate isn't moving at all, and every basis point change in the level of rates also changes the slope of the curve. We already calculated that the 2s/10s yield beta was –56:100 and scaled that beta to the maturity of the cheapest issue. In our example above, the maturity for the cheapest issue was the 7-year point, but it's worth noting that the maturity of the cheapest issue can change! The beta for the 7-year versus 10-year was –27:100; therefore the only thing left to do is to draw a line of the appropriate slope on the basis matrix.

F I G U R E   1–28

Net basis value at expiration with yield beta path overlay

30y	Flatter					10s/30s Slope			Steeper					
	-10	-5	0	5	10	15	20	25	30	35	40	45	50	55
5.50	0	0	0	0	0	1	2	7	14	31	54	80	105	130
5.45	0	0	0	0	0	0	1	4	11	26	48	74	99	124
5.40	0	0	0	0	0	0	1	3	8	21	41	68	94	119
5.35	0	0	0	0	0	0	1	2	5	16	35	61	88	113
5.30	0	0	0	0	0	0	0	1	4	12	29	55	82	108
5.25	0	0	0	0	0	0	0	1	2	8	23	49	76	102
5.20	0	0	0	0	0	0	0	1	1	5	18	42	69	96
5.15	0	0	0	0	0	0	0	0	1	3	13	36	63	90
5.10	0	0	0	0	0	0	0	0	1	2	9	29	56	84
5.05	0	0	0	0	0	0	0	0	1	1	6	22	50	77
5.00	0	0	0	0	0	0	0	0	0	1	3	16	43	71
4.95	0	0	0	0	0	0	0	0	0	1	2	11	36	64
4.90	0	0	0	0	0	0	0	0	0	1	1	8	29	58
4.85	0	0	0	0	0	0	0	0	0	0	1	4	22	51
4.80	0	0	0	0	0	0	0	0	0	0	1	2	15	44
4.75	0	0	0	0	0	0	0	0	0	0	1	1	9	37
4.70	0	0	0	0	0	0	0	0	0	0	1	1	6	30
4.65	0	0	0	0	0	0	0	0	0	0	0	1	3	23
4.60	0	0	0	0	0	0	0	0	0	0	0	1	1	15
4.55	0	0	0	0	0	0	0	0	0	0	0	1	1	8
4.50	0	0	0	0	0	0	0	0	0	0	0	0	1	4
4.45	0	0	0	0	0	0	0	0	0	0	0	0	1	1
4.40	0	0	0	0	0	0	0	0	0	0	0	0	1	1
4.35	0	0	0	0	0	0	0	0	0	0	0	0	0	1
4.30	0	0	0	0	0	0	0	0	0	0	0	0	0	1

As Figure 1–28 makes apparent, the optimal path for a short basis holder, who doesn't want delivery option to go in-the-money, doesn't lie along our expected yield beta line but is slightly flatter. History has shown that yield betas are rarely strong enough to ensure that delivery option stays out-of-the-money, and short basis trades don't always work out. Yield beta movements do help a delivery option seller; but they're rarely strong enough to turn a bad trade into a good trade. However, this type of movement may stave off losses in a trending market. After quite a bit of analysis, we end at our original conclusion: nonparallel shifts may delay CTD switches and lower the value of delivery option, but in most cases they simply delay the inevitable. If a trader is counting on yield beta movements to keep an issue from becoming CTD, then she is likely in the wrong trade.

FEAR ARBITRAGE: SQUEEZES AND WHAT GOES WRONG

The first two sections imply that the behavior of the contracts can be weighed and measured in an orderly way, but there are periods when none of these rules apply. As useful as arbitrage trades can be to ensure that prices remain close to their fair value, poor regulation can provide an incentive for traders to wreak havoc in the market. During some of the squeezes in 2005 there were as many failures to deliver in the Treasury market as there were after the terrorist attacks in New York and Washington in 2001. During these periods the market can become so distorted that buying in the contracts lowers their price, a contradiction that can be found in no other class of securities. As terrifying as these episodes are to the users of the contracts, there are ways to predict the circumstances that can lead to these types of problems, just like we might predict a dam bursting if the water is rising. Although squeezes are not in the long-term interests of the market, they do cause volatility that can be taken advantage of by short-term trades. It seems that as long as contracts have been around there have been people willing to game the system, and we now look at ways of alternatively avoiding and exploiting these periods.

The graph in Figure 1–29 shows failures to deliver in the cash Treasury market since 1990; these failures indicate a primary dealer selling notes or bonds to someone but subsequently failing to transfer possession of them. Two things should leap off the graph. First is that the spikes in 2005 caused by squeezes were of the same magnitude as the spikes from September 2001; the figure is even more startling considering that in 2001 there were failures all across the yield

F I G U R E   1–29

Delivery failures in the cash Treasury market since 1990

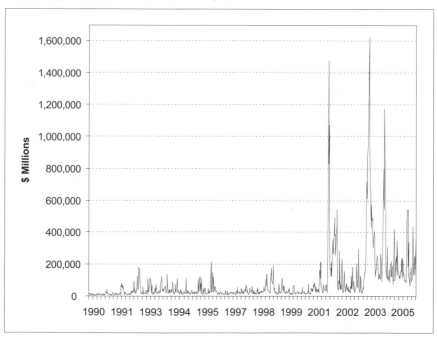

curve but those in 2005 stemmed from a single off-the-run 10-year note. Second is that there were relatively few failed trades prior to 2001, an average of $36 billion per week; but after 2002 they have been persistently higher, an average of $210 billion per week. There has been a clear regime shift in the market where it's become more acceptable for primary dealers to fail to transfer possession of the notes and bonds they sell. Not every failed trade is an insidious effort to disrupt the market, because if someone fails to deliver bonds to a dealer, this causes the dealer to fail when he subsequently sells those bonds. In this way a single break in the delivery chain can mushroom hundreds or perhaps thousands of times. It's worth noting the scale of the chart in Figure 1–29. The average weekly failures to deliver in June 2005 were as high as $550 million, which is around 23 times the amount outstanding of Feb '12, which was the cheapest bond at that time, the scarcity of which caused nearly 100% of the fails. The point being that a $24 billion issue can cause more than half a trillion dollars' worth of failed trades. It's also worth noting that the spikes in the series from 2005 come and go with quarterly expirations, starting in the beginning of the delivery month but normally clearing up after trading stops during the third week of the month.

The fact that Treasury futures are settled via physical delivery is the key element to understanding squeezes. There is a fixed supply of each Treasury issue, and the basic idea during a squeeze is for the long to force more contracts to go through delivery than exist of the cheapest issue. If there are $20 billion of the cheapest issue outstanding, then forcing $25 billion through delivery guarantees receiving at least $5 billion of bonds that are not the cheapest issue. In this case the holder of short contracts would have to buy not just the cheapest issue, but some of the second or third cheapest issues as well. Of course, these bonds have higher prices than the cheapest issue, and the hope is that the long gets a basket of bonds worth more than the price of the contracts she paid for. There are spectacular examples of these trades succeeding in recent history, such as Fenchurch in 1993, but none have escaped subsequent legal action. What are the conditions that allow for a squeeze in the first place?

Recalling first principles of Treasury futures, we know that the maturity of the cheapest issue follows the direction of rates and the slope of the curve. We might suspect therefore that a very low and very flat yield curve environment would not only make the shortest bond in the basket the cheapest issue, but that it would have a converted forward price far below every other bond in the basket. This was in fact the case leading up to the squeezes at the end of 2004 and 2005. In response to the terrorist attacks in 2001, the Fed lowered short-term interest rates to just 1%, and deflation concerns were the topic of the moment, pushing long-term rates to 40-year lows. The Fed mentioned the risk of falling prices in the statement after its May 6, 2003, meeting and then Federal Reserve governor Ben Bernanke used warnings of falling inflation or deflation and unconventional measures to fight it to garner publicity that launched him into the spotlight, and eventually the chairman's seat in 2006, in spite of the fact that deflation never materialized. These warnings sent 10-year rates tumbling to 3.5% during the summer of 2003 and were still a topic of conversation a year later in 2004. The Federal Reserve did more than set the table for speculators to gorge on the chaos that was to follow; it rang the dinner bell!

Jawboning on deflation lowered long-term rates while direct action from the Fed on short-term rates kept the yield curve very steep, widening the gulf in price between the cheapest note and every other issue in the basket. There was no "straw that broke the camel's back," but rather a growing realization among traders that the Federal Reserve was being more permissive about allowing failures in the payment system. Prior to 2001 no one was sure what would happen to the market if there were a massive spike in failures. Unfortunately, firms were so efficient at clearing up fails in this instance that it provided a vivid illustration of how a completely frozen market could be resuscitated in short order, which had never been attempted before.

This was again illustrated in 2003, when the May '13 on-the-run 10-year issue started failing in the repo market because financing rates dipped into negative territory and sell-off handed quick losses to the holders of the new issue. Negative financing rates often cause exceptions that are kicked out of the automated clearing systems, which are often unable to accommodate negative values. Ironically, when these systems were built, no one envisioned a world where general collateral rates were 1% and a special rate could be 0% or negative. A negative repo rate means that you can be paid to borrow money as long as you post a certain Treasury issue as collateral. As the number of exceptions piled up, they were harder and harder to cope with and the cycle fed on itself. Additionally, even foreign accounts that normally lend their bonds in the repo market stopped doing so because they were simultaneously terrified of not getting them back and having anyone find out that they bought a 10-year note at a 40-year low yield of just 3.50%. Eventually, these fails were cleared up, but even 2 years later the May '13 issue continued to trade at a premium to surrounding bonds, which is a testament to the influence of the integrity of the payment system on the market.

Twice since 2001 traders witnessed massive clearing problems that have brought portions of the Treasury market to its knees, only to see them cleaned up in a matter of weeks. It's worth bearing in mind that this had never happened before, as illustrated by the low and stable values in Figure 1–29. Eventually, a light went on in somebody's head that a payment system could be used opportunistically. Strategically freezing up portions of the market could manipulate the price of target securities in a magnitude that hadn't been done before 2001. At the same time this was happening, a new type of trade emerged in the repo market called *prompt delivery,* or PD for short. In the PD market delivery is made within 15 minutes or the trade is canceled, but initially PD markets were only for overnight repo trades. The cost of a PD rate could be anywhere from 15% to 25%, which is staggering in a market where the Fed Funds rate was around 4%.

The idea for the PD market appears clear-cut at first; if a trader has a significant enough economic incentive to take possession of a bond, he should be willing to pay. For example, if a trader is going to lose 5 ticks if she doesn't have a bond, she should be willing to pay up to 4.9 ticks, because a 0.1-tick savings is better than nothing! This is the story many traders would have you believe. It's the job of Wall Street to price things, and the story goes that this is just another way to price the imperative of taking possession of a note. In this way one might argue that the PD market helps to clear up fails and facilitates the orderly operation of the payment system. However, a less benign version of the story might go like this: what if a repo trader is intentionally causing failures in a particular bond and simultaneously offering the bond in the PD market so that instead of earning a 4% rate, he can earn 15%? In this scenario the PD market creates an incentive to cause fails, and its existence is a detriment to the Treasury market. So which is it?

Interestingly enough, the popular press singled out the CBOT as the source of problems in the Treasury market, failing to understand that the exchange operates more like a referee than a goalie. *The Wall Street Journal* and *Financial Times* both printed multiple stories asserting that the exchange was to blame for price spikes in the cash Treasury market and isolated collapses of the clearing system. None of these stories mentioned the repo market or prompt delivery, and the chatter on Wall Street was completely off base. Many of the stories alluded to the millions of dollars made and lost because of unexpected behavior of the contracts, which is closer to the truth. The problem is that these stories did not present a clear overview of the problem, leaving readers and students of the market to try to piece together half-truths from fragments of anecdotal evidence. It is worth pointing out that there was also a great deal of anecdotal evidence offered by traders who had a financial interest in the outcome.

While it's true that the price action of CBOT products signals a significant problem, the root cause has to do with the primary dealer system, not the futures exchange. It's easy to understand why some may initially suspect that problems in the Treasury market are caused by the CBOT, since problems are often first evident in futures because of their unique "keystone" position in the fixed income markets. In these markets, hedging is done with incrementally more liquid products. One wouldn't hedge a Treasury note with a corporate bond, but the opposite is usually true. Futures are linked to prices in the Treasury market via physical delivery of Treasury notes at expiration of the contracts. As Figure 1–30 illustrates, growth in Treasury futures has outstripped that of Treasury notes, and traders have mistakenly blamed this dynamic for unusual price spikes in both markets. The reasoning, so it goes, is that more futures mean more deliveries, and more deliveries mean that the supply of notes to satisfy them is increasingly scarce and that their prices should increase.

During March, June, and September of 2005 certain bonds became so scarce that dealers simply ceased to deliver them. Although it was possible to buy the bond, it was impossible to take possession of it, and every sale created a failure to deliver. Since Treasury futures prices reflect prices in the notes or bonds that can be used to settle them at delivery, their price jumped as well. Unanticipated price jumps were problematic for hedgers interested in continuity and orderly markets. CBOT products that had faithfully reflected their risk in the past were

FIGURE   1–30

Futures growth contrasted with supply of available notes and bonds

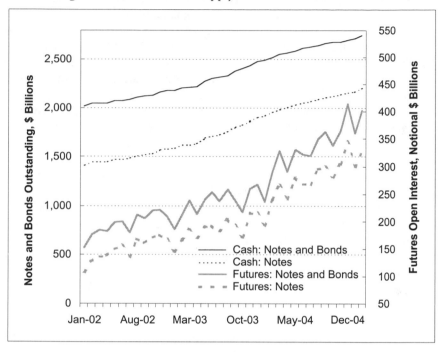

suddenly acting erratically. How do we prove that growth in futures trading was not behind the recent price spikes?

Numbers make the story concrete. In June of 2005, the 4 3/8% coupon Treasury due in February 2012 was the least expensive note that satisfied delivery for the 10-year Treasury futures contract. There is $24 billion of this issue outstanding, and on a normal day it's possible to buy and take delivery of several billion dollars at once. However, on March 1, 2005, deliveries of the issue entirely stopped. At the time, it appeared as if more than $24 billion worth of Treasury futures would need to be offset and that this issue wasn't big enough to go around. The common explanation for the complete breakdown in the delivery system was that people who were in possession of the notes withheld them from the market to satisfy delivery against Treasury futures. Although this is certainly a legitimate reason to withhold notes from the market, at least some of the people offering this explanation were not telling the truth, because only $11 billion of deliveries actually took place.

Were those in possession of the remaining $13 billion of the notes intentionally withholding them from the market to drive up their price? If so, the

CBOT would not be to blame for the price spikes of its product; the blame for the problem was on a breakdown in the mechanism for deliveries between primary dealers. Theoretically, it is possible that the $13 billion in question were no longer available for trading in the market for one reason or another, whether they were pledged at a bank or held in a mutual fund. Since it's impossible to know exactly how much of the $24 billion was available for trading, it's also theoretically possible that the payment system broke down for a legitimate reason: there were exactly $11 billion of the bonds available for trading, and everyone who withheld bonds was doing so to offset Treasury futures.

At the time, this explanation seemed perfectly plausible. Subsequent events, however, proved it was not true. While there were $11 billion of deliveries in March, 3 months later a staggering $15 billion of the same issue carried through to delivery. The June delivery proved that the "fail problem" from March couldn't have been due to the legitimate withholding of notes consuming the entire available supply, because an additional $4 billion were delivered just 3 months later. It seems unlikely that $11 billion could represent 100% of the tradable supply if $15 billion of the same issue changed hands during the next cycle. Who profits from delivery failures in the repo market?

It isn't a coincidence that when the system for deliveries broke down, a new market sprung up: prompt delivery. In this market, delivery is guaranteed within 15 minutes or the trade is cancelled. The cost associated with the privilege of possession is sometimes exorbitant, and has been as much as 14% for 1 day (in a market measured in basis points, a 1,400-basis-point cost sticks out when the Fed Fund's rate is only at 400 basis points). This prompt delivery market ended up being both a blessing and a curse, since it may help to alleviate failures to deliver in certain circumstances but create them in others. Anyone who is willing to pay up in the prompt delivery market can gain possession of the notes; however, the delivering individual may intentionally fail on earlier obligations where she is earning a lower return. A two-tiered market for delivery isn't in the long-term interests of the Treasury market, because it may provide at least some incentive for the holders of notes to break delivery obligations and create fails.

Transparency is one of the beauties of futures. Although it was impossible to prove at the time, the complete histories of the March, June, and September 2005 futures delivery cycles illustrate the strategic behavior of traders intentionally causing delivery failures to drive up the price of their notes, or creating an opportunity to profit from a two-tiered market for delivery. The Treasury Secretary requested large position reports for holdings of 10-year notes in order to fire a warning shot, indicating that the Treasury would begin monitoring who has possession of these notes and what is done with them. Creating a record of ownership is often the first step in any prosecution, and the market received the message loud and clear. There was subsequently a dramatic cheapening of both the 10-year Treasury note and futures contract, but the situation never had to get as bad as it did. Prior to September 11, 2001, there were barely any failures to deliver notes among primary dealers, and anyone who purchased a note could reasonably expect to take possession of it. Of course, there was a sharp increase in failures in 2001, but as traders saw these problems clear up, they also saw an opportunity.

As we mentioned earlier, from 1990 to 2001 the cumulative average weekly failures to deliver in the Treasury market was $36 billion worth of notes. From 2002 to the present, this value jumped almost sixfold to $210 billion. Once traders saw that a market could be manipulated this way, they decided to opportunistically wreak havoc. Certainly, it's not the domain of the CBOT to regulate deliveries between primary dealers, and the exchange should not be the focus of the ire of fixed income traders. If there is a legitimate criticism of the exchange, it was that it "fiddled while Rome burned" by working on position limits to address a perception problem, rather than attacking the substantive issues facing markets related to its products. Until the Treasury requires that in addition to bidding on new notes, primary dealers have an obligation to promote an orderly market, which explicitly includes making delivery and promoting an unbreakable chain of possession from one note holder to another, these types of problems will continue. The days of voice brokerage are over, and perhaps the market has forgotten an important lesson from the Chicago trading pits: my word is my bond.

In spite of the pressures on the market, there were no multi-issue deliveries in 2005, and every trader who went long the contract at a negative net basis and held it through delivery ended up losing money. This was true in December of 2004 as well as in March, June, and September of 2005. It's understandable if the market isn't able to anticipate the proportion of deliveries between the cheapest and second cheapest issues before the fact, but in this instance every single time there was a threatened multi-issue delivery, it never panned out. In spite of this, the market continued to price the contracts as if the squeezes had succeeded. Figure 1–31 paints part of the picture by illustrating the relative sizes of the deliverable issues in the 10-year basket. The Feb '12 was the cheapest issue in March and June of 2005, while the Aug '12 was cheapest into September and December contracts.

Whether or not a repo trader is intentionally withholding bonds from the market to cause fails, the task is certainly easier when issue sizes fall. Aug '12 is just a $19 billion issue compared to Feb '12, which has $24 billion outstanding, a 26% increase. Does that extra $5 billion make that much of a difference? No! The experiences gained in 2005 show that more than half of the supply of even a relatively small issue can materialize for delivery. Obviously it's slightly easier to come up with chunks of a larger issue than a smaller one, but in terms of the fears that a small issue instills in the market, the psychological difference is gigantic. History shows this fear is irrational, but in spite of this, most traders will parrot the traditional story that small issues are "put away" and can't come back into the market and a futures delivery relying on smaller issues is bound to cause the short holder of the contracts problems when he goes out to try to find the bonds, making it more likely that he delivers some of the second cheapest.

FIGURE 1–31

Amount outstanding of deliverable 10-year notes

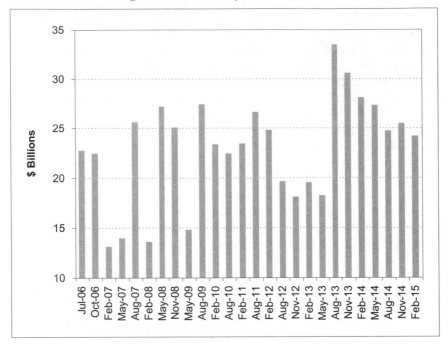

Another dimension here is that regulators such as the Commodities Futures Trading Commission (CFTC) and the CBOT Office of Investigation and Audit also play a role during these times. The CFTC has explicit rules governing the behavior of traders during these periods, and it has broad emergency powers to limit trading to position liquidations, impose or reduce limits on positions, require liquidation of positions, extend delivery period, or close a market. Of course, the CFTC carries the big stick in this arrangement, but to its credit, has only used emergency powers four times between 1977 and 2005. Just as the threat of delivery is normally enough to force the contracts to trade close to fair value, the threat of legal action is normally enough to get traders to behave, following the letter and spirit of the law.

The case of Fenchurch Capital Management is illustrative of the behavior that typifies a squeeze. (This case is available to the public through the CFCT.) Fenchurch was a money manager who acquired a substantial position in the June 10-year Treasury futures contract in 1993. On the last day of trading, Fenchurch's position was about 12,700 contracts, which was 76% of the open interest of the contract. More important than its proportion of the total remaining open interest, was the size of their futures position relative to the size of the CTD issue. At the time, the cheapest issue was 8.5% Feb '00, which was a $10.7 billion issue. It's interesting to note that a little over a decade later the issue sizes in the 10-year basket have more than doubled, reflecting growth in the Treasury market and the Federal budget deficit. Also at the time, 12,700 contracts was the third largest delivery to take place in the history of the contracts, representing $12.7 billion face amount of Treasury notes. A squeeze revolved around the inability to offset the entire open interest with the cheapest issue, and by owning almost $2 billion face more contracts than there were of the Feb '00, Fenchurch was guaranteed to receive at least this amount of a second and more expensive note.

Short holders of contracts on the other side of Fenchurch's trades couldn't anticipate that there wouldn't be enough of the securities to go around prior to the delivery month, because there are normally more contracts in open interest than notes to offset them before the last month of trading. The difference between a squeeze and business as usual is the amount of contracts that roll from one quarter to the next, as illustrated in Figure 1–32. At the first day of the delivery month, it's impossible to guess what open interest will be on the final trading day, about 3 weeks later. Most people assume there will be no squeeze and price the contracts with the anticipation of receiving 100% of the cheapest issue. The short

F I G U R E   1–32

10-year Treasury futures declining open interest during a squeeze

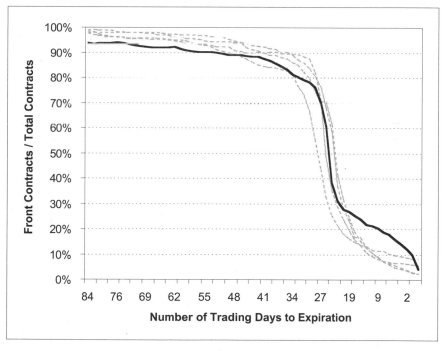

basis holder buys the note, lends it out on term repo, and then sells contracts. There is no guarantee of receiving the issue when the term repo is over, and it's always possible that she could be "failed to," meaning that she would not able to take possession of notes she was promised. However, if the short holds contracts past the last trading day, she must deliver something to the CBOT, and if she doesn't get the cheapest bonds back, she must buy a more expensive issue in the deliverable basket. Only as time goes by does it become apparent that open interest isn't falling in line with historical patterns and that there may not be enough of the cheapest issue to go around.

There are generally two ways to ensure that a squeeze succeeds; although it's also worth noting that this conduct is illegal. The first is through the repo market, which is the method Fenchurch employed, and the second is with Treasury STRIPS. The holder of short contracts is also long the cash note, but normally these traders don't purchase the note outright, rather borrowing money in the repo market to pay for them. To collateralize their loan, holders must give up possession of the note, and their risk is that they won't get the bonds back in time to make delivery to the CBOT. If holders of long contracts can ensure that there are a number of repo counterparties that take possession of the notes, but subsequently fail to deliver them back, then they have effectively reduced the supply of notes. In Fenchurch's case it controlled around $1.4 billion of the repo market with counterparties who agreed to withhold them from the market.

At the same time Fenchurch was entering into repo trades with counterparties it knew would not re-lend the notes, it was intentionally failing on other repo trades. Whenever Fenchurch took possession of the notes, the firm wouldn't give them back no matter the rate. This single action, more than the size of their intended delivery, attracted regulatory attention. It's debatable as to whether or not anyone should use Treasury futures to take possession of the notes in the normal course of business, since traders are guaranteed to get the least valuable notes possible (by design). Failing to deliver bonds in a repo trade when the rate on the bond is zero means that traders were giving up the opportunity to borrow money interest-free and instead paying higher general collateral rates. The fact that the firm was doing something that was explicitly not in its financial interests on one portion of the trade was proof positive that the activity had to be linked to another trade, where it hoped to make enough money to offset its loss on the repo leg.

A second way to drain supply of deliverable notes from the market is to buy principal STRIPS. Stripping notes means that the individual cash flows are broken apart and become their own bond, to be traded separately. For example, a 10-year note would create 21 separate bonds, composed of 20 coupon pieces and a principal piece. In Treasury STRIPS, coupon are interchangeable with any other coupon falling on the same day from any other note, but this is not true of principal pieces. Principal pieces are distinct, and in order to reconstitute a coupon bond from a series of zero coupon strips, it's necessary to buy the correct principal piece; not just any bond will do. If the holder of long futures contracts

T A B L E   1–7

How to Price a Multi-Issue Delivery

Feb '10	100	66%
May '10	110	33%
Contract price with 100% of the cheapest issue	100	
Contract price with one-third the second cheapest issue	103	

also buys a block of principal strips for the cheapest issue and doesn't lend them out to the market, then the holder is ensuring that the supply of that note is diminished.

In Fenchurch's case it ended up receiving $480 million of notes that were not the cheapest issue, or approximately 4,800 out of its 12,700 contracts. It's interesting to see that even in this case of overt manipulation, Fenchurch was able to secure only the second cheapest issue for about one-third of its position but made no money on two-thirds of its position. To see why receiving one-third of its position with the second cheapest issue is desirable, consider the converted forward prices in Table 1–7:

If 100% of the Feb '10 were received, the contracts would be worth 100. However, since one-third of the deliveries were made with the second cheapest, the contracts are now worth 103. In fact, the value of a squeeze depends on the price spread between the cheapest and second cheapest issue. If the spread were just 1 tick, rather than 10, it would make receiving the second cheapest much less valuable.

This brings us back to the economic environment as the single most important factor enabling or preventing a squeeze. If a single issue dominates the deliverable basket so that there is a large price gap between the cheapest and second cheapest issues, this sets the stage for problems. This normally happens when interest rates are either very low or high, and significantly different from the 6% notional coupon on the contract. On the other hand, if the deliverable is in the middle of the basket and the price spread between the adjacent issues is relatively small, there is little risk of a squeeze because the holder of short contracts can simply satisfy delivery obligations with adjacent bonds for a relatively small penalty. The Fenchurch experience of 1993 shared the most important characteristic of the squeezes of 2005—intentional fails in the repo market. If the economic conditions enable a squeeze, then it's the failure of the Federal Reserve to exert pressure on primary dealers that facilitates these types of trades.

Squeezes lead to the most interesting phenomenon in any market: the more the contracts are bought, the lower the price falls. The reasoning is clear-cut, but just as we said at the very beginning of the chapter, a few simple rules can lead to complex behaviors. Suppose that as the delivery month winds down, open interest, like that diagrammed in Figure 1–32, ends up stalling and not dropping down in the usual pattern with about 19 trading days to go before expiration of the contract. Further suppose that the number of contracts is greater than the available supply of the cheapest issue. The term *available supply* is hotly debated among traders because not 100% of the amount outstanding of the issue is available. Common reasons that bonds are drained from the market include pledging them at a bank as collateral against a loan or stripping and using them to defease municipal issues or the fact that the bonds are held as cash equivalents by a foreign central bank that will not lend them out or resell them, no matter the rate. By and large though, the Treasury market is astoundingly deep and liquid, and in 2005 more than half of the amount outstanding of an issue was delivered through the CBOT without incident. How high is high? If the face value represented by the contracts constitutes 75% of the amount outstanding of the cheapest issue, could that much be delivered? It's never happened to date, but a value around 75% is probably too much, in which case the short would need to deliver some of the second cheapest issue.

Let us suppose though that we have an unambiguous case, where the face value represented by the contracts is $20 billion compared to the $18 billion outstanding of the cheapest issue. If open interest hangs at $20 billion, then the short holders of the contracts are stuck. Each day that passes where open interest doesn't fall the contract price will rise, but it won't be the sort of orderly trading that happens after an economic number, and it may jump higher. There will still be people who don't understand the situation and will be willing to sell into the spike in prices, and it's quite possible these people may sustain massive losses. During the squeezes in June of 2005, the price on the contracts spiked by 11 ticks when it became apparent that a large delivery was likely. To date, the contracts have behaved as designed—rallying on information that some of the second cheapest issue may be delivered, in a similar fashion to what is presented in Table 1–7. In a sense, there is nothing wrong with a multi-issue delivery because the contracts were designed to allow this. But practically speaking, an 11-tick jump is too much volatility for the typical hedger to handle.

Here we are, a week before the last trading day, and open interest is at $20 billion, which is $2 billion more than the amount outstanding on the issue. There are only two possible outcomes: either the entire $20 billion goes through delivery or it does not. It's at these times that the CBOT and CFTC will ramp up their jawboning efforts to make sure that there are no manipulative practices occurring. During the September 2005 cycle the Treasury Department lent a hand by asking for large position reports of the cash issue, creating a paper trail that could be used in litigation in case there were manipulative practices. Essentially the tactic of the regulators is to terrify enough of the holders of long contracts so that they liquidate their positions. This is a case of good regulation. If the contracts are 11 ticks rich, why isn't the long realizing that profit? This is a legitimate question, and parallel to what regulators were asking Fenchurch. Why would they rather not lend their bonds and pay a general collateral rate instead of lending them and paying a zero interest rate? If the price of the futures contract has gone up in accordance with the expected proportion of cheapest and noncheapest issues and if the futures contract is priced fairly given the price of the issues received, then why would the long ignore this opportunity to take delivery? The list of possible excuses, other than manipulating the price of the contracts, is short. Even if the longs are intractable and refuse to sell their contracts at any price, there is another way for the price to fall.

Suppose the long holders of basis, those who are short the contracts, unwind a fraction of their positions. Open interest can fall just as easily from a short selling as from a long; and if the long basis holder is trying to get the price of the contracts to fall, that holder has control over some portion of the open interest and can just unwind a fraction of the contracts at a loss with the hope of making a profit on the remaining portion. In this case, buying to cover short contract positions, which are held against long cash positions in a long basis trade, will drop the price of the contract because as open interest falls it will become easier to cover the remaining contracts with a greater proportion of the cheapest issue. This is that the strangest dynamic of any market: buying of the contracts reduces open interest, making it easier to cover existing contracts exclusively with the cheapest issue, which drops the price of the contract!

Early delivery is another way for the long basis holder to try to escape a squeeze from the long. Aggressive metaphors often find their way into the bond business, but the best description of early delivery is like trying to eat a spiny animal—it may not stop the predator, but it makes the whole experience that much more unpleasant. The long holder of contracts is counting on the fact that the short can't get enough of the cheapest issue to make delivery with, but the reality is that the long contract holder doesn't want the cheapest issue. The only reason to go through delivery from the long side is if you think you're not going to get the cheapest issue. Put another way, the long is asking for a bond with the hope of not receiving it. If the short can get any of the cheapest bonds and deliver them, two things are accomplished: first, the short forces the long to take a loss if the contracts were purchased at a negative net basis; second, the long will have to lend those bonds back out again because he is also a levered player, and by lending those bonds back out, it becomes more likely they will be recycled and clear up fails in the payment system. The important question, from the perspective of the short holder of contracts trying to break the squeeze, is how many fails does a dollar's worth of the cheapest bonds delivered early clear up?

Most large fixed income firms clear their trades through the Fixed Income Clearing Corporation (FICC), which was originally set up to clear government securities trades but has since expanded to clear mortgage-backed securities. If two counterparties trading a government security both use the FICC, then trades are compared, confirmed, and netted all within the system. An early delivery of the cheapest bond would likely clear up an enormous volume of failed trades; but not all counterparties use the FICC, and there are normally some bonds that leak out of the system. To estimate the proportion of bonds that leak from the FICC, we can roughly estimate that in the year ending in November 2005, the FICC cleared $221 trillion worth of Treasuries, including repo transactions. We also know that the Federal Reserve reports that $147 trillion worth of Treasuries traded at primary dealers during this same time. The FICC data include purchases and sales of the outright notes and bonds as well as repo transactions, and if we guess that about a third of this value comes from repo transactions, then the value is deflated to $146 trillion, which just about matches the primary dealer volume. One rule of thumb to estimate the multiplier effect of an early delivery of the cheapest issue is to divide the face of the bonds delivered early by 1 minus the proportion of bonds cleared at the FICC:

$$\$100 \text{ million}/(1-0.9) = \$1,000 \text{ million}$$

Suppose that 90% of the CTD bonds clear at the FICC, which means that $1 of delivered securities would clear up $10 in fails. The reality is that the vast majority, likely into the high 90% of all failed trades for the cheapest issue are between primary dealers who clear through the FICC, which would make the ratio closer to 50 or 100:1. It's clear that if the long is relying on failed repo trades to create a scarcity bid for the cheapest bond, then early delivery is a painful prospect. This is exactly what happened during the September 2005 10-year squeeze, where $100 million worth of Aug '12, the cheapest issue, were delivered 3 days before the last trading day. Although this delivery alone wasn't enough to break the squeeze, it certainly contributed. Our rudimentary estimation of multiplier effects indicate that this $100 million in notes probably cleared up several billion dollars' worth of failed trades.

Experienced traders will recognize that forgone carry income is one problem with delivering early. If we are long the cash Treasury and short the contracts in a positive carry trade, then delivering the notes early eats into the income of the trade. In fact, if the note is special in the repo market and is financing close to zero, as it will undoubtedly be during a squeeze, then a few days of carry can be substantial. There are no easy choices when the holder of short contracts is caught in a squeeze, but the general idea with delivering early is to punch the long holder of contracts in the nose just hard enough so she gives up the chase, without completely destroying your own profits. From the short's perspective, early delivery is only realistic with a small proportion of his overall position, say 10%. However, it's better to take a loss of 10% on your position and have 90% work out rather than have the whole thing turn into a loser.

If the long is relying on failed trades to create the illusion that more bonds are going through delivery than actually exist, the short is trying to jam the long with bonds before the last trading day to break the squeeze, and everyone is disseminating self-serving anecdotes, what information can you trust? There is one source of data that's unambiguous; it is collected by the Federal Reserve Bank of New York (FRBNY). As we suggested, the Federal Reserve's administration of the market doesn't always make sense, but it does a fine job collecting repo data from primary dealers for the System Open Market Account (SOMA). Every day the FRBNY publishes the notes and bonds that are financing more than 100 basis points through general collateral rates, and during squeezes these data are an invaluable lifeline. The way that SOMA works is that it buys notes at auction and later through open market operations as part of a portfolio that was worth approximately three-quarters of a trillion dollars at the end of 2005. These bonds are available to lend in overnight repo trades if the rate is ever more than 100 basis points special. If this threshold is met, then the Fed lends the bonds overnight and publishes the amount and average rate at which they were lent.

Figure 1–33 uses SOMA data to illustrate the pattern of a CTD bond getting special leading up to the last trading day. It's apparent that there are significant jumps in the series, when the bond richens in repo by more than 275 basis points from one day to the next. Paradoxically, in the middle of the series there are 30 days when the bonds are not lent at all by the Fed, indicating the overnight rate is less than 100 basis points special. The one caveat is that basis trades are normally done with term repo to the end of the delivery month, whereas SOMA data only show overnight rates. Normally these two rates move together, and it's rare to see a rich overnight rate but cheap term rate. Consider what an amazing

FIGURE   1–33

Overnight repo rates jump lower during a squeeze

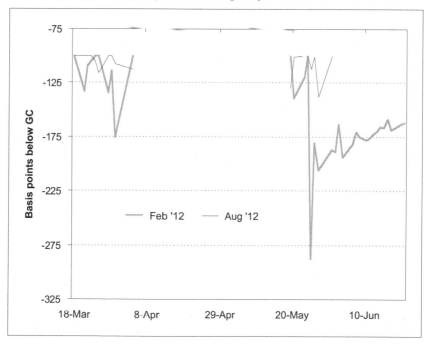

window onto the market SOMA data provide; we can look at not only the data for the cheapest issue, but the second cheapest as well. Remember why we're here in the first place; pricing squeezes and multi-issue deliveries.

A multi-issue delivery means that the short is going to have to buy not just the cheapest issue, but some bonds that aren't cheapest as well. Presumably, the first place the short would look would be to the second cheapest issue. Of course the converted forward price of this bond is higher than it is for the cheapest issue since it has the second lowest net basis in the basket. Using the SOMA data, we can see if the second cheapest bond is special in the repo market. If the futures market is implying a two-issue delivery, then wouldn't the repo market price in special rates for the issue as well since it is going to be delivered? Not necessarily. Remember that during each of the squeezes during 2005 the futures price implied a two-issue delivery, but it never ended up happening.

SOMA data provided one clue that suggested no one was considering delivering the second cheapest issue and the squeeze would break. Throughout the September delivery month Nov '12, the second cheapest issue, was never more than 100 basis points special and never showed up in SOMA lending operations. The contradiction was that the futures market was pricing in a multi-issue delivery but no one was withdrawing Nov '12 from the market in preparation for making delivery with it. People were saying that there was going to be a multi-issue delivery, but no one was acting on it. It's these contradictions that can make squeezes profitable for traders who know where to look for the clues. Although Aug '12, the cheapest issue, was trading very special in the repo market because of the threat of record deliveries, Nov '12 was never special enough for SOMA to take notice. This wasn't proof positive information that the squeeze was going to break, but it was a critical clue.

Why so much discussion about squeezes? It's important to realize that futures contracts don't always survive squeezes. There have been cases when the pressures on a contract, and more specifically on the hedgers and speculators who trade it, have been so extreme that both sides decided to walk away. The 10-year municipal contract at the CBOT is a perfect example. This contract was priced to a survey of municipal bond prices in the cash market by various dealers on the last day of trading. These dealers used the muni contract to hedge their position, and the CBOT relied on them for quotes to settle the contract. In hindsight, it doesn't take a genius to figure out that the dealers had an incentive to twist their prices and manipulate the value of the contract. It was routine in the market for dealers to go long the contracts settlement, or at least cover short positions, and then give quotes that were higher than the true value of bonds in the cash market to increase the settlement price of the contract. In fact, this was so regular that even the typical users of the contract came to expect it, except at the time there were no real alternatives to hedging municipal credit, and most users accepted this as the price of doing business. In most cases, the price change that might be chalked up to manipulation was relatively small in comparison to the losses that would have been caused by using another hedging vehicle. Here too, Wall Street traders might say that they were simply serving a pricing function; if muni hedgers need to use the contact badly enough, they will have to pay for the privilege.

The story ends predictably. During one expiration, some dealers reported prices on their cash instruments that were much higher than they should have been, trying to squeeze too much from the futures contract, and enough users griped loudly enough to make the CBOT redesign the contract. Unfortunately, it was too late, and open interest fell from more than 20,000 contracts to zero as depicted in Figure 1–34. Death of the muni-bond contract left a hole in an important part of the fixed income futures market, but it wasn't the first time that a squeeze led to the collapse of a contract. The Chicago Mercantile Exchange, with its traditional focus on short-term products, used to list and trade a T-bill contract. As bill supply dwindled in the 1990s and Treasury finances improved, it was evident that this contract was also vulnerable to squeezes. In an attempt to rectify the problem, the CME implemented position limits that increased as the time to maturity dwindled. The idea was to try to prevent a concentration of ownership in the few days leading up to the settlement of the contract. The result? The end of T-bill futures. Based on these two examples of once vibrant markets that were subsequently destroyed by squeezes, one might guess that the exchanges and regulators would have developed new tools or methods for dealing with manipulative practices. Not so! The response from the CBOT during the June and September

F I G U R E   1–34

Death of the muni bond contract

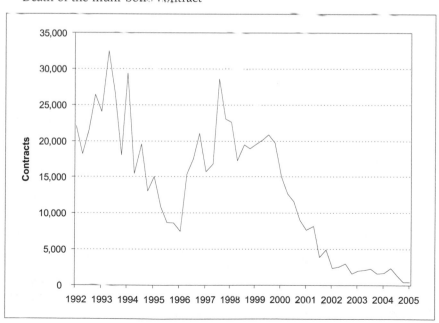

2005 10-year squeezes was to implement position limits, which were the same in-effective remedy for the T-bill contract at the CME.

One Problem, Three Solutions

The problem of fails in the repo market dramatically affects only a handful of securities but has the potential to bring the broader market to its knees. What were the proposed solutions? It turns out that there were three answers to the same question, each from a different market participant. The CBOT elected to implement position limits that prevented any one firm from holding enough contracts to create a squeeze. The Bond Market Association recommended repo "flip" rates, which would arbitrarily double the cost of failing in some cases. The Federal Reserve Bank of New York expanded its already popular SOMA program for lending securities that are trading special in the repo market. There has rarely been a more revealing instance about the mindset of each institution than how it responded to this crisis.

The CBOT was the first responder to the problem, and it implemented position limits, preventing a firm from holding more than roughly one-quarter of the amount outstanding of a deliverable bond or note, and going into effect 10 trading days before the expiration of the contract. In 10-year futures the limit is 50,000 contracts, or $5 billion notional value, which means that it would take at least three people doing the same trade to effectively squeeze the contracts. The rules do prevent any one firm from holding enough long contracts through delivery to individually impact the price. However, the rules don't prevent two or more people from doing the same trade and taking 50% or more of the face value of a deliverable issue through expiration. The impact of the limits was unclear to many traders, and it's easy to see why. The CBOT intended the limits to restrict any one individual's ability to squeeze the contracts; and while explicit collusion is illegal, the exchange is implicitly saying that a small group of people is less likely to all stay in the same trade and any tacit cooperation to squeeze the contract is likely to fall apart. What if you consider the same situation flipped on its head by saying that the position limits give traders a defense against the exchange or the CFCT claiming that they are manipulating the market as long as they are within the defined limits. There is a certain beauty to ambiguity from a regulator's perspective. Laws that create explicit rules are eventually going to be gamed, and the beauty and curse of the traditional system of jawboning by the exchange and regulators was that situations were evaluated individually and subject to varying interpretations.

A number of savvy traders have postulated that all squeezes are bound to fail and that there is a rational framework that proves it. But this is not strictly true! While there is a rational framework to evaluate the decision making of individuals involved in a squeeze, it's not a foregone conclusion that rational players will always choose to unravel early and unwind their positions before going through delivery. This question is of particular importance to futures traders judging the

TABLE 1–8

Prisoners' Dilemma, Payoffs, and Choices (Where S < P < R < T)

	Collude	Defect
Collude	R, R	S, T
Defect	T, S	P, P

potential impact of position limits on prices. Beginning on December 1, 2005, no individual could hold contracts with a face value of more than approximately one-quarter of the size of the deliverable issue. Does this mean that it will only take four people to collude to force an uneconomical delivery, driving up certain Treasury prices?

Table 1–8 illustrates how a squeeze involving futures is like the prisoner's dilemma, a famous example that illustrates a conflict between individual and group decision making. A group whose members pursue self-interest may end up worse off than a group whose members act contrary to their individual interests. The math isn't intuitive, but the story is. Suppose two bank robbers are caught and individually offered a deal where they either are released with 100% of their loot if only one robber implicates the other, receive a heavy sentence if they both implicate each other, or are both released and have to split the loot if neither says a word. Does only one robber turn on the other, do both robbers turn on the other, or do they both stay silent? This is the most basic example of competitive strategy, and the rational choice for each individual is to defect and implicate the other in the crime, although it means that both will do so, resulting in a heavy punishment that neither of them wants.

The implication for trading futures is that if the payoff for defecting and unwinding the trade early is larger than the payoff for colluding, the squeeze will collapse. This is a *Nash equilibrium,* and a player can only do worse making another choice. However, this result hinges on the payoffs we detail in Table 1–8: S < P and R < T (Silence is less than Punishment, and Reward is less than Temptation), where temptation (T) offers the greatest payoff of any of the choices. Mapping this framework to futures markets implies that the payoff from one trader defecting, choosing not to squeeze the contract and unwind his position early, is greater than the payoff from going through with the squeeze. Does this make sense? At some points in the Sep 10-year cycle the contracts were pricing in the chance of receiving not just the second cheapest issue, but some of the third cheapest as well. If traders know that successfully carrying out their squeeze will only succeed in receiving the second, but not the third cheapest, then it makes sense to unwind their position early.

What if the contracts are priced so that the payoff from unwinding early is the same as following through with a squeeze? If S < P or R < T, then the situation

TABLE 1–9

Player 2's Payoffs, Given Player 1's Choices

	Collude	Defect
Collude	R <	T
Defect	S <	P

is slightly changed. In this case, it's not a given that a squeeze will fail since a player can do at least as well by colluding and going through with delivery. The bottom line is that it will normally be rational for traders to break a squeeze by unwinding their positions prior to delivery, but there are payoffs and market prices where this is not true.

If Player 1 colludes with Player 2 and stays silent S, they both go free and split the loot in half receiving reward R. If only one player turns on the other (defects), he is set free and keeps all of the money while the other rots in jail, which is temptation T. If they both turn the other in, then both receive moderate punishment P. Neither player controls the choice of the other, and both see their payoffs the same way. If Player 1 colludes and stays silent, then the choices of Player 2 are as shown in Table 1–9.

Here, it's the optimal strategy to defect since the payoffs are higher no matter what Player 1 does.

What if the payoffs between two of the choices are not strictly larger? If the payoff is equal to or larger than the original choice, it's denoted by the underscores in Table 1–10.

In this case it's not a given that a player colludes or defects, since the payoffs might be the same. If the CBOT is basing its position limits on this type of analysis, the results are indeterminate at best, because it's not clear that there is an incentive for any individual to break or not break the squeeze. The important conclusion to take away from this analysis is that squeezes are not automatically doomed to fail and that there is really nothing that the CBOT can do, outside of jawboning and regulatory enforcement, that can provide an economic incentive

TABLE 1–10

When Payoffs Are Not Strictly Different $(S \leq P \leq R \leq T)$

	Collude	Defect
Collude	R ≤	T
Defect	S ≤	P

not to manipulate the price of its contracts. In spite of the fact that we've found evidence that quasi-market programs cannot replace the necessary duty of a regulator to enforce fair play, that doesn't keep people from coming up with new schemes, as we see with the second proposed solution to the fails problem from The Bond Market Association (BMA).

The Bond Market Association has proposed that Treasury traders agree to enter into repo "flip" rate agreements to prevent fails. The BMA proposal may have a chilling effect on trading in issues that have some chance of failing, and it could effectively end trading in some off-the-run issues. The proposal is that traders agree to change the terms of repo trades so that if one fails to deliver collateral into the opening leg of a trade, where she is "paying" a negative rate, the rate would change signs and "flip" so that the trader is paying a positive rate. For example, a trader in possession of a note that is in high demand who enters into a repo trade where she is borrowing money and "paying" a rate of –2% would earn 2%. Under the current rules, if the trader fails to deliver the collateral, the trader earns nothing, and there is an opportunity cost of 2%. The BMA guidelines would mean that rather than paying –2%, the sign would flip and the trader would be paying 2%, creating a 4% swing in the trader's costs. Why arbitrarily flip the sign of an interest rate?

Opportunity costs are real costs! Forgoing 2% in interest won't show up in accounting profits or losses, but it's certainly an economic cost. The BMA proposal would double the opportunity cost and impose it as an explicit cost, implying that forgone income isn't enough of a motivator as a hard dollar charge. The BMA is searching for a quasi-market system for clearing up fails, which might be justified if there were problems all across the curve. However, the only issues subject to significant fails in 2005 were off-the-run 10-year notes that were cheapest-to-deliver into futures contracts. Rather than address the problems surrounding deliveries to the CBOT in a small handful of issues, the BMA is treating this as if it were a systemic problem. Figure 1–31 also illustrated that the fails problem was related to issue sizes after the notes that were CTD into 10y contracts, and by the second half of 2006 the problem would take care of itself, because the upcoming issues are larger and there's less chance of their being scarce in the repo market.

The third solution to the fails problem, which comes from the Federal Reserve Bank of New York (FRBNY), builds on an already successful program and is likely to deepen liquidity in off-the-run issues. The FRBNY change will affect the System Open Market Account (SOMA) by changing the dealer per issue limit from $200 million to 20% of the theoretical available supply of an issue with a cap at $500 million. The dealer aggregate limit will also grow from $1 billion to $3 billion. SOMA lends bonds from its portfolio when they are more than 100 basis points special in the overnight repo market, and traders typically perceive issues with large holdings at the Fed to have a limit as to how rich they can get. In the past SOMA lending has helped put the brakes on idiosyncratic richening of individual issues, and beefing the program up is certainly positive for

the market by ensuring there's an additional supply of notes when they're needed most. The dramatic change in the SOMA program has gone a long way toward
preventing squeezes in the future, but there is a limit to how large SOMA holdings can grow before they begin to cause the kind of scarcity they're meant to
prevent.

At this point the CBOT, the BMA, and FRBNY have all responded to the
fails problem in different ways, but only the FRBNY was able to respond in a way
that neither restricted trading nor was punitive. At the beginning of our studies
of the Treasury and futures markets the fails problem may have appeared so vast
as to be impossible to get a hold of. The response of three different organizations
to this problem, a problem brought about by attempts to manipulate the market,
draws in sharp relief who the different players are and the tension between
laissez-faire policies and forcing an even playing field. Markets aren't about
equations or prices, but rather these things transmit the intentions of the players.
Traders, regulators, and exchanges don't always get it right, but understanding
their decisions means understanding the foundations of a market.

EURODOLLAR FUTURES

Eurodollar futures at the Chicago Mercantile Exchange (CME) are currently the most actively traded and liquid fixed income instrument in the world. They were originally misunderstood and used solely as a tool to control money market risk; few traders initially seized on the versatility of the product. Although Eurodollar futures had been introduced in 1981, more than a decade passed before such trading gained a critical mass. Two related trends during the late 1990s were key in the development of this market: improving government finances leading to lower Treasury supply, and growth of the retained portfolios of government-sponsored entities (GSEs) like Fannie Mae and Freddie Mac. These trends turned out to be cyclical, and both were eventually reversed in the early part of the next decade. By this time Eurodollar futures had gained enough of a foothold in the market to retain the liquidity they enjoyed during the days of heady growth.

It wasn't an accident that the GSEs aggressively grew their portfolios at a time when the supply of Treasury debt was shrinking. The GSEs viewed falling Treasury supply as an opportunity to create a new benchmark in the market, against which every other instrument could be referenced. In fact, the concept was so important to the GSEs that it became part of the sales literature of the two largest, Fannie Mae and Freddie Mac. Both entities sought to standardize their issuance patterns using the Treasury market as a model. Rather than opportunistically pitting their traders against buyers of their debt, only coming to market with structures they believed were expensive, the idea was that predictable issuance would deepen liquidity and reduce borrowing costs in the long run. Although individual notes might not come at the optimal time, the program as a whole would benefit as Agencies became the new standard "risk free" rate. In the late 1990s it wasn't clear whether Agencies or interest rate swaps would become the new benchmark; Agencies took an early lead, but then it appeared as if interest rate swaps were the clear winner as the new fixed income benchmark. As it turns out, neither product assumed that mantle.

Wall Street is unique in the fact that many people who work there feel completely comfortable taking the last 15 minutes of history and projecting it out 15 years! Falling Treasury and growing Agency supply turned out to be a singular landmark in the history of fixed income markets, because the situation was quickly reversed, as illustrated in Figure 2–1. Although no one could have predicted the specific reasons for a return to federal budget deficits, the general pattern should not have surprised anyone. Budget surpluses of the late 1990s were short lived,

FIGURE 2-1

Growth of the fixed income market

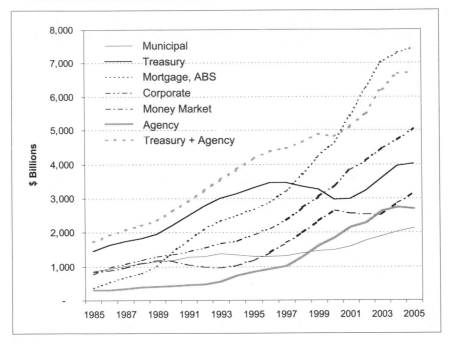

and government finances inevitably deteriorated after 2001. Once again there was a glut of new Treasury supply that would slowly crowd out borrowing by private companies. Specifically, it was increased spending on security that ballooned government borrowing and accounting errors that put the brakes on Agency growth. This is all relevant for the Eurodollar market because of the way in which the Agencies were growing; using high leverage to buy mortgage securities.

Leverage amplifies financial results. Even small fluctuations or discrepancies in hedging can have significant dollar values attached to them in leveraged strategies. By statute, Fannie Mae and Freddie Mac were originally required to hold just $2.50 for every $100 in mortgages they retained in their portfolios. This implied that the leverage of the GSEs could be considerable at 40:1. Compare this to Long Term Capital Management, a hedge fund that failed in 1998 and was famously bailed out by the Federal Reserve, employed around 100:1 leverage at its peak. Since mortgage securities are ultimately credit products, and there is no guarantee that the borrower will make good on her home mortgage loan, there has always been a slightly higher hedging correlation between mortgages and other credit products than between mortgages and Treasuries. Practically speaking, most people would do anything to avoid losing their homes, and most mortgages that meet certain criteria are guaranteed by the Agencies. One interesting aspect of this market is that the institutions that guarantee mortgages are also the largest investors in them, which undermines the strength of their obligation since rising defaults would drain an Agency two ways, through higher payouts on defaulted loan guarantees as well as lost earnings in their retained portfolios. Given that every small difference in correlation between Treasuries and mortgages could be amplified 40 times over in the GSE portfolios, the demand for products with greater hedge effectiveness grew. In fact, the demand for these hedges grew in proportion to the amount of mortgages held at high leverage. Interest rate swaps, which amount to synthetic corporate bonds issued by Wall Street dealers, grew into the instrument of choice for the Agencies to hedge their mortgage risk. The only problem for the dealers was where to put all of the risk from the other sides of the trades.

This is the point in the story where Eurodollars come to the forefront, because as much as three-quarters of trading in these futures is done by interest rate swap dealers. As it turns out, there are frequently times when a Wall Street dealer will trade an interest rate swap but can't find a customer to take the opposing view, which means that they have to hold the other side of their trade. Eurodollars can be used to hedge that risk, because even though each contract covers only a 3-month period, a string of consecutive contracts behaves like a fixed-rate interest rate swap. In fact, most interest rate swap contracts are written to make them easy to hedge with Eurodollars, including payment dates matching up to futures expirations. The genius of the design of these contracts is that instruments that settle to a floating rate, in this case 3-month LIBOR, can be combined in a string to create a synthetic fixed-rate bond. Depending on how they're combined, these contracts can represent any spot or forward period. They can be held individually to replicate short-term floating interest rates or in groups to create a fixed-rate note, and as we'll see, there is an enormous amount of information embedded in the price of each Eurodollar contract, including the yield of the group as a whole and the interest rate risk that it represents.

Eurodollar futures are cash settled to 3-month LIBOR, and their simple structure belies a subtle implication that makes them well suited for mortgage hedging. Originally conceived as a means of hedging money market risk, Eurodollar futures are cash settled to 100 minus the 3-month LIBOR rate 2 days before the third Wednesday of the expiration month. Each Eurodollar contract represents just 3 months of risk beginning on the expiration date and there are currently 40 contracts listed, representing 10 years of possible interest rate exposure. There is no physical delivery or explicit embedded option as with Treasury futures; however, a convexity bias in these contracts makes them behave as if the contract were short an embedded option. As with any option, the value of this bias increases with time to expiration, and it is worth more for deferred contracts expiring in 5 years than it is for contracts with just 3 months to live. This aspect of the contracts was widely ignored in the early years of trading because so much of the activity was focused on the front end of the curve, with virtually no trading beyond 2 years.

While the first 2 years' worth of contracts remain the most liquid, there is grow-ing open interest in longer maturities, and the first 20 contracts, representing 5 years' worth of risk, are routinely executed as a bundle of staggering size. It could be many years before all 10 years' worth of contracts are liquid enough for the average trader; but convexity bias is an important consideration for the contracts that are actively traded today, and it can significantly impact the value of contracts with expirations past 2 years.

The convexity bias in Eurodollar futures stems from their discount style pricing, where they settle to 100 minus 3-month LIBOR quoted as an add-on interest rate. Since prices and yields move 1:1 in this framework, these futures have no convexity. When used to hedge a fixed-rate swap, there is a systematic advantage to being short contracts with no convexity, and long a fixed-rate swap which is positively convex. Suppose that one were receiving fixed coupon pay-ments on a 5-year swap and had sold a package of Eurodollars with a final matu-rity 5 years in the future, effectively creating a synthetic fixed-rate offset for the swap and a duration-neutral position. It's normal for rates to move by some small amount every day, with major news periodically causing substantial jumps. Whenever there is an interest rate move, the positively convex swap is going to appreciate by just a little bit more than 1:1 between price and yield, as duration would predict, but the price of the Eurodollar contracts move 1:1 with changes in yields. If the position is marked to market every day, profits will slowly accumu-late to the holder of the fixed-rate bond based on the size of the daily moves.

There's no free lunch! Since this phenomenon is well known, the market lowers the price of the futures contracts to account for this bias. In essence, the market requires that the seller of contracts pay a higher rate to compensate for the advantage of selling instruments with no convexity. Though there is no explicit option, these mechanics operate very much like a straddle because the prices of deferred contracts have to be lowered by an amount that is based on anticipated volatility in both up and down moves, but the actual convexity advantage will be determined by realized volatility. The same is true of naked options that are priced on implied volatility, which is the market's expectation of future volatility. The true value of the options depends on realized volatility, which is only known after the fact. In this way Eurodollar and Treasury futures are more alike than differ-ent, since both behave as if they were short options. The same is true of many types of mortgages, which makes futures an excellent choice to mirror the perfor-mance of these securities.

However, Treasury and Eurodollar futures are dissimilar along another dimension—their underlying risks are different. While a Treasury futures contract will respond to changes in Treasury rates, and perhaps be occasionally influenced only by changes in credit conditions during flight to quality trading, Eurodollar contracts are directly tied to the London Interbank Offer Rate (LIBOR), which is a credit product. This rate is much like the Fed Funds rate in the United States since it too is a credit product representing unsecured interbank loans and serves as an international benchmark. Every day the British Bankers' Association polls

16 banks with an average credit rating of AA– for money market rates with maturities from 1 day to 1 year. If the credit quality of these banks or their counterparties deteriorates, that will certainly raise LIBOR rates, dropping Eurodollar prices.

To make sense of the 40 listed contracts, the Chicago Mercantile Exchange (CME) organizes contracts into annual groups, each with a unique color code. There are 10 annual groups, and Figure 2–2 illustrates open interest by each contract and color code. By far, the vast majority of activity is in the first few contracts, though over time trading interest has been growing farther out the curve, and the past few years have seen a marked increase in the Green and Blue contracts. The Eurodollar futures market has also developed a somewhat unique terminology, referring to annual color codes as *packs* and groups of two or more annual packages as *bundles*. A *strip* of contracts is more generic, denoting only a series or adjacent expirations that may not fall into annual color codes. The terminology aids in quotation since it's often more convenient to quote changes in four consecutive contracts as a whole, rather than individually.

Equally convenient is the fact that the dollar value of a 1-basis-point change in rates is constant, at $25 per contract. By contrast, the potential duration drift of

FIGURE 2–2

Eurodollar futures volume and open interest

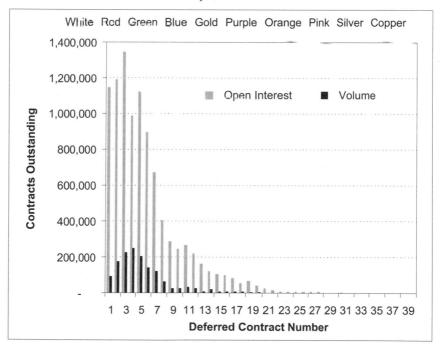

FIGURE   2–3

Hedge effectiveness versus net carry costs

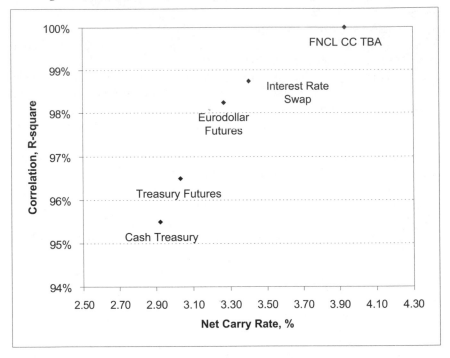

Treasury contracts means that the dollar value of a 1-basis-point change in yield, the DV01, may change. Quick and dirty hedge ratios require far less work with Eurodollars, but as we'll see these seemingly simple contracts require quite a lot of analysis in order to realize their full usefulness. From the perspective of mortgage hedgers there is a second advantage having to do with the fact that Eurodollars are a LIBOR-based instrument: they offer higher correlations to mortgage rates than do Treasuries. Figure 2–3 shows the correlation of 5-year instruments to generic mortgage rates, in this case 30-year TBA mortgage pass-throughs, against their net carry rate. The higher the net carry rate, the more costly an instrument is to sell short. Though LIBOR instruments have higher correlations, which may lead to greater hedge effectiveness over time, they also tend to have higher net carry rates, and are relatively more costly to sell short. The choice of a futures hedge is very much determined on a quality spectrum, with less effective but less costly alternatives based on Treasuries, to more effective but more costly instruments based on LIBOR. The old trader's joke asks, how do we hedge a bond? By selling it! This is apropos of Figure 2–3, since it's possible to achieve a perfect correlation to new-issue mortgage rates by selling TBA collateral forward.

The problem is that this is also the most costly solution, and futures may allow a mortgage hedger to maintain a reasonably effective duration offset while earning more positive carry from a relatively high mortgage yield. Ultimately mortgage hedging, whether it's coming directly from portfolios holding them at high leverage, or indirectly from dealers offsetting risk from swaps done with mortgage hedgers, remains the most important class of users for Eurodollar futures. In fact, the growing trend away from long-term fixed-rate mortgage pass-throughs toward hybrid ARMs, dubbed the "hybridization" of the mortgage universe, plays right to the strengths of the Eurodollar market. Hedging for these products relies mainly on the front end of the curve, where Eurodollars have traditionally been the most liquid and have become the product of choice.

AN EMPIRICAL APPROACH TO CONVEXITY BIAS

Even novices know that Eurodollars settle to 3-month LIBOR, but consider what this rate represents: an unsecured short-term deposit between large money center banks. While few might imagine that one of these large international banks might fail, defaulting on its short-term loan, there have been spectacular exceptions in the past. Large money center banks as well as brokerages, including Barrings Bank and Drexel Burnham Lambert, have seen their fortunes change in as little as a 3-month period. Although the default risk of short-term interbank loans is small, it's not zero, which makes LIBOR a credit product. Short- and long-term loan rates are related, since stringing together consecutive terms of LIBOR deposits creates a synthetic fixed-rate corporate bond that the market perceives as being interchangeable with interest rate swaps. Understanding how interest rate swaps are constructed will make it clear how Eurodollars are their ideal hedging instrument, as well as what we're really after: an empirical approach to model convexity bias and to determine fair value for each contract.

The easiest way to understand interest rate swaps is to pick up where we left off with a levered Treasury position. Borrowing money to buy a Treasury means paying some rate in the repo market. Although repo terms can be anything from overnight to 1 year, most trades are done with standardized dates on the last day of each quarter. In this case the holder of the Treasury note earns the interest from the long-maturity fixed-rate leg of the trade but pays some financing cost in the repo market. What if we decided that the Treasury note we are buying needs to be financed for the remainder of its life, with individual repo terms no longer than one-quarter of a year? In this case we would essentially create a synthetic floating-rate repo note, the cost of which would be weighed against the yield-to-maturity of the Treasury. A financed Treasury has exactly the same economics as an interest rate swap: long-maturity fixed-rate leg and a short-maturity floating-rate leg. Not only are the reset dates for the floating-rate leg standardized in the swap market, but so too are conventions for pricing the fixed-rate leg. One of the original selling points for the swap market is that the 3-month LIBOR leg could never go special like the financing for a Treasury, but experience has shown that swaps do move in sympathy to prices in the Treasury market, although the movements aren't perfectly correlated.

Just as Treasury notes and bonds have their coupons fixed when they are auctioned, the same is true with interest rate swaps. In fact, the most common type of swap is a *par swap*, meaning that the initial price is fixed at 100 and the coupon is changed to match the yield. This convention makes the terms of a new interest rate swap easy to understand: a fixed-rate leg with the coupon equal to the initial yield to maturity, against a floating-rate 3-month LIBOR leg. If a trader either pays or receives the fixed-rate leg, he will do the opposite in the floating-rate leg. Another simplifying aspect of this market is that there is no initial exchange of principal on a par swap, since the present value of the fixed and floating rate sides are the same. How could that be if the 3-month LIBOR rate is different from the yield and coupon on the fixed-rate leg of the swap?

If we accept the premise that a long-maturity interest rate swap is merely a series of 3-month deposits, then the present value of the two should be equal. The ingenious observation that lets this market function is that future 3-month LIBOR rates should be priced as implied forward rates from the interest rate swap curve. The British Bankers' Association (BBA) publishes LIBOR fixings from overnight to 1 year, including 3- and 6-month rates. There is no ambiguity about where the front Eurodollar contract will settle, since the BBA explicitly publishes the rate, but what about the next contract? The BBA doesn't publish the 3-month rate, 3 months forward, but it does publish the 6-month rate. Knowing the rate for the first 3 months and the entire 6-month period means that we can imply the rate for the second 3-month period:

$$R(n) = \frac{r(n) \bullet n - r(n-1) \bullet (n-1)}{(n) - (n-1)}$$

If the 6-month BBA rate is 4.65 and the 3-month rate is 4.45, then the 3-month rate in 3 months is 4.85:

$$4.85 = \frac{4.65 \bullet 0.5 - 4.45 \bullet 0.25}{0.5 - 0.25}$$

This is an elementary conclusion that every first-year finance student learns, but the implication for the Eurodollar market is profound because it allows for the pricing of the deferred contracts with great precision. However, what happens when we run out of BBA fixings, since they're only published out to 1 year? This is the point where we run into "chicken or egg" problems.

Do deferred Eurodollar contract prices determine swap rates, or is it the other way around? We can't calculate implied forward rates unless we know the rate for the entire term, as with the equations above. We couldn't, for example, determine the prices for a sequence of 3-month contracts out to 2 years without knowing the 2-year swap yield. But if swap rates are merely the sum of a sequence of 3-month LIBOR deposits, don't we have to know all of the rates to determine the 2-year yield? This is the fundamental problem when pricing Eurodollar contracts: the convention is to assume that they are implied forward rates from the swap curve. Although the term *implied* gives the idea that Eurodollar rates are a derivation from the swap curve, Eurodollars help to determine the swap curve so, in fact, these rates are not "implied" at all. Whatever the case may be, the convention is to interpret Eurodollar rates as implied forward rates, so that the average yield on a string of them will equal the yield on a swap of the same maturity. Even though no one knows what future 3-month LIBOR rates will be, they are derived from the swap curve so that at initiation of the trade the present value of the fixed and floating rate legs are equal.

Unfortunately, there is an additional complication before we can prove the point, because Eurodollar rates are quoted in a different basis from the Treasury or swap market and are not annual percentage rates. Rather, Eurodollar rates are quoted as add-on interest, which is slightly lower than money market rates, quoted in actual/360-day count. For example, a contract price of 96.00 implies:

Contract price:	96.00
Add-on yield:	4%
Add-on interest:	$1mm • 0.04 • 91/360 = $10,111
Discount price:	$1mm − 10,111 = $989,889
Money market yield:	$10,111/$989,889 • (360/91) = 4.04%

In this case the money market yield is just 4 basis points higher than the add-on yield, but this difference grows as rates rise. For example, the spread between the two if the add-on yield were 7% would be 13 basis points. Although 7% is 1.75 times our original 4% number, the difference between add-on and money market rates is more than 3 times larger, and precision counts when the dollar values grow.

Consider the pieces we have at this point. The first is our leap of faith that an interest rate swap is interchangeable with a series of 3-month LIBOR deposits. The second is a calculation of implied forward rates for at least the first year's worth of Eurodollar contracts. Finally we have a way of translating the add-on interest from a LIBOR deposit into a standard money market rate quote. These pieces allow us to build a synthetic fixed-rate bond with the first four Eurodollar contracts. Table 2–1 illustrates the process in reverse, taking the first year's worth of BBA fixings and calculating implied forward rates. Knowing that these rate quotes are in a different basis from the Eurodollar rate quote, we have to translate money market rates in add-on interest. Finally, Eurodollars are quoted as 100 less the add-on interest rate in the last column labeled *MMR*. The last column (*Strip Yield*) shows the average yield for a string of Eurodollar contracts, beginning with the first expiration and ending with each successive contract.

Figure 2–4 expands on the table and illustrates the synthetic fixed-rate bond yields that we've built with Eurodollars, showing how the strip yield, the average

TABLE 2–1

Building a Synthetic Interest

Contract	Expiration	Settle Price	100-Price	Change	Convexity Bias, Bp	Adjusted Rate	MMR	Strip Yield
EDZ5	Dec. '05	95.50	4.50	–	0.03	4.50	4.55	4.55
EDH6	Mar. '06	95.23	4.77	0.50	0.30	4.77	4.82	4.69
EDM6	Jun. '06	95.12	4.88	1.00	0.58	4.87	4.93	4.77
EDU6	Sep. '06	95.13	4.88	1.50	0.88	4.87	4.93	4.81

money market yield for the contracts, is going to lag behind the yield of the longest maturity contract, as would any average. In this example, the yield of the final contract is 4.93, but the average yield, including all four contracts, is 4.81. This is an important consideration since two things happen as the futures contract expiration becomes more distant: rates are typically much higher than the average yield of all of the contracts to that point, and each new contract has less and

FIGURE 2–4

Simple Eurodollar strip hedge construction

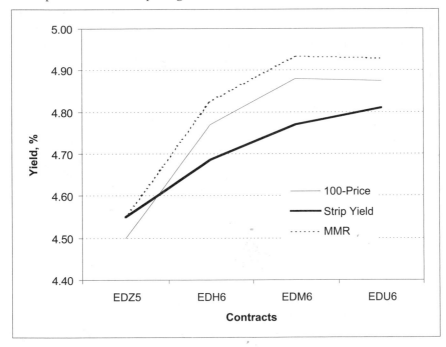

FIGURE 2–5

Eurodollar curve and convexity bias

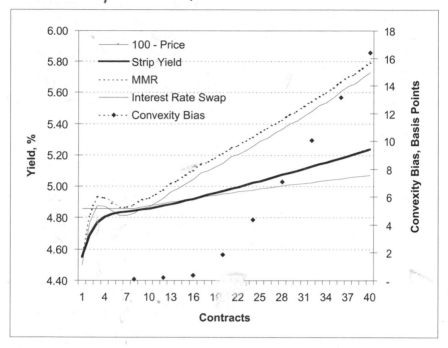

less influence on the yield of the strip as a whole. This point will be discussed again in the final section of this chapter on hedging, which uses a mathematical decomposition to test for the amount of pricing information contained in each contract. Although that approach is analytically robust, an explanation for why only the first few years' worth of contracts are traded need be no more complicated than an understanding of the average yield. As the number of contracts grows by including distant expirations, the individual contribution of each falls, and so does the trading in that issue.

While Figure 2–4 is illustrative of the mechanics of determining strip yields, it belies the depth of the market. Figure 2–5 illustrates all 40 Eurodollar contracts, out to 10 years, as well as the strip yields and interest rate swap yields. What's interesting about this graph is that there is a growing and apparently systematic discrepancy between the strip yield and swap rate. As the maturity grows, the synthetic swap rate derived from Eurodollar contracts is uniformly higher than the interest rate swap rate observed in the market, and the dotted line illustrates this difference distinctly. Although there is little difference between the Eurodollar and swap market in the first 2 years and only a small difference at the 5-year point, at just a few basis points, from that point on the difference grows substantially.

What are 2 basis points worth? Considering that there are more than 5 million contracts open and that back-month contracts trade in 1/2-basis point increments, this difference amounts to paying four times the bid/ask spread, or $250 million across all of the contracts. Although very few contracts with 10-year expirations actually trade, the difference is quite high at this point. What's going on?

Initially we mentioned that the contract design was 100 less the add-on interest rate for that particular 3-month period. With a 1:1 trade-off between price and yield, Eurodollars have no convexity. Of course, coupon bonds have convexity, as illustrated by the axis on the right in Figure 2–5. If an interest rate swap has the same economics as a sequence of 3-month LIBOR contracts, what happens when one instrument has convexity but the other doesn't? There is a systematic advantage to owning an instrument that has positive convexity and being short a duration- and maturity-matched instrument that has no convexity. However, it's the value of this advantage that's difficult to quantify. In Eurodollars this difference in yield between the synthetic fixed-rate bond created with a strip of contracts and a swap of the same maturity is called the *convexity bias*.

Suppose that we are long a 5-year interest rate swap and short the first 20 Eurodollar contracts. Every day it's normal for interest rates to change slightly, even when there is no economic news, because prices are determined by transactions and it's almost never the case that buyers and sellers come to the market at exactly the same time. Since futures are marked to market every day, the interest rate swap will appreciate by slightly more than 1:1 in a rally, and depreciate by slightly less than 1:1 in price/yield in a sell-off than the strip of contracts. Of course, the price difference is small on a daily basis, as illustrated by Figure 2–6, but it adds up over time. From 1990 to 2005 the average daily yield change for a 5-year interest rate swap was 4.8 basis points and the average yield was 5.96%. From the chart we can estimate, as a rule of thumb, that a 100-basis-point change in yield would have caused the performance of the two to drift apart by just a small fraction, around 0.1175 points. Since the average daily change was 4.8 basis points, a simple ratio indicates that the daily convexity advantage of the interest rate swap was 0.0056 points. With 252 trading days in the year, this also indicates that the yearly value would be around 1.42 points, which is quite substantial.

This approach isn't bad as a rough estimate, and it certainly explains the convexity bias in an intuitive way, but it has some problems, not the least of which is that we pulled the value off of a graph rather than directly measuring it! This first approach is valuable though because it does highlight another element that's not always evident in analytical solutions: the price/yield line in Figure 2–6 is not perfectly symmetrical, meaning that the price value of yield changes isn't exactly the same for a 100-basis-point move up in rates as it is for the same move down. Although the difference in direction of rate changes is small, it's noticeable if we are considering how to value a contract that will last almost 5 years. How about a contract that is going to last 10 years? In this case it's necessary to rely on a computer to keep track of all the decimal dust accumulated by rate changes on a daily basis. As we'll see, not all volatilities are the same.

FIGURE 2–6

Roots of convexity bias—1:1 changes in Eurodollar price to yield

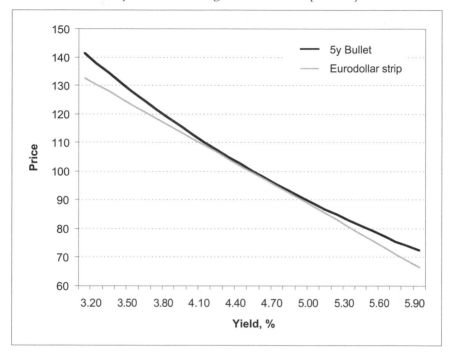

Figure 2–7 graphs the cumulative value of daily convexity by year, and it's obvious that there are substantial differences across time. Although this is a result we might expect, what's unexpected is that even in years where the standard deviation is quite close, the cumulative dollar value can be significantly different. What this chart is picking up is that there are different price patterns that could produce the same standard deviation. Lots of little changes or a few gigantic changes might have the same aggregate standard deviation but produce different cumulative dollar values for convexity. Part of the difference can be explained by the asymmetry between "up" and "down" moves in rates, but this is a small difference. The real driver of these differences comes from the growing distance between the straight and curved lines in Figure 2–6 due to convexity of the coupon bond. Put another way, a 10-basis-point move in rates is worth more than 2 days worth of 5-basis-point moves.

Figure 2–7 illustrates that over time, even though there are years when the same volatility produces different values, there are clear trends across years and maturities. This chart is the key to understanding convexity bias because it provides a road map to link predicted volatility to the price impact of convexity differences. Remember that the ultimate goal is to determine how much lower the

FIGURE 2–7

The link between yield volatility and convexity advantage

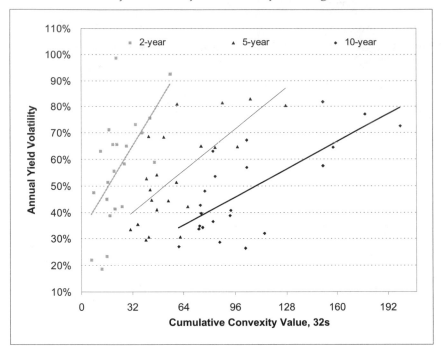

prices of deferred contracts should be so that traders are indifferent between being long one and short the other in a duration-neutral interest rate swap and Eurodollar strip position. Rather than produce a closed-form solution, which may or may not be consistent with the empirical evidence, it's possible to directly observe historical values and use those as a foundation for predictions.

Just as a string of 20 Eurodollar contracts creates a synthetic fixed-rate bond, we can estimate the convexity bias using the results from Figure 2–7. This value must include the 5-year bond for 1 year, a 4-year bond for 1 year, and so on. Over the life of the bond we can sum up the changing value of the convexity difference and construct a model curve to estimate all of the points in between. We are able to estimate what the dollar value of the convexity bias is not only for a 5-year bond, but also for all of the Eurodollar contracts along the curve that create it. The *x* axis in Figure 2–7 is in thirty-seconds, which means we have to multiply them by $31.25 to turn them into dollar amounts (the "ticks" in this table are arbitrarily calculated with $100,000 face). If we know the dollar value per year of a convexity mismatch and we know what the term structure looks like (the shape of convexity bias across maturities), then we can determine the quarterly values applicable to each futures contract with a simple interpolation.

Take the 2004 value or the 5-year swap as an example. The value that year was 30.7 ticks, which is a dollar value of $959.38. As a rule of thumb we might simply divide that value by 4, knowing that there are four quarterly contracts that make up the 5 year point, which implies that each contract would be lower in price by $239.85. Of course, Eurodollars trade in basis points that are worth $25, so this is the equivalent of 9.6 basis points. If we had calculated the implied forward rates for the swap curve, starting with the BBA fixes and working our way out, this implies that we would have to drop the price of the four 5-year contracts by 9.6 basis points each before we were indifferent between owning the Eurodollar contracts with no convexity and a fixed-coupon swap covering the same period. Although the yield of the Eurodollar strip is higher than the implied forward rate, the long holder of contracts would never realize this extra income because we calculated that 9.6 basis points of it would come from daily volatility. If the Eurodollar contracts were each priced less than 9.6 basis points below the implied forward rates and the same volatility from 2004 occurred again, then it's easy to say that they are mispriced.

There are a few things we can do to make our estimate of fair value in the contracts more precise. The obvious next step is to take advantage of the fact that we have volatility information at the 2-year and 10-year points, and we don't have to simply divide the $959 by 4 for each contract. Figure 2–7 takes the 2-, 5- and 10-year volatility information from 2004 and interpolates a curve around the 5-year point. Not surprisingly, the curve is slightly upward sloping, indicating that the value of convexity bias should be a little lower for the shorter expiration contract and a little longer as the expiration extends. Based on the curve we drew, the average of all four is 9.6 basis points, but in essence, we've taken the original estimate of $959 for the year and spread those dollars across each contract, assigning a little less for the front months and a little more for the back months.

The second thing we can do to increase the odds that our predictions based on historical evidence more accurately predict future results is to return to the median volatility lines in Figure 2–7. As we pointed out before, even a year with the same annual volatility can produce different dollar values for the convexity bias depending on the specific price action. Years with lots of outliers are likely to generate larger dollar values (values to the right of the regression line in the chart) than years with heavy but steady price moves (which would register to the left of the regression lines in the chart). Even if we knew with absolute certainty what the annual volatility of a particular part of the curve was going to be, we couldn't determine the dollar value of the convexity bias with certainty because we don't know the specific characteristics of that year's movements. The benefit of historical measurements is that even though any one particular year may have unique characteristics, there are shared patterns across years that we can take advantage of by measuring something like a "central tendency" for convexity bias to revolve around.

Finally, this approach means that we aren't saddled with simply using the previous year's volatility as our prediction of future values. The regression lines in Figure 2–7 allow us to estimate the convexity value for any volatility level, and if last year was a particularly quiet year, but we have some sort of information leading us to believe that next year will be a blowout at double the level of last year, we have a way of measuring that as well. In fact, what might be the best way to implement this approach is to use a rolling history of some length, perhaps 90 or 180 days, to get an indication about the trend of future volatility. Taking these volatilities and then mapping them to a convexity bias value is the most forward-looking approach to estimating fair value for the Eurodollar strip. While the implied forward rate calculation is mechanical and relatively straightforward, the convexity bias calculation took some time to develop. What is the end result of all this work? We can now revisit our original table and add another dimension of realism to the calculations.

Table 2–2 contains all of the ingredients necessary to cook up a synthetic fixed-rate bond with Eurodollars, which would be necessary if we were hedging a 2-year interest rate swap and there were no other way for a trader to shed the risk with an offsetting transaction. As before, we begin with the BBA fixings for the first year to calculate the first four quarterly rates (the first rate we use is the spot 3-month LIBOR rate and the next three are implied). Ignoring the causality issue we outlined earlier about whether Eurodollar rates lead to swap rates or the other way around, suppose that we are able to observe swap rates in the spot market from 1 to 2 years. Knowing that these rates are quoted as money market rates, we have to translate them into add-on interest rates, which is the convention for quotations in Eurodollars. It's at this point that we apply the convexity bias determined with our empirical observations from Figure 2–7. At this point we have determined the fair value for each of the eight contracts and we know where each should be priced, assuming the market shares our expectations about future volatility. After much effort we have determined what we should be paying for each of the contracts individually, but there's another lens through which to perceive value in this market.

What if we go in the opposite direction and put our futures fair values back into money market rates to calculate a strip yield so we can compare it to the 2-year swap rate? Because most contracts are traded as either packs or bundles against them, it may make more sense to view them in aggregate against interest rate swaps rather than individually. Assuming an equal weighting of all eight contracts, we can take the average of all the money market yields in Table 2–2 and, if the work to this point is correct, we should get a value that's identical to the 2-year interest rate swap yield. The strip rate we calculate from the table is 4.899 compared to the 2-year swap rate of 4.900, which the same to 1 basis point. At this point in the curve the differences are individually insignificant, but even 0.1 basis points can be an enormous gulf when multiplied millions of times over. Remember that although each trader faces the profit or loss of only her whole position, this analysis is on fair value for the whole market, and even a small mispricing implies a massive transfer of wealth between the long and short holders of contracts. Worse still, the strip yield we calculated is below the 2-year swap

Synthetic Swap Rates and Convexity Bias for the Whole Curve

Contract	Expiration	Settle			Convex. Bias, Bp	Adj. Rate	MMR	CMS	Strip Rate	Sprd Bps	CMT	CMS-CMT *TED*
		Price	Rate	Chg.								
EDH6	3/13/06	95.185	4.815	2.5	0.1	4.81	4.87					
EDM6	6/19/06	95.075	4.925	4.0	0.4	4.92	4.98					
EDU6	9/18/06	95.075	4.925	3.0	0.3	4.92	4.98					
EDZ6	12/18/06	95.115	4.885	3.0	1.1	4.87	4.94					
EDH7	3/19/07	95.175	4.825	3.0	1.5	4.81	4.88					
EDM7	6/18/07	95.200	4.800	3.5	1.3	4.78	4.85					
EDU7	9/17/07	95.210	4.790	4.0	2.3	4.77	4.84					
EDZ7	12/17/07	95.200	4.800	4.0	2.3	4.77	4.85	4.90	4.90	0.0	4.49	38.0
EDH8	3/17/08	95.195	4.805	3.5	3.3	4.77	4.86					
EDM8	6/16/08	95.175	4.825	3.0	3.9	4.79	4.88					
EDU8	9/15/08	95.150	4.850	2.5	4.5	4.80	4.90					
EDZ8	12/15/08	95.105	4.895	2.5	5.2	4.84	4.95	4.90	4.90	0.1	4.47	37.6
EDH9	3/16/09	95.085	4.915	2.0	6.0	4.86	4.97					
EDM9	6/15/09	95.050	4.950	2.0	6.7	4.88	5.01					
EDU9	9/14/09	95.020	4.980	2.0	7.5	4.91	5.04					
EDZ9	12/14/09	94.980	5.020	1.5	8.3	4.94	5.08	4.93	4.93	0.1	4.44	40.8
EDH0	3/15/10	94.965	5.035	1.0	9.1	4.94	5.09					
EDM0	6/14/10	94.940	5.060	1.0	9.3	4.96	5.12					
EDU0	9/13/10	94.915	5.085	0.5	10.5	4.98	5.14					
EDZ0	12/13/10	94.875	5.125	0.5	11.4	5.01	5.18	4.95	4.97	1.7	4.45	41.0

TABLE 2-2

(Continued)

Contract	Expiration	Settle Price	Settle Rate	Settle Chg.	Convex. Bias, Bp	Adj. Rate	MMR	CMS	Strip Rate	Sprd Bps	CMT	CMS-CMT *TED*
EDH1	3/14/11	94.860	5.140	0.0	12.2	5.02	5.20					
EDM1	6/13/11	94.835	5.165	0.0	12.9	5.04	5.22					
EDU1	9/19/11	94.810	5.190	-0.5	13.6	5.05	5.25					
EDZ1	12/19/11	94.780	5.220	-0.5	14.3	5.08	5.28	4.97	5.01	4 3	4.46	41.0
EDH2	3/19/12	94.770	5.230	-0.5	14.9	5.08	5.29					
EDM2	6/18/12	94.740	5.260	-0.5	15.6	5.10	5.32					
EDU2	9/17/12	94.715	5.285	-1.0	16.2	5.12	5.34					
EDZ2	12/17/12	94.685	5.315	-1.0	16.8	5.15	5.37	4.99	5.06	6.9	4.48	41.5
EDH3	3/18/13	94.675	5.325	-1.5	17.4	5.15	5.38					
EDM3	6/17/13	94.645	5.355	-1.5	18.0	5.17	5.41					
EDU3	9/16/13	94.620	5.380	-2.0	18.6	5.19	5.44					
EDZ3	12/16/13	94.590	5.410	-2.0	19.1	5.22	5.47	5.01	5.11	9.8	4.49	42.4
EDH4	3/17/14	94.585	5.415	-2.5	19.7	5.22	5.48					
EDM4	6/16/14	94.550	5.450	-2.5	20.2	5.25	5.51					
EDU4	9/15/14	94.520	5.480	-3.0	20.7	5.27	5.54					
EDZ4	12/15/14	94.485	5.515	-3.0	21.2	5.30	5.58	5.02	5.15	12.8	4.51	43.5
EDH5	3/16/15	94.480	5.520	-3.5	21.8	5.30	5.58					
EDM5	6/15/15	94.445	5.555	-3.5	22.3	5.33	5.62					
EDU5	9/14/15	94.415	5.585	-4.0	22.8	5.36	5.65					
EDZ5	12/14/15	94.380	5.620	-4.0	23.3	5.39	5.68	5.05	5.20	15.3	4.52	44.8

yield, and just like any other instrument with embedded options, the Eurodollar yield should be higher than the swap yield, not lower. Is all lost?

As it turns out, we're close to being finished, but the devil is in the details. Our simple average of all eight contracts is not quite the right way to go about building a synthetic fixed-rate bond with a string of Eurodollar contracts. A more accurate way is to set the present value of each contract against the present value of its comparable cash flow in the interest rate swap. Normally, one might use the simple present value formula:

$$\frac{1}{(1 + \text{rate})^\wedge \text{time}}$$

This equation uses compound interest calculations, since the annual rate is raised to the number of years. Discount factors calculated this way fall exponentially, but the convention in the Eurodollar market is to use the following equation for discount factors:

$$\frac{1}{(1 + \text{rate}) \bullet \text{time}}$$

Here the discount rate is multiplied by time in years, rather than being raised to that power. This makes the discount factors linear, rather than exponential, and there's no compounding. The rationale for such an approach is that the duration of the strip should fall at the same rate as the fixed-rate bond it is meant to hedge. If the number of contracts dropped in each month exponentially, the duration of the strip would fall faster than a fixed-rate bond, but if an equal number of contracts were used, then the duration of the strip would fall too slowly and we would underestimate the falling duration of a note. As it turns out, dropping the number of contracts by a discount factor calculated by multiplying time to the rate produces a ratio of each contract that will best match the duration of a coupon bond as time passes. As each quarterly contract expires, the DV01 of those remaining should equal that of a note with a maturity equal to the longest contract. By dropping the number of contracts in each expiration, the strip is more heavily weighted to the shorter contracts, and the resulting weighted average yield is slightly lower as well. It makes a small difference in our example with a 2-year rate, since it's such a short maturity, but the difference grows the farther out on the curve we travel. See Table 2–3.

Once again we return to the same table of rates, except that this time we add a column of discount factors based on the add-on interest rate directly observed from the market. These discount factors become the weighting for each Eurodollar strip we calculate. No matter how many or few contracts we use, we will use them in this proportion. Returning to our Eurodollar strip yield versus 5-year interest rate swap comparison, we recalculate the strip yield as a weighted average of each

TABLE 2-3

Historical Dollar Value of Volatility along the Curve

Year	2-year			5-year			10-year		
	Yield Vol. (Stdev)	Avg Daily Chg	Yearly Total	Yield Vol. (Stdev)	Avg Daily Chg	Yearly Total	Yield Vol. (Stdev)	Avg Daily Chg	Yearly Total
1982	194%	0.44	113.0	164%	0.78	201.0	151%	1.12	290.4
1983	59%	0.18	46.1	65%	0.38	97.4	57%	0.58	151.1
1984	92%	0.22	56.0	80%	0.49	127.5	73%	0.77	199.8
1985	76%	0.17	43.1	83%	0.41	105.6	77%	0.69	177.8
1986	65%	0.11	28.3	65%	0.32	83.4	64%	0.61	157.4
1987	73%	0.13	33.9	81%	0.34	88.3	82%	0.58	151.2
1988	58%	0.10	26.9	42%	0.26	66.5	32%	0.44	114.6
1989	70%	0.15	38.3	65%	0.29	75.0	57%	0.40	103.2
1990	42%	0.10	25.6	31%	0.24	61.9	27%	0.40	102.7

TABLE 2-3

(Continued)

Year	2-year			5-year			10-year		
	Yield Vol. (Stdev)	Avg Daily Chg	Yearly Total	Yield Vol. (Stdev)	Avg Daily Chg	Yearly Total	Yield Vol. (Stdev)	Avg Daily Chg	Yearly Total
1991	66%	0.08	19.5	54%	0.18	47.5	37%	0.32	82.1
1992	56%	0.08	20.5	51%	0.23	59.6	39%	0.36	92.9
1993	19%	0.05	12.8	30%	0.16	40.2	35%	0.29	73.9
1994	98%	0.08	22.0	81%	0.23	60.1	67%	0.40	103.5
1995	66%	0.09	22.5	58%	0.20	52.0	63%	0.32	82.5
1996	41%	0.08	21.4	44%	0.21	54.9	41%	0.36	93.5
1997	23%	0.06	13.2	31%	0.16	42.2	34%	0.28	73.5
1998	51%	0.06	16.4	53%	0.16	41.1	43%	0.29	74.6
1999	45%	0.06	15.9	48%	0.17	43.4	48%	0.30	77.3
2000	39%	0.07	18.0	45%	0.17	44.2	40%	0.29	74.7
2001	71%	0.07	17.4	41%	0.18	47.3	29%	0.33	86.5
2002	63%	0.05	12.1	69%	0.16	42.4	53%	0.32	83.7
2003	22%	0.03	6.6	35%	0.14	35.3	34%	0.29	75.9
2004	47%	0.03	7.9	33%	0.12	30.7	27%	0.24	61.3

of the contracts using the discount factors as the weights. What this does is put slightly more emphasis on the front contracts with the closest expirations, and slightly less on the back contracts with deferred expirations. In an upward sloping yield curve as we have in this example, this change will lower the weighted average yield of the contracts, lowering the strip rate, which should match the 5-year swap rate. This is in fact what happens. The 5-year swap rate is 4.95 and the strip rate, including our convexity bias adjustment and discount factor weightings, is within 1.7 basis points at 4.97. Although it's not exactly the same, it's close, and if we believe that our estimate of future volatility is correct, then this difference represents a mispricing.

As an aside, the duration of the Eurodollar strip position also depends on these discount factors, and there is an enormous amount of information contained in each Eurodollar price. Each contract price has to satisfy a handful of criteria: It is a forward rate, its money market yield equals that of a swap when held as part of a strip, and the yield provides a guide about the ratio of contracts to use in order to create a strip with duration dollars that falls at the same rate as a fixed-rate bond, as well as the difference in convexity between the two and how that convexity difference is allocated across contracts. Remember that this is not just true for an individual contract but for all 40, and the price of each takes into account how it will fit into the group. When viewed in terms of the convexity bias calculation, which is in essence determining a no-arbitrage price, these contracts represent a remarkably complex system. Increasingly capable computers are no doubt behind some of the growth in trading of back month contracts.

This exercise should give us confidence that the market views value in Eurodollar contracts in a way that's largely consistent with our empirical convexity bias calculations. Hedging with Eurodollars is systems intensive, since it takes a computer to keep track of all of the calculations in real time, but each individual step is straightforward. Figure 2–8 illustrates the Eurodollar strip hedges for $100 million face of the most actively traded Treasuries, which are on-the-run bonds and CTD bonds into Treasury futures. No matter the face value of the note we are hedging, the Eurodollar contracts are always used in the same proportion. It is also worth noting here that we did make an additional assumption regarding calculation of the strip hedge. Eurodollar futures settle to the rate beginning on the settlement day, meaning that a contract expiring on December 19 covers the 3-month period beginning with that day. Except on the last day of trading, Eurodollar futures do not hedge against changes in spot rates, from settlement to expiration of the contract. While this term must be less than 3 months by definition, since the contracts are quarterly, it can make a small difference depending on how the hedges are constructed. Although 1-month LIBOR contracts do trade at the CME for this very reason, most of the time hedgers ignore this short period, also known as the *stub rate,* and spread that duration risk evenly along the contracts.

It is interesting that so many traders develop intricate models of fair value only to use a rule of thumb at the end. Although a perfectly riskless trade would

FIGURE 2–8

DV01 versus PV01, illustrating how the duration of a strip falls with time to mirror the falling duration of a swap as it matures

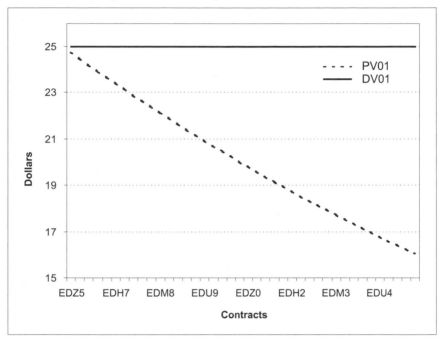

necessitate hedging the stub rate, most traders are comfortable with using all 3-month contracts to capture their risk and spread the risk represented by the stub evenly among the contracts they use. The strip hedge calculated in this way never needs adjustment and can be executed efficiently all in the same market, rather than having to trade 98% of the risk in Eurodollar contracts and then 2% in a 1-month contract. Although it misses a small amount of the risk in the stub, the value of which depends on maturity, it's significantly more accurate than the popular alternatives, which usually involve either taking that risk and putting it all on the front contract or using an equally weighted number of contracts.

Does the market agree with all of our efforts? Unfortunately, the results are indeterminate. While it's encouraging that we can readily measure the phenomenon and it's of the same magnitude that we model, it appears as if the market is judging the convexity bias to be roughly linear, with only small variations from one quarter to the next. Our empirical model of delivery option is nonlinear since the slopes in Figure 2–7 are not all the same, although they are close. For example, the slope of the 2-year and 10-year regression lines in Figure 2–7 could be reasonably approximated with the slope of the 5-year line. It looks like the market

FIGURE 2–9

Model and market values of convexity bias

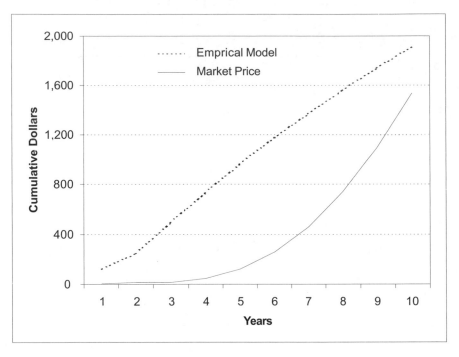

might be doing just this, using a single point on the yield curve as an approxima-tion for the value of convexity all along the curve. While this isn't perfectly accu-rate, and Figure 2–9 proves this, it's likely that the market is now at a stage of sophistication that lags behind our empirical work. This is more of a condemna-tion than a self-congratulatory statement, because in order to be useful to traders, the analytics need to reflect the realities of the market today, not where it was 5 years ago or where it might be in 5 more years.

As we mentioned earlier, there was a similar phenomenon in the early days of Treasury futures. During their first decade of trading, there was relatively little computer power available to throw at the problem by today's standards, and there were certainly times when delivery options were wildly mispriced. What good would it have done to have precise valuations of what delivery options should be? One use would have been in arbitrage trades, where mispricings could be exploited in relatively short order, in the front contract expiring no later than 3 months from now or in the back contract with a 6-month expiration. Arbitrage in Treasury futures is a parallel, but slightly different, problem, because if it seems as if a 6-month horizon on a trade is impossibly long, then arbitrage in Eurodollars may appear impossible. Remember that Treasury futures are short-lived contracts on long underlying bonds while Eurodollars are the opposite. Each Eurodollar contract exists for 10 years, even though it will eventually settle to a 3-month LIBOR. In order to realize the full value of a mispricing in Eurodollars, one would need to create a duration neutral strip position held against an interest rate swap and (unrealistically) hold it all the way to maturity. "I know the trade is going to go my way; just give me another 9 years to prove it!" Needless to say, there are few arbitrage traders who would make such a claim to their bosses or investors.

Determining how the market should be pricing Eurodollar contracts is of value. Although it would be necessary to hold the contracts until they expire to realize the entire mispricing, there is no reason to say that a trader couldn't put the position on with the expectation that it will revert to fair value before expiration. The subtle difference between the Treasury arbitrage discussed in the first chapter and arbitrage in Eurodollar futures is the length of time it would take to force the prices to converge. Due to the time horizons involved there is certainly more potential for Eurodollar contracts to drift in value compared to Treasury futures, but to a small handful of traders even a 10-year horizon isn't too long. Many non-levered investors have been around for many decades (which is rarely true with levered traders), and if they can go long a mispriced string of Eurodollars that will eventually outperform the equivalent duration interest rate swap, they would be happy to do it for virtually unlimited size. The key to arbitrage trades is the eventual opportunity to enforce the no-arbitrage price, and there is a case to be made that the horizon over which this enforcement takes place is of relatively little concern. For this reason the most accurate empirical valuation of convexity bias possible will be of great use to traders, although no one knows whether these are the kind of traders that can wait 3 months or 10 years.

HEDGING HYBRID ARMS

Eurodollars are most often used as an outlet for interest rate swap dealers to offset the risk they accumulate from trading, and most of this risk comes from trading with mortgage accounts. However, as mortgage hedgers become more sophisticated, they are increasingly bypassing swap dealers and accessing the Eurodollar market directly. If dealers are going to rely on futures as their ultimate source of liquidity, why should a mortgage hedger pay to use an over-the-counter product, when the trader on the other side is going to end up accessing the liquidity of the futures markets anyway? It does take some expertise in the products to match what's available in an interest rate swap since futures are building blocks rather than finished products. Accounts large enough to gain economies of scale are increasingly finding that it doesn't make sense to pay a dealer for the convenience of using over-the-counter products if they can bring to bear expertise of their own. This section details four examples of Eurodollar/hybrid adjustable-rate mortgage (ARM) hedges, each one slightly more accurate (but complex) than the previous one.

The first step to tackling the challenge is to understand the risk in the mortgage we are trying to hedge. Since this is not a book about mortgages, we'll take the risk numbers on this side of the hedge as given, but an overview is necessary in order to accurately hedge hybrid ARMs, which have at times been as much as half of the total mortgage originations. These mortgage structures have a relatively brief period when their coupons are fixed; then a longer period when the coupon floats based on some reference rate, often 1-year constant maturity Treasury (CMT) rates. For example, a 5/1 ARM has a fixed rate for 5 years, then floats based on a 1-year CMT for 25 years thereafter. Hybrid ARMs take advantage of the fact that most of the time the yield curve is upward sloping by combining fixed- and floating-rate loans into one instrument with a fixed rate for some period of time, after which the interest rate floats. There are periodically limits on how much the floating rate coupon can change in any one period as well as lifetime limits.

As one can imagine, there are different formulas for the trade-off between the rate charged for the fixed- versus floating-rate periods. Often there is a low "teaser" rate in the beginning, after which the rate charged jumps higher. There is normally a large increase in prepayments when the loan flips from fixed to floating interest rates, and for this reason the vast majority of owners prepay their loans before the coupon resets. Traditionally these structures have been compared to short-term balloons, even though they don't have a hard final payment date. Hybrid ARMs are popular in times when the yield curve is very steep, since the initial fixed rate is far below the rate of a 30-year fixed-rate loan. By the end of the lockout date, when the loan turns from fixed to floating, only a small fraction of the borrowers actually pay the floating interest rate, and this portion of the structure is called the *tail*. These bonds are a combination of fixed- and floating-rate structures, and, as with other fixed-rate products, these bonds have positive duration until the reset date and then negative duration during the floating-rate period. Since most of the pool prepays prior to the reset date, the positive duration dominates, but a 5/1 ARM will have a little lower duration than a 5-year bullet, because there is some floating-rate risk in the tail.

The worst hedge that we could come up with for an ARM is to use an equally weighted pack of Eurodollar contracts so that the DV01 of the pack matched that of the mortgage. For example, if the DV01 of a new 5/1 were $350 per million, and we needed 20 quarterly contracts to span the fixed-rate period to the reset date, we would need 70 contracts in each month per $100 million face of the mortgage:

$$\frac{350 \cdot 100}{20 \cdot 25} = 70 \text{ contracts each for the first 20 contracts}$$

A very glaring omission is that we used an equal number of contracts in each expiration, although we know from our Treasury/Eurodollar hedge that we were supposed to diminish the number of contracts as the expirations became more distant so that the risk of the Eurodollar hedge will match the cash flows of the underlying instrument (which is the ARM in this case). The cost of simplifying the execution with an equal number of contracts is that we ended up introducing some curve risk by using too many deferred Eurodollar contracts. In fact, we didn't even drop the number of contracts in a way that would be appropriate for a nonamortizing note, let alone an ARM that will be subject to prepayments. In a long ARM/short Eurodollar position, this would mean that we would make money in a steepening, even if rates perfectly pivoted around the average maturity of the two instruments, with the front end rallying by 1 basis point and the back end selling off by 1 basis point. This point about diminishing the number of contracts used, as we diagrammed in Figure 2–8, would be true for any nonamortizing bond, but with mortgages we should always have at the back of our mind that prepayments are likely. The number of contracts used in a Eurodollar strip to hedge a mortgage should be below the number of contracts used to hedge a nonamortizing bond. Even if we hold the ARM for a short amount of time, we have to be concerned about the projected future cash flows. As a footnote, we once again ignored hedging the stub rate, but this is an insignificant omission.

Figure 2–10 illustrates the prepayment patterns of three of the most popular hybrid ARM structures. It compares the strip rate to constant maturity swap rates. All of these structures float on 1-year constant maturity Treasury rates, but the fixed-rate period is different, either 3, 5, or 7 years. There are also shorter and longer lockout structures, but the mechanics are the same and so are the prepayment

F I G U R E   2–10

Hybrid ARM projected cash flows

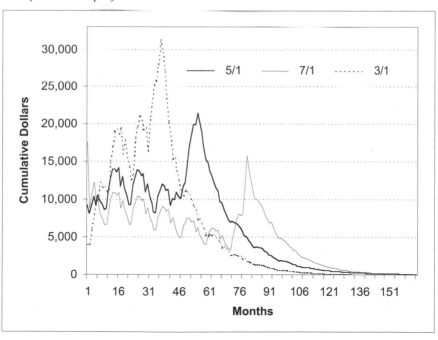

patterns. Most of the pool is paid off before the loans go to floating rates, but there is always some small number of loans left over, either because the borrower can't refinance because of credit impairment or it's on such a small balance that it's not worth paying the fees involved in refinancing. Although these bonds are hardly bullets, this chart provides some defense for traders who hedge them as if they were bullets. As with all rules of thumb, treating a 5/1 ARM like it's a 5-year bullet Treasury misses some nuance, but such a hedge would cover most of the risk.

What if nuance were important? Investors in a levered fund might not agree that "close enough" should be the objective when it comes to hedging these types of loans, and even banks that typically employ very modest leverage from 8 to 10 times aren't normally willing to have their hedging discrepancies amplified if it can be avoided. The next step to make our hedges more accurate (but also more difficult to implement) is to match the amortization of the mortgage with the number of contracts in our Eurodollar strip. Figure 2–10 illustrates that after 1 year in a 5/1 ARM about a quarter of the pool is expected to be paid off, which means that unless we taper off our hedge, we will end up mismatching the cash flows and risk between the two. These prepayment speeds change over time and are very much dependent on the general macroeconomic environment. A popular first step is to execute packs of contracts, each with the same number of contracts in them, but then slowly dwindle the number of packs used in each year until they mirror the amortization of the bond we're hedging. For example, if only 80% of the face amount of a pool is expected to be left after 1 year (this would be true with a prepayment rate of 20% per year), then we can "stair step" each year's worth of contracts in Eurodollars. The first year would have 100% of the original duration dollars, the second year just 80%, then 60%, and so on. This is a relatively easy way to "amortize" the hedge instruments while keeping execution simple, since Eurodollar packs are easy to execute.

In terms of accuracy this is a major step forward, since it's more likely that diminishing the annual number of contracts according to the expected amortization of the mortgage will better match the curve risk between the two. If there is a steepening curve and we've matched the dollar duration at the 2- and 5-year points, for example, there should be little resulting change in profit or loss. On the other hand, if we had implemented our original hedge, in which we used the same number of contracts in each month, it could have led to a substantial profit or loss. Using the stair-step approach is the single biggest gain to hedge accuracy that we can make, but it misses a portion of the hedge effectiveness that could be gained by more precisely matching the amortization of the mortgage by changing the amount of contracts used each quarter. Once again we've missed the floating rate tail after the end of the lockout period as well as the stub rate.

The only thing holding back a hedger from matching the quarterly cash flows of her mortgage with the Eurodollar hedge is knowledge of the underlying security. If we are confident that the cash flows from the ARM can be modeled with some degree of precision, then it makes sense to do as good a job as possible mirroring those cash flows. The most common mistake with this implementation is for traders to treat a mortgage hedge as if it were somehow distinct from a Treasury hedge and only amortize the Eurodollar strip by the projected cash flows of the mortgage. If the number of contracts we use for a nonamortizing bond falls by the linear discount factor mentioned above, we have to use this as a starting point for building a hedge on a nonamortizing bond. It turns out that the appropriate hedge requires discounting twice; once by the same factors we used to determine a hedge for a bullet bond and once by the projected amortization of the mortgage.

Figure 2–12 illustrates the situation by using the information from Figures 2–10 and 2–11 to develop a Eurodollar strip hedge for an ARM. From the cash flows we are able to back out a factor for the pool, a series representing the fraction of the face value of the mortgage left outstanding after cumulative prepayments. Once we know the percentage of the face value of the bond that is expected to be remaining at any month, then we aggregate the months by quarter to match up with the contract expirations. Multiplying these percentages by the discount factors that we would use to determine the hedge for a Treasury gets us to our end result. Why discount the number of contracts twice? The motivation for the first discounting is the same as it was with the Treasury hedge, to match

FIGURE   2–11

Hybrid ARM hedge construction

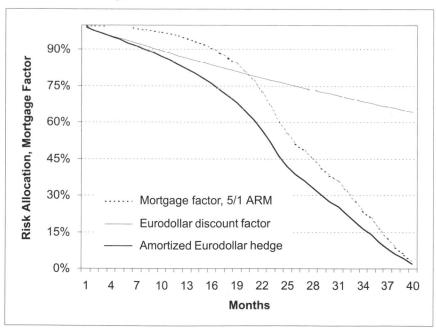

FIGURE 2–12

Strips with the same risk, but with different allocation along the curve

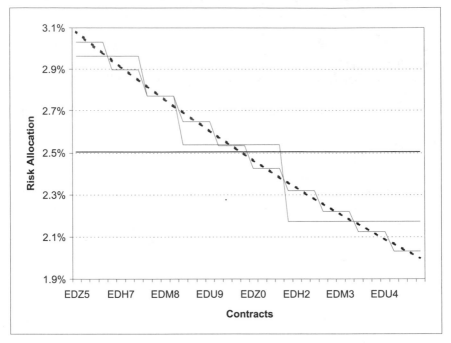

the DV01 of each cash flow so that the risk of the ARM and Eurodollar strip will be the same as time goes on, with the contracts expiring at the same time as pre-payments hit the mortgage. The second discounting according to expected amor-tization determines the face amount but not the interest rate sensitivity. Although the two are related, a hedge that only falls according to the factor of the mortgage is going to use too many deferred contracts, introducing a steepening bias in a long ARM/short contract position. Figure 2–11 is useful because it represents the Eurodollar hedge as a shape, and no matter how the DV01 of the ARM changes, the shape of our strip does not. If we model the DV01 of the ARM to be 10% higher from one day to the next, all we do is use more Eurodollar contracts in the same proportion so that the total duration dollars of the strip matches the risk of the mortgage.

In order to know how much to shift the strip hedge up or down to use more or fewer of the contracts, we need to be able to calculate the aggregate duration dollars and then find a way to set up a system to automatically scale our hedge to match the duration of our ARM. The aggregate of duration dollars is simply $25 multiplied by the number of contracts and summing this value. The reason that it's likely necessary to do some fine-tuning with the strip is that even if the notional values every quarter in the Eurodollar match those expected in the mortgage, the two have different yields and different durations. The only change from a Treasury hedge is that the number of contracts drops off more dramatically the farther out the curve we go. One can imagine implementing this in a spreadsheet using some of the same tools from our Treasury futures modeling. If we know the DV01 of the ARM, then why not have the computer search for a scaling factor so that the sum of the squared difference between strip and mortgage is zero? Put another way, the computer can shift the number of contracts in Figure 2–11 in parallel, up or down, until the duration dollars of the Eurodollar strip and mortgage are the same.

Figure 2–12 compares the alternatives discussed so far, and it's important to keep in mind that although the distribution of contracts is different, each of the strips displayed represents the same interest rate risk. The horizontal line was our first pass at an ARM hedge, but it put too much interest rate exposure far out on the curve, introducing some curve risk. The stair-step pattern is evident in the second hedge, in which the same number of contracts is used each year in an attempt to strike a balance between ease of execution and an accurate reflection of the amortization of the mortgage. Finally, the curved line is the best representation of the face value of the ARM in each quarter, based on expected prepayments. It's worth noting that if interest rates remain range-bound, this third approach will be the most accurate. However, when interest rates change, so will the cash flows we're attempting to replicate. The more finely we match the hedge to expected cash flows, the more often it's going to be necessary to readjust the hedge if interest rates change. Accuracy, it's evident, comes at a price, not just in terms of interest rate cost but also maintenance. Commissions are a small cost for futures users, but if the quantities of contracts need to be changed on a daily basis because of wild swings in interest rates, they will add up and become a drag on performance. Additionally, none of these decisions happens automatically, and someone must dedicate considerable time to the analysis.

In spite of the realism that we've been able to capture with our Eurodollar strip, all the time making our Eurodollar contracts perform more like the mortgage we're trying to hedge, we are still omitting one risk. Even after matching the amortization of the ARM during the fixed-rate period, we have yet to address the floating-rate tail risk after the loans reset. It's true that the risk of a floating interest rate bond is less than a fixed rate, but many hybrid ARM structures float to 1-year constant maturity Treasury rates, which do have some interest rate sensitivity. The fact that this floating-rate period is so long, possibly lasting the balance of 30 years (and there are often periodic and lifetime caps on how high or low the rate can float) also has the potential to add duration to the mortgage. We mentioned earlier that Eurodollar open interest and liquidity fall off past the first few years, and contracts aren't even listed past 10 years. Hybrid ARM hedgers typically use two methods of getting around this problem; deciding which method to use is a matter of strategy.

With liquidity Eurodollar contracts falling off past 5 years, hedgers rely on either Treasury futures or 15-year mortgages. It's an interesting pairing since they share similarities and differences. Broadly speaking, Treasury rates are default risk-free and principally subject to macroeconomic factors, but we have also detailed the structure of Treasury futures that allow their duration to drift along with changes in interest rates. Mortgage pass-throughs, on the other hand, are subject to substantial interest rate risk and are the least structured of all products. The 15-year collateral doesn't have any structure either; the final maturity date is much closer, and borrowers who take out these kinds of loans exhibit consistent behaviors. Although it's not necessary to repay these loans until 15 years in the future, it's typical of these types of borrowers to make prepayments so that the bulk of the cash flows come in the 5- to 10-year portion of the curve. Sound familiar? Ten-year Treasury futures have a window for eligibility of deliverable issues that's between 6.5 and 10 years, which means that the duration drift of a pool of 15-year loans and 10-year Treasury futures echo one another.

What distinguishes the risk of a Treasury futures contract from mortgage collateral is that one is a spread product and one is not. Treasury prices should have no response to changes in general credit conditions, but mortgages are responsive to the credit climate to some extent (although all of the loans are collateralized with houses and many are guaranteed by the GSEs, a guarantee is only as strong as the entity making it, and every private institution is subject to some default risk, even if it is small). In addition to credit risk there is quite a bit more optionality in mortgage collateral than in Treasury futures. Even though the observed behavior of mortgage borrowers is similar to that of Treasury future borrowers, it's possible that the mortgage collateral performs in unexpected ways under extreme circumstances. In a typical rate environment, the bulk of the cash flows will come at the 5-year point, but if interest rates rally substantially, there's nothing preventing 100% of the loans from coming due immediately! Similarly, it's not impossible for rates to rise by 500 basis points and for each borrower to be quite reticent about letting go of what turned out to be extremely low interest rate loans. In this case there's nothing preventing all of the loans from coming due in 15 years, without any prepayments. Neither of these scenarios is likely, but they are possible, and it's this possibility that the market picks up on when comparing the optionality of a mortgage with Treasury contracts.

Both differences in credit and optionality lead to changes in the valuation of mortgage collateral and Treasury futures, and it shouldn't be surprising that the yield spread between the two changes. Remember that we first touched on this topic as a means of hedging the floating-rate tail risk of hybrid ARMs and mentioned that traders treat their choice of hedge instrument strategically. A trader who is adding duration and who thinks that the spread between 15-year collateral and Treasuries will widen should favor Treasury over mortgage hedges. When the yield spread between the two is already quite wide, the focus is on being long mortgages, in anticipation of mortgage rates falling compared to Treasury rates. Of course, the decision about whether to be long a Treasury or mortgage in anticipation of a relative value move depends on whether we need to be long or short to hedge our ARM. In a newly minted ARM, where the limits on the floating-rate leg are far away (caps or floors), the duration risk of the floating-rate tail is normally negative, meaning that a hedge for a long ARM position might include a short Eurodollar strip and long 10-year Treasury or 15-year mortgage. In an aged pool of ARMs that were issued at substantially higher or lower rate levels, the period or lifetime caps may come into play, effectively turning these cash flows from floating to fixed and adding significant duration. In this case, the appropriate hedge for a long ARM position would be a short Eurodollar strip and short 10-year Treasury or 15-year mortgage.

Figure 2–13 illustrates a time series of the yield spread between 15-year mortgage yields and 5-year Treasury rates. It's revealing to look at how this spread changes over time because it shows the frequency of moves. At the time of this writing the spread between the two is relatively narrow, indicating that new short hedge positions should be made with mortgages in anticipation of their underperformance compared to Treasuries. However, the spread between the two has been narrowing since 2002, and we would have been building a short mortgage position for quite some time without any validation of the strategy. While

F I G U R E   2–13

15-year pass-through mortgage versus 5-year Treasury

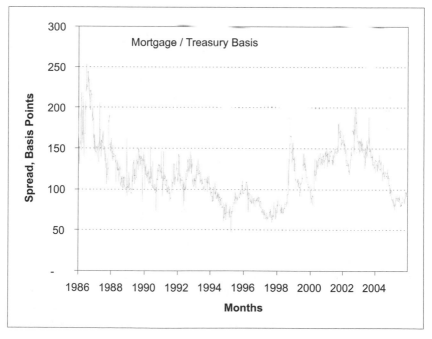

it's quite likely that the spread will widen again, it's evident that this reversion can sometimes take many quarters or even years. The average number of days between crossing the average of the series, which is one rule of thumb showing mean reversion, is 74 days. This implies that in 5 years' worth of hedging we might only switch from favoring one over the other 17 or so times.

There is a second dimension to consider in the choice of a hedge for the tail of the cash flows in a hybrid ARM having to do with carry. Whenever we switch from using a Treasury to a spread product, one of the questions we should be concerned with is what will be the differences in net carry rates. Just as with on-the-run Treasury issues (and sometimes notes that are cheapest-to-deliver into futures) particular mortgage coupons and months can become quite special in the financing market. Using our earlier rule of thumb, we can guess that the net carry cost, the difference between the yield of the mortgage and it's financing rate, would be around $0.27 per basis point, per million, per day. Suppose that the yield on a 5% coupon 15-year collateral were 5%, meaning that this is the current coupon TBA bond. If the price drop over the next month is 10 thirty-seconds, then we can imply a carry rate:

$$\left(\frac{p_2 - p_1}{p_1} \right) \bullet 12$$

$$\left(\frac{100 - 99.6875}{100} \right) \bullet 12 = 3.75\%$$

All this equation does is move the price drop from one month to the next $(p_2 - p_1)$ in percentage terms and turn it into an annual interest rate. As in any other market, when there is more selling pressure, the price drops and the implied net carry rate increases. This parallels the calculation with a Treasury, except we made a simplifying assumption in this case by using the current coupon mortgage. If the yield were different from the coupon, the equation would change slightly in recognition of the fact that we are paying the coupon on the face amount of the bond and earning the financing rate (whether it's repo for a Treasury or LIBOR, plus or minus some spread in a mortgage) on the full dollar amount. In all likelihood this value will be different from what it is for the Treasury futures contract, which is our alternative hedge vehicle. What does it matter?

Figure 2–13 provides information about historical patterns of mortgage/Treasury basis moves. Every basis point change in this chart has a corresponding dollar amount, and once we can translate everything to dollar values, the trade-off is clear: trading the basis may mean paying some extra carry costs. Is it worth it? Perhaps, but it's difficult to know ahead of time because one can imagine three moving pieces. If the note that is cheapest-to-deliver into Treasury futures has a net carry rate of 100 basis points and the price drop on a current coupon 15-year mortgage implies a carry rate of 55 basis points and the mortgage/Treasury basis is very low by historical standards, perhaps 50 basis points below the long-run average, then the trade probably makes sense; but we have to measure just how much carry we give up against what we expect to earn on the cheapening of the mortgage compared to Treasuries:

$$50 \text{ bps for } 30 \text{ days} \bullet 0.27 = \$405$$

This was the easy scenario where the richness of the basis indicated that we needed to be short the bond with the lowest carry rate. What if the current coupon mortgage were extremely special? In this case it wouldn't make sense to trade the basis since we would likely incur more costs in carry than we would expect to make in a relative value move.

There is another method of analyzing the basis that might shorten the time horizon over which we would expect it to mean-revert. Rather than waiting for the line to pass the average value, which would have been a horizontal line in Figure 2–13, plotting a regression line takes out the trend in the series. If there are long periods of narrowing or widening of the spread, then a regression line is going to capture that trend. This begs the question, "what about even shorter trends within trends?" The bottom graph in Figure 2–14 makes a fairly simple segregation of the data into two simple categories according to Federal Reserve rate regimes: tightening and easing. The hypothesis here is that the mortgage/Treasury basis responds differently during changes in monetary policy. Rather than simply lump the whole past into one category, why not organize it according to simple rules, whether the Fed Funds rate is rising, falling, or stable?

This chart decomposes the mortgage basis into each Fed cycle, and the results are worth studying, since it is more accurate in some ways and less accurate in one important way. When doing empirical analysis, it's a useful rule of thumb not to throw out available information, and in this case the "cost" of determining what type of monetary policy the Fed is following is very simple. We just have to look at a history of the target rate, which is overlaid on the chart. While this segmenting by rate cycles made each prediction appear more accurate, it's important to keep in mind that our goal is to develop fair value methodologies that are useful from a trading perspective. Unfortunately, no one knows at the time what the inflection points are, meaning that the change from tightening to easing cycles is usually a surprise to the market.

While it's true that the Fed tries to use expectations as much as actual changes in the Fed Funds rate, expected changes have less of an impact on employment and prices than do unexpected ones. For this reason the Fed tries to surprise the market when it is cutting rates so that the moves have the maximum possible impact to tamp down prices and pricing expectations. On the other side, when the Fed is going to raise rates, it tries to broadcast the moves so that they don't utterly decimate employment. Greenspan's Fed was the first to harness expectations as a policy tool, even though it's an idea that owes its existence to academic economists. Much of the credit for "increased transparency" during Greenspan's tenure is amusing, since policymakers are using

FIGURE 2–14a

Mortgage basis deconstructed by Fed cycle

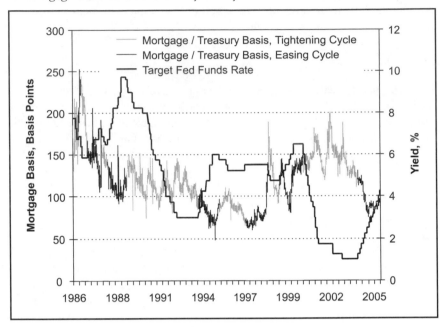

FIGURE 2–14b

R-squared by the Fed cycle compared to the entire period

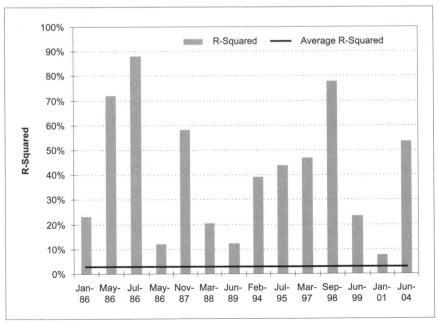

their comments as a method of manipulation. Inevitably when the Fed is raising rates, there are mountains of news stories about how much better communicators Fed officials have become, but then there are shifts to more opaque language when they are cutting rates. The switches from one era to another are entirely predictable.

These shifts are the major problem with Figure 2–14. How do we know when there is a shift coming during an easing cycle when policymakers are intentionally trying to surprise the market? Broadly speaking, the transition from easing or tightening can be a rocky one in the market. Although segregating the mortgage basis by Fed cycle increases our predictive capability in one sense, it leaves us open to major mistakes unless we know the inflection points. Suppose the Fed is in the middle of a tightening cycle and we expect rates to continue to rise and the basis to narrow in the short term, but there is an unexpected speech by a Fed official that the end of the rate hikes is at hand. It's likely that the hedger will not be able to shift gears fast enough to catch the next shift in the basis. At least when we're in the middle of tightening or easing cycles, it's more apparent what the next move is going to be. Figure 2–15 illustrates that over the long run the mortgage basis has been well behaved, and we are seeking to exploit relatively

FIGURE 2–15

Mortgage basis has been relatively well correlated with rates

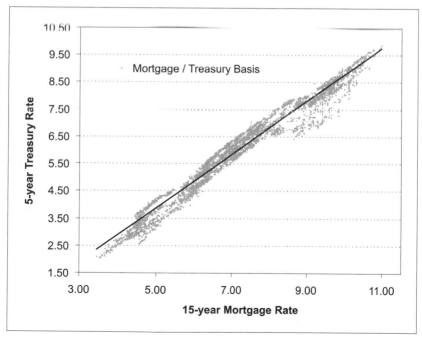

small differences. What if rates are stable and there is a surprise cut? It's possible that the extra income we would have picked up by trading the basis might be given back in one quick dislocation. As a practical matter, it may make more sense to use these "micro" predictions after a new cycle has begun, putting less emphasis on them as the cycle wears on.

As one might expect, 15-year collateral has a higher correlation to ARM rates than to Treasuries, and this constitutes another element of the hedge decision. In a highly levered situation, where small differences might be amplified 10 or 20 times, a pickup in correlation can be quite important. There are also some hedgers who are not allowed to make judgment calls about what they think the mortgage basis will do, and so they're limited to using just Eurodollars and mortgages as hedge instruments, which brings our analysis full circle to Figure 2–3, illustrating the relative cost and correlation of each hedging choice. It is possible to incur fewer hedging costs by using vehicles with lower correlations, but it's necessary to develop an expertise with these products to prevent implementation mistakes from consuming the available savings.

IS PERFECTION THE ENEMY OF THE GOOD?

Financial analysts are sometimes at odds with practitioners when it comes to hedging. A veteran trader may have an intuitive sense of what's "good enough" that is quite different from the modeled interest rate risk. In these instances, analysts may not appreciate the complexity of implementing a "perfect" hedge or its relative costliness. Hedges involving multiple instruments, and lengthy analysis may not be well suited to an active trading desk. If a hedge has enough moving parts, it may introduce as much risk in the execution as it seeks to reduce. However, there is analytical evidence to span the divide between analysts and practitioners and to support many traders' assertion that sometimes "good" hedges turn out to be quite a bit better than they seem.

Figure 2–16 illustrates the modeled interest rate risk for a 5/1 hybrid ARM. Though there is nothing particularly exotic about this bond, the interest rate risks are quite complex. One possible solution to shedding risk would be to short a series of Eurodollar contracts with a maturity out to 5 years, as well as go long enough 10-year swap futures to match the duration dollar risk at that point. Unfortunately, we can't stop there because the string of Eurodollar futures can't be equally weighted if it's going to match the partial duration in Figure 2–16. The heaviest concentration of contracts is at the 2-year bucket, but none of the points are equally weighted. Equally weighting groups of Eurodollar contracts is important because it eases execution, and orders can be taken as packs or bundles. On the other hand; a string of contracts with varying weightings must be executed individually. Without even addressing convexity, a "perfect" hedge involves buying and selling multiple maturity points, each with varying quantities. Imagine how difficult it could be to implement this strategy for dozens, or perhaps even hundreds, of pools of loans.

FIGURE 2–16

Hybrid ARM duration and convexity along the curve

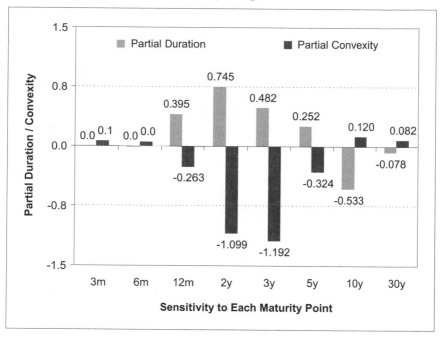

The first step toward building an analytical framework in support of a simpler hedging approach, more in line with trader intuition, is to understand the basic movements of the yield curve: level, slope, and curvature. The curve doesn't always move in parallel, but when it does, this registers as a "level" effect. Similarly, a change in the slope of the curve represents the second basic element, and curvature the third. If we had no empirical evidence and we found ourselves at the beginning of time trying to rank the three effects in order of importance, it would be impossible. Although no one knows what the future may hold, empirical evidence can at least tell us what has happened and provide a jumping-off point to form expectations about upcoming periods. The problem of estimating each of the three effects from historical measurements is that they all happen at the same time!

Wouldn't it be convenient if traders all decided that Monday would be the day to set the level of rates; Tuesday might deal with the slope, and Wednesday with the curvature. Our problem of finding evidence to support a trader's intuition would be much easier in this case, since it would be possible to measure each of the effects one at a time. Unfortunately, information is reflected across the yield curve concurrently. In this case, it's necessary to decompose changes in rates into

FIGURE 2–17

5 years' worth of Eurodollar yields

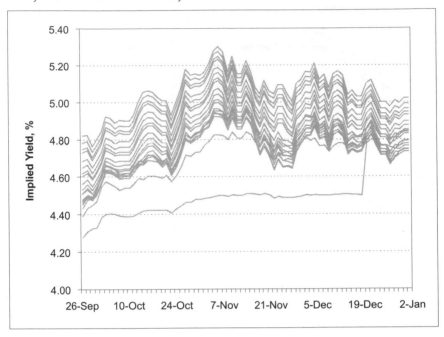

pieces, and principal component analysis (PCA) is a way to do just that. Without getting bogged down in the minutia, it suffices to say that this procedure can turn a simple rate history, like the one shown in Figure 2–17, into an orderly series of pieces like the ones illustrated in Figure 2–18. The information represented in Figure 2–18 isn't a time series of rates, but rather a depiction of the relative importance of each of the types of movements of the yield curve: level, slope, and curvature. Figures 2–17 and 2–18 represent the same data, but in different ways.

Figure 2–17 illustrates a yield history for the first 20 Eurodollar contracts, which constitutes 5 years' worth of interest rate risk. The discrete jump in the lowest series is due to the Fed hiking the funds rate, which also influences LIBOR and Eurodollar pricing at expiration. The longer the time to expiration, the less a contract is directly influenced by changes in Fed rates. Since there are 20 Eurodollar contracts in Figure 2–17, there must also be 20 principal components listed in Figure 2–18. Principal component analysis reorganizes the information behind yield changes in Figure 2–17 into groups. Imagine that each of the rates represents buckets made up of different colored sand and that all the colors are mixed in each bucket. What if we assigned the computer the monotonous task of organizing the sand by color, so that each bucket holds only one color of sand?

FIGURE   2–18

Principal component decomposition: level, slope, and curvature

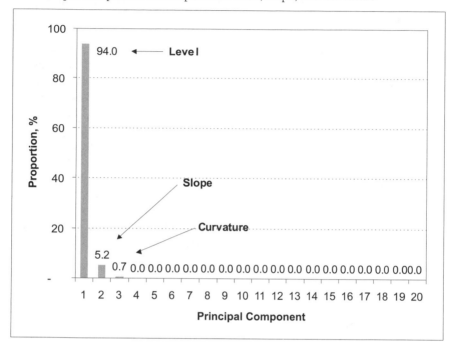

What we would be left with are 20 buckets of different colored sand. Each bucket would have different amounts of sand, each one a unique color. Similarly, there is a multitude of reasons behind changes in each of the rates listed in Figure 2–17. If we group these forces so they are distinct from one another, the result would be a history of 20 different effects, each of which would represent a unique source of information. In a sense, principal components pull out not only the three factors we are interested in—level, slope, and curvature—but also 17 others that are more difficult to describe in the context of yield curve movements.

The first three components in Figure 2–18 represent the three primary yield curve movements, level, slope, and curvature, respectively. This plot illustrates that these three effects are not of the same magnitude. To extend our analogy, most of the sand we end up with is one color. When distilled into primary components, the level effect dominates all the others, representing 94% of the changes in rates, while changes in the slope account for just 5% and curvature another 1%. Is it any wonder that duration calculations, which assume parallel movements in rates, remain the single most important risk measure in the bond market? Even though traders know that the curve can move in nonparallel ways, their intuition is that hedging along the single dimension of level effects captures the majority of their risk. This alone may not be enough evidence to support a simple hedge approach that is satisfying for practitioners, but the story doesn't end here. This level effect can be further decomposed to show why the Eurodollar futures market looks the way it does.

Suppose that we focus on this first driver of yield movements, the level effect, and ask: Does each Eurodollar contract contribute equally to this effect? While parallel movements are the most important single driver behind curve movements, it would make sense that some Eurodollar contracts were more important than others, since traders can't focus on all 40 listed contracts simultaneously. Does one contract in particular receive a majority of the attention? Figure 2–19 compares the sensitivity of the first principal component (PC1) to changes in individual Eurodollar contracts. As it turns out, there is a distinct difference in the sensitivity of each of the contracts to the first principal component. The general pattern is that sensitivity to the level effect falls as the expiration date of the Eurodollar is more distant, and it falls dramatically so after the first four contracts.

These differences in sensitivity between contracts have an important implication for the market: not only is the level effect the most dominant force in the

Contribution of each contract to first principal component (level)

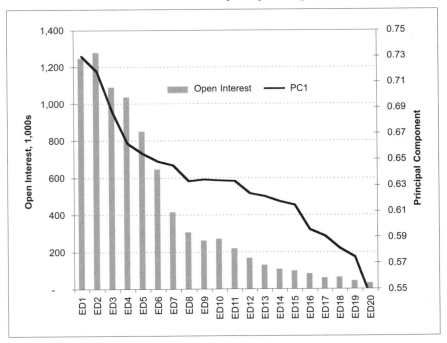

yield curve, but a few contracts turn out to be the most sensitive to these changes. Focusing on just the first four contracts gives traders the bulk of what they may need in terms of risk management. The second overlay in Figure 2–19 compares open interest in each contract with its sensitivity to changes in the level effect from our PCA. Another strong pattern emerges in open interest to show that by ignoring some of the details of the "perfect" hedge, traders are responding to empirical evidence in quite a sophisticated way.

Open interest in Eurodollar futures falls in a similar pattern to the sensitivity of each contract to level effect. Remember, this first principal component refers to the level effect in Eurodollar curve movements. Without explicitly replicating our calculations, Eurodollar futures traders intuitively discern that the first four contracts in the white pack dominate the rest of the others in terms of pricing information. While some information is missed by focusing only on the first four contracts (at least 6% as represented by the slope and curvature effect), it's clear that the white pack contains the majority of pricing information, and open interest is concentrated in these few contracts. Complex hedges that take into account the interest rate sensitivity of a mortgage to changes on each part of a curve may be as close to "perfect" as is humanly possible, but they can be costly in terms of analysis requirements and execution costs.

Rather than a sign of haphazard guessing, simple hedges using just a few contracts may be relatively effective. While not addressing the full spectrum of modeled risk, the choice of a simple hedge may be a sophisticated reaction to empirical evidence. Experience with these hedges teaches two lessons:

- Changes in the level of rates are by far the most important to understanding yield curve movements, compared to changes in the slope or curvature of the curve.

- The first few Eurodollar contracts are the most sensitive to changes in the level effect, and the majority of trading is concentrated there.

What's astounding is that individuals are able to develop an intuitive feel for such a complex phenomenon, simply based on observation and experience. Focusing on just a few contracts is always going to miss the fine distinction between risks along the curve, and these omissions may have serious consequences. Our analysis explains why many traders feel comfortable shedding the bulk of their risk with a simple hedge, while leaving the details for secondary consideration.

EURODOLLARS AS PREDICTORS OF FED POLICY

So far we have dealt with the risks of Eurodollar futures hedges and how they interact with other securities, but there's another perspective on value in this market that echoes Fed Funds futures. Rather than viewing value in terms of other securities, it's possible to link Eurodollar prices directly to expectations of Fed Funds changes. While Fed Funds futures are designed to directly express market expectations of monetary policy, they are often not traded actively enough out on the yield curve to imply expectations for more than the next few months. Since all Eurodollars listed at the CME settle to a short-term rate and there are 10 years' worth of listings, they provide a wider window through which to view market expectations. All of the concepts in this book are related, and the harder we look at the relationship between Eurodollars, Fed Funds, and market expectations, the more precisely we define the leap of faith traders have made by agreeing that a series of 3-month LIBOR deposits is interchangeable with a long-term interest rate swap. In order to analyze the situation, we rely on some of the same tools developed to evaluate fair value in Treasury futures, and the work ultimately highlights the technical complexity that prevents most people from using Eurodollars to extract market expectations of Fed policy.

Before contrasting Eurodollar behavior with Fed Funds futures, it's important to review how Fed Funds contracts work. Like Eurodollars, Fed Funds share discount style pricing and settle to 100 less a rate. In the case of Fed Funds, this is the average effective Fed Funds rate for the month in question. It's important to remember that this is not the target Fed Funds rate, but rather an actual overnight rate determined by the market that may drift slightly from the target. This wrinkle was introduced to keep traders interested in the contract, even when the Fed wasn't active, and it harkens back to the tradeoff between appealing to hedgers or speculators when designing contracts. Unfortunately, this choice of settling the contracts to the effective, rather than the target, rate limits their usefulness, as we'll see later on. In those months when the Fed has no meetings, normally 4 out of 12 months a year, the pricing of the contract simply depends on the probability of a move in the prior month as well as the expected difference between target and effective Fed Funds rates. In this case the calculation is a simple weighted average, where X is the probability of the Fed changing rates at a prior meetings and $1 - X$ is the probability of the Fed doing nothing at the prior meeting:

$$FF_{start} \bullet X + FF_{new} \bullet (1 - X)$$

Here FF_{start} is the incoming rate at the beginning of the prior month, and FF_{new} would be the new rate after the Federal Open Market Committee (FOMC) meeting. There are 4 months out of the year when it is quite simple to imply probabilities for rate moves since there are no meetings scheduled. For example, a June contract with no meeting would be priced based on the probability of a move in May, if there were a FOMC meeting scheduled that month. If the rate alternatives in the May meeting were either 4% or 4.5%, then the June contract would be priced as:

$$4 \bullet X + 4.5 \bullet (1 - X)$$

Here X stands for the probability of no move and $1 - X$ is the probability that the Fed changes rates, assuming that we start from 4%. This is a rule of thumb to determine probabilities for the immediately prior 4 months of FOMC meetings, since the probability of rate moves in these months must be equal to the probability of the moves in the prior month.

The more interesting question is how to price these contracts in months when there is a Fed meeting. Fed Funds contracts settle to a weighted average for the month, and the days before the meeting are easy enough to calculate by simply taking the average of the effective rate for each day. It's what happens after the Fed meeting that is in question. The reality is that there are many possible outcomes of a Fed meeting. The Fed could decide to do nothing and keep the rate the same. Or it could decide to raise or lower the rate, in an increment of its choice. Additionally, there could be an intermeeting move, as has sometimes happened in the past. Although anything is theoretically possible, it would be unusual and probably counterproductive for the Fed to move erratically in a way that couldn't be hedged with Fed Funds futures. After all, the Fed is as interested in promoting stability in the financial market as anyone else since it regulates the banking industry.

The Federal Reserve is painfully aware of its long history of needlessly inflicting pain on the banking system with bad policy, dating back to the Great Depression, and policymakers have learned the hard way that they have to be careful not to regulate industries out of existence. It was also uncharacteristic of the Greenspan Fed to shift from 25-basis-point to 50-basis-point moves very frequently. There have been times when the Fed has gotten behind the curve in terms of its policy accommodation or aggressiveness, but it's unusual for its perception of the underlying economy to hop from one extreme to the other, necessitating a quarter point move one month, then a half point move the next, and so on. It is similarly unusual for the Fed to immediately move from a tightening to easing without at least a few months' pause. Figure 2–20 makes the case that although the Fed has left some wiggle room in terms of its policy decisions, they are not impossible to get a hold of.

From historical patterns of Fed decisions, it's possible to make a handful of assumptions to reduce the degree of freedom that policymakers have in order to price these contracts while still being relatively realistic. First we assume that there are no intermeeting moves. It is impossible to anticipate surprises! For this reason we stick to the FOMC schedule. In the real world the Fed could do anything, but practically speaking the Fed is doing one of two things: continuing with a tightening or easing cycle or not: on or off. If the Fed is raising interest rates, then we can assume that the two possible movements are for Fed Funds to either increase rates or not, and we can ignore the possibility of a rate cut. While that rule would rarely have been violated in the past, the next is slightly more controversial. In order to limit movements to a two-dimensional, rather than a three-dimensional universe, we assume that rates will move by the same amount at every meeting, either 25 basis points or 50 basis points. In this model the Fed only has one speed, once it starts moving. Out of the past seven tightening or easing cycles, the Fed has mixed moves of 25 basis points with 50 basis points in five instances. This indicated that our single-speed constraint of either a 25-basis-point or a 50-basis-point change might be too restrictive at times.

Experience shows that no matter how realistically we construct a model, there are always going to be people willing to argue the absurd. If the Fed begins

FIGURE 2–20

Effective and target Fed Funds rates

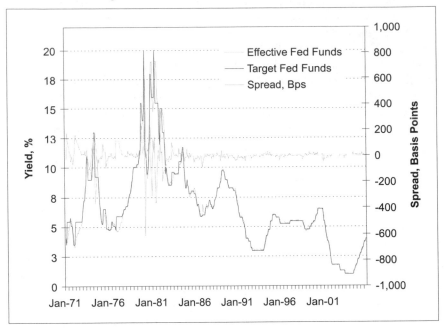

a cycle of 25-basis-point hikes, there will be times when the market expects them to jump 50 basis points, and there will inevitably be chatter about a 75-basis-point hike from people looking to grab headlines for themselves. There are even people who believe that you can't interpret Fed Funds probabilities because of the chances for surprise intermeeting moves. This idea, of course, is silly. There probably are individuals who are paralyzed by the knowledge that something unexpected might happen, like an asteroid plummeting out of the sky and into their living rooms, but such an event is unlikely and impossible to predict, and most people are able to live their lives in relative calm. Assuming that our two assumptions regarding timing and proportion of Fed moves are acceptable, we can tackle the second part of our equation, which determines how to price the second half of a month when there is a Fed meeting.

If the Fed only changes rates on the meeting date, which is the 15th of a month with 30 days in our example, then it's clear that the effective rate should be within a few basis points of the target rate for these days. On the 15th, the Fed will either continue with its current cycle or pause; this means that if the Fed is in a tightening cycle, then we assume that it can either increase rates or keep them the same. Suppose the probability of increasing rates is X; then the probability of not hiking rates is $1 - X$ so that the sum of the two is 100%. It should be clear how to put together a pricing formula for Fed Funds futures at this point:

$$\frac{\left(FF_{start} \bullet Days_{before}\right) + \left(FF_{start} \bullet X + FF_{new} \bullet (1 - X)\right) Days_{after}}{Days_{before} + Days_{after}}$$

The variable names aren't mysterious: FF_{start} is the effective Fed Funds rate for the days before the meeting, and we can assume this will equal the target rate ahead of time. $Days_{before}$ is the number of days until the FOMC meeting. $Days_{after}$ is the number of days after the FOMC meeting. FF_{new} is the target rate plus 25 basis points (or 50 basis points depending on what "speed" you run the changes at). Obviously, if you add $Days_{before}$ and $Days_{after}$, you get the total number of days in the month.

If the FOMC meeting date is on the 15th of a month with 30 days, then half of the change in percentage probability will be reflected in the price. This trade-off is different for every contract, since the FOMC date is normally different for each month and so are the number of days in the month. The equation does highlight the probabilistic nature of the contracts, but there's a wrinkle that escapes many traders. What if we were trying to price a deferred contract two meetings from now? In this case the contract price at that second meeting is harder to get a handle on because we don't know with certainty what the beginning Fed Funds rate will be for that second contract, since it depends on what the rate decision for the first month will be. In a very real way the price of the second contract hinges on the decision concerning the first contract. The price of the second contract should have something to do with the chance of a move in that second month and the chance of rates moving in the first month. We can illustrate the situation conceptually:

			5%
4.5%	4.5%	4.5%	
4%			4.5%
			4.5%
4%	4%	4%	
FF_{start}	$FOMC_1$	FF_{end}	$FOMC_{2F}$

Once we begin to layer on probabilities of multiple meetings, where the pricing of one contract depends on the pricing of another, the situation becomes more complicated. As the figure above hints, it's necessary to build the same type of binomial lattice that we did to evaluate Treasury futures; but rather than allowing the cheapest-to-deliver issues to float, we let probabilities of FOMC decisions be the independent variable. This is all relevant to Eurodollar futures because our analysis is going to work in much the same way.

Imagine all of the different paths that could be constructed from the above rate choices. Each time there is an FOMC meeting, there is the possibility for rates to change. If we live (by assumption) in a world of 50-basis-point rate hikes, then the probability of moving from 4.5% to 5% depends on the probability of moving from 4% to 4.5%. In fact, the number of paths grows exponentially with the number of FOMC meetings. If we have one meeting, there are two possible paths. If we have two meetings, there are four paths. If there are M many meetings, then there are M^2 paths. It may seem impossibly complicated to solve a problem like this, but it is more tedious than complicated. To solve the system, all we have to do is define each of the possible paths Fed Funds could take, subject to our original two assumptions, and then we could take two possible paths, either implying FOMC rate moves from market prices or market prices from FOMC rate moves. Since the market provides prices, our job is to search for the unique set of probabilities that will reproduce those prices, given that the timing and magnitude of moves are fixed.

Figure 2–21 illustrates all the possible paths that Fed Funds could take during 6 months and 4 FOMC meetings. As we mentioned before, the number of paths is the squared value of the number of FOMC meetings, but Figure 2–21 isn't as complicated as it may look. At each meeting we've narrowed the outcomes to just two: no move or move. To put it another way, X or $1 - X$. Since there are 4 columns, there are also 16 probabilities, but the number of probabilities is the squared value of the number of meetings. It stands to reason that the probability of any one rate during a month without meetings must equal the probability of a

FIGURE 2–21

Most likely path of Fed Funds based on implied futures prices

	Jan-06	Mar-06	May-06	Jun-06	Probability of Path
		4.25	4.50	4.50	4.50	0.0%
		4.25	4.50	4.50	4.75	0.6%
		4.25	4.50	4.75	4.50	0.2%
		4.25	4.50	4.75	4.75	3.9%
		4.25	4.75	4.50	4.50	0.1%
		4.25	4.75	4.50	4.75	0.9%
		4.25	4.75	4.75	4.50	0.4%
4.25	4.25	4.75	4.75	4.75	5.9%
		4.50	4.50	4.50	4.50	0.3%
		4.50	4.50	4.50	4.75	4.4%
		4.50	4.50	4.75	4.50	1.8%
		4.50	4.50	4.75	4.75	28.6%
		4.50	4.75	4.50	4.50	0.4%
		4.50	4.75	4.50	4.75	6.7%
		4.50	4.75	4.75	4.50	2.7%
		4.50	4.75	4.75	4.75	43.0%
						100%

rate move in the prior month. In essence it's possible to boil down the table into just 16 probabilities, since there are four FOMC meetings during the period.

Although it's impossible to know with 100% certainty what the path of Fed Funds will be, it is quite useful to calculate a most likely path, based on market expectations. If there is greater than a 50% chance of a rate hike, then we can assume Fed Funds will move to that point. We can repeat the exercise at each point to determine a probable path from Figure 2–21, although this brings about an interesting question: how much confidence do we have in the deferred market estimates? It may seem as if we're building a house of cards, because the market has no concrete guarantee upon which to base its conclusion and is only able to make its best judgment based on the available information. This calculation has more to do with proving how uncertain the market is in its assertion about future rates than it does in relaying any sort of concrete information. To put it another way, even if the market were priced in 100% probabilities about future rate movements, that's no guarantee that they will happen because no one, not even the FOMC meeting members, will know the results of the next ballot on rate changes. FOMC voting members may know their own individual votes, but not everyone else's.

In order to determine the probability of realizing any path, we multiply all of the probability of choices at each point together. Suppose that in Figure 2–22

F I G U R E   2–22

All possible Fed Funds paths

the probabilities are all hovering around 90% over 6 months with 6 meetings. The chance of that path being realized is just over 50%. It's amazing how just a little bit of uncertainty about each decision can erode our confidence in realizing a particular path. In most endeavors, 90% would give most people a great deal of confidence. In finance, however, just that 10% chance of being wrong severely limits the usefulness of the results. This analysis also highlights just how weak the evidence is that commentators are often relying on with Fed Funds futures for a likely path of FOMC rate decisions. Normally market prices represent the point where all gains from trade have been exhausted. Is that also the market's "best guess" about the future? It's certainly the point where no one else is willing to bet on a different outcome, given the price he or she would incur to do so, but it's also not clear that this is equivalent to a best guess.

One of the problems with these contracts is anticipating the difference between the target and effective rates. Normally there are enough days in the month after a possible rate move where it doesn't really matter what we anticipate that difference to be, but there are instances when an FOMC meeting might be on the 29th of a month with 30 days in it, in which case even a high probability of a move will have a relatively small impact on the price of the contract. In fact, it's possible that the price impact from expected rate moves is below the expected difference between the target and effective rates. What happens in this instance is that the contract turns out to be effectively useless for backing out market expectations, since there is no way to accurately judge what happens to the effective Fed Funds rate on any given day. It is possible to get around this problem by looking at the next month contract if it happens not to have a meeting scheduled. In this case we can back out the simple probability of a move using a simple weighted average. Unfortunately, if the next month has a meeting scheduled, the information conveyed in these contracts is unclear.

What does all this have to do with Eurodollars? There are 1-month LIBOR contracts traded at the CME that facilitate hedging the stub for many Eurodollar trades, and if we assume a constant spread between Fed Funds and 1-month LIBOR, we can perform exactly the same pricing procedure we just detailed. Fed Funds and LIBOR are quite similar, since both are unsecured interbank deposits. Just because of the term structure of interest rates, a 1-month deposit normally has a slightly higher yield than an overnight rate, and for this reason 1-month LIBOR contracts normally have a slightly higher yield than Fed Funds. Figure 2–23 details how the spread between 1- and 3-month LIBOR contracts over Fed Funds has performed over the past 15 years. Over this period the average has been 30.7 and 39.8 basis points respectively, although the relationship has been somewhat volatile. Given these spreads, we can imply the same sorts of probabilities from LIBOR contracts that we do from the Fed Funds market by adding these fixed spreads to the target Fed Funds rate, and not surprisingly the implied probabilities of FOMC moves are quite similar.

F I G U R E   2–23

Short-term LIBOR closely follows Fed Funds

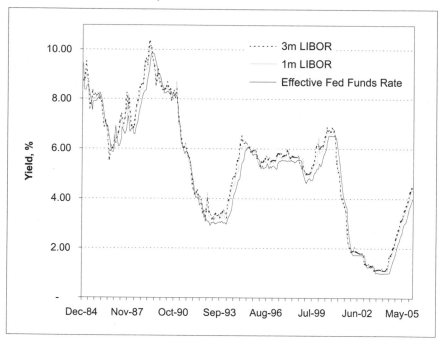

The important question now is how do we translate this work to Eurodollars? The problem is that Eurodollars are 3-month forward instruments and potentially cover two FOMC meetings, since the typical schedule is to have eight meetings a year. One way to apply similar arithmetic to what we've already developed for single-month contracts is to assume that the probability of Fed moves is the same during each of the months covered by the contracts. This assumption makes the arithmetic slightly more involved than in our original case, but saves us from introducing an additional probability variable, which would make the problem unsolvable since there would be one equation and two unknown variables. The only real change is that the denominator is different in the day-count calculation. Rather than representing the total days in the month, we are now calculating probabilities over the entire 3-month period, and there are normally 91 days between Eurodollar expiration dates. The trick to understanding the iterative nature of the equations is that we are using the outgoing probability-weighted yield in the prior month as the incoming rate for the current month.

Suppose that the current Fed Funds rate is 4%, the meeting is halfway through the month, and we are currently in a tightening cycle. If there is a 50%

chance of a Fed Funds rate increase from 4% to 4.25%, then the arithmetic is simple:

$$4.00 \cdot \frac{15}{30} + (4.00 \cdot x + 4.25 \cdot (1 - x)) \cdot \frac{15}{30}$$

We know the 4% Fed Funds rate with certainty since it's the declared target, and we can determine the price of the contract by knowing either the probabilities for a rate hike or the price of the contract. If we assume a constant 9-basis-point spread between Fed Funds and 1-month LIBOR, then we can simply add this many basis points to each of our rates: 4% goes to 4.09% and 4.25% goes to 4.34%. If there were another FOMC meeting the next month, but no meeting in month 3, the equation would look a little different because we would use the probability-weighted rate from the first month as the incoming rate for month 2, and this second-month rate would hold through the end of the 3-month period. For example:

$$4.00 \cdot \frac{15}{90} + [4.00 \cdot x + 4.25 \cdot (1 - x)] \cdot \frac{15}{90}$$
$$+ [4.00 \cdot x + 4.25 \cdot (1 - x)] \cdot \frac{15}{90} + [4.25 \cdot x + 4.50 \cdot (1 - x)] \cdot \frac{45}{90}$$

If the first and second FOMC meetings are 15 days into the month and the entire period is 90 days, then the rate determined at the final meeting will last for the remaining 15 days of that month plus the full 30 days of the next month. The calculation for the following contract would begin with the final rate from the prior month, the value multiplied by 45/90 as its starting rate.

There is a slightly different interpretation to this calculation compared to the original one we did for Fed Funds futures. In Fed Funds futures the contract price directly implied a probability of a Fed move at a single meeting. Since Eurodollars can span several meetings, we have to interpret the calculated probability as the change that rates reach the final target level by the time the contract expires. Again, there is a critical distinction since Fed Funds settle at the end of the month that they cover, whereas Eurodollars cover a 3-month period beginning at the expiration date. The market relies on past observations to settle Fed Funds, and while it's simple enough to observe the spot 3-month LIBOR rate on the Eurodollar expiration date, there is some guesswork involved about what that 3-month rate should be. While there's no ambiguity about how to settle the contract—simply 100 less the spot 3-month rate—it is possible for the market to misprice the 3-month rate if the Fed does something unexpected. Frequently in the financial press there are people who comment on "what the Eurodollar market is telling us about the Fed," but it would be interesting to see if these same people understand the details and assumptions involved in the calculations.

CLOSED-FORM SOLUTION VERSUS MLE

What if we turned the problem on its head? Rather than specifying a closed-form solution, it is possible to employ the tools developed to value Treasury futures to value these contracts. Even though it was a very simple one, the equation we specified earlier for Fed Funds and Eurodollar futures was a closed-form solution. The complexity involved by adding multiple Fed meetings to value Eurodollar futures is just a taste of the complexity involved when we take a formulaic approach and try to make it more realistic. Alternatively, we could set up the same logical rules in a spreadsheet and let the computer spin its wheels, randomly searching for probabilities of Fed moves to create contract prices that match what we observe in the market. Granted, this approach is massively wasteful of computer calculations in contrast to the relative ease with which we can solve the closed-form equations above; but the point of this book is to leverage modern resources to keep abreast of futures contract performance, and this is a perfect example.

The details of computer search algorithms are all a little bit different, but an artillery man from Napoleon's time would recognize the pattern. Without knowing the exact range to a target, a cannon crew would simply take a guess with their first shot, then look to see if it hit in front of or in back of the target. If the shot hit in front of the target, they estimated too short a range, and the second shot would be slightly longer. If any of the shots landed in back of the target, the crew knew they were using too great a range and would shorten their next shot somewhat. As long as the target didn't move (or run away!), this was a reasonable algorithm of searching for the exact range. Although there is an element of randomness, the process is structured and isn't entirely trial and error.

A computer can do exactly the same thing. Without knowing exactly what the value should be, the computer will simply "fire a shot" and guess a value to start with. The computer then will check to see whether it has "hit the target" and whether the resulting value satisfies the criteria we established, in this case matching market prices. If the first value resulted in a match to the market price, then the algorithm scored a "hit" and stops. Otherwise it will try a second value and check the results again. If they are closer to the goal, then the second value was in the correct direction, or at least closer to the right answer, and the computer knows to keep searching in that direction. The algorithm zeroes in on the target and eventually finds it after hundreds or even thousands of wrong answers. Why rely on such a wasteful process? Because a computer can process a thousand wrong answers in the blink of an eye. Given how fast machines are, there's little reason not to rely on this approach, since it lets us add criteria like maximum and minimum constraints that are difficult to represent in a closed form solution.

TABLE 2–4

Backing Out Probabilities from Fed Funds Futures Contracts

Contract	FF1
Exp	1
Month	Jan
Days	31
Meeting	31
FDTR	4.25
x	100%
$1-x$	0%
Start	4.25
New	4.50
Old	4.25
Days old	30
Days new	1
Predicted	4.26
Actual	4.29

What if we added a third criterion to the original two from the last section—that the Fed would move only on meeting days and would stick to either 25-basis-point or 50-basis-point moves? The third criterion could be the probability that a move could never be below 0% or above 100%. This is a simple real-life constraint that could easily be violated by our original equations, which used market prices to back out probabilities.

Table 2–4 illustrates the implied probability problem for Fed Funds futures using this new method. It shouldn't be hard to see the links to the previous work since we've visually laid out the periods in chronological order from left to right. The first 15 days are at the beginning Funds rate of 4%, and the rate for the remaining 15 days of the month will be determined at the FOMC meeting, whose members have the choice of keeping the 4% rate or moving to 4.25% (we're assuming that the Fed is in a 25-basis-point tightening cycle for this example). The next month the incoming rate is the probability-weighted average of 4% and 4.25%, which happens to be 4.15% using a 60% probability of a rate hike. Of course, the computer could search for probabilities that matched the market price of the Fed Funds contract covering the month and the process is much the same, month after month, and the only change in formula between our front month contract and back months is that the Fed Funds rate is known for the front month, but we use probability-weighted averages for distant contracts.

The boundary conditions for the search must limit probabilities to between 0 and 100%, but as we mentioned before, there are going to be times when traders start to price in the absurd. For example, during the 14 rate hikes from 2004 to 2006 there were traders and economists who expected the Fed to move by 50 basis points at each meeting. Even after the 13th time when the Fed moved 25 basis points, there were long discussions on Wall Street about what the 14th move would be. Even after the Fed moved by the same 25 basis points it had in the past, there were those whose predictions became more absurd, claiming 75-basis-point moves. If the market prices in some chance of a 50-basis-point move but we've limited the Fed by our assumptions to 25-basis-point moves, we could easily put an upper boundary on our computer search for a probability to match the market price. In this instance a market price implying a 50-basis-point move would be assigned a 100% chance of a 25-basis point move, but no more, even though we run the risk of throwing off subsequent probability calculations. There is a way around this problem that we discuss at the end of the section, but it involves two-stage estimation, which we haven't done so far in our examples.

Even if we ignore the chance of the market violating our steady rate hike assumption of always moving by the same amount, how do we know if the next two choices should be between 4.25% and 4.5% or between 4% and 4.25%? Most often the market will price in some chance of either happening, but it's reasonable enough to put in a logical "switch" that moves the next two rate choices higher if the probability of a hike is greater than 50%. If the probability of a move is less than 50%, then the choices in the next month will remain the same as in the prior month. As we add in logical statements like this one and limits on the probabilities, it should become apparent how difficult this problem would be to solve with a closed-form solution like the one we originally started out with. The work in Table 2–4 on Fed Funds is necessary to illustrate the individual pieces of the analysis, which we need to combine in a slightly different way before gaining useful probability information from the Eurodollar market.

Determining implied probabilities from Eurodollar futures with numerical analysis gives us a degree of freedom to make our model more realistic, but as with all of the prior work, this realism comes at a price. Table 2–5 illustrates all of the same pieces as in our prior work with Fed Funds, except this time we aren't searching for weightings to match an individual market price, but rather a set of weightings that will re-create a market price. Conceptually, the difference is between a ratio of 1:1 or 3:1, whereas in Fed Funds and 1-month LIBOR contracts there is one probability that the Fed will move (the X variable), which is determined by one market price for the month in question. In Eurodollars we are searching for up to three probabilities, depending on the FOMC schedule, to match to one market price. The mechanics of the calculation share elements of both 1-month LIBOR and Fed Funds futures. It is necessary to assume some fixed spread between LIBOR and Fed Funds in order to build a bridge between the two

T A B L E   2–5

Determining a Set of Implied Probabilities from Fed Funds Futures

Contract	FF1	FF2	FF3	FF4	FF5	FF6	FF7
Exp	1	29	60	88	121	151	182
Month	Jan	Feb	Mar	Apr	May	Jun	Jul
Days	31	28	31	30	31	30	31
Meeting	31	–	28	–	10	29	–
FDTR	4.25						
x	100%	0%	100%	0%	9%	89%	0%
$1-x$	0%	100%	0%	100%	91%	11%	100%
Start	4.25	4.50	4.50	4.75	4.75	4.77	4.97
New	4.50	4.75	4.75	5.00	5.00	5.00	5.25
Old	4.25	4.50	4.50	4.75	4.75	4.75	5.00
Days old	30	–	27	–	9	28	–
Days new	1	28	4	30	22	2	31
Predicted	4.26	4.50	4.53	4.75	4.77	4.79	5.00
Actual	4.29	4.50	4.54	4.70	4.76	4.79	4.81

markets. As with Fed Funds futures, the incoming rate will be the probability-weighted average of the outgoing rate for the prior month.

The intermediate stages of the calculation are displayed at the top, where the number of days is multiplied by the probability-weighted rate for those days. What we're really doing here is setting up a structure for the computer to search within, but not specifying anything about the functional form of the equation to solve for probabilities that match market prices. The process is analogous to setting up the rules of a game without specifying the steps players should take. In this case we've unrealistically assumed that there are three FOMC meetings in 3 months and that each meeting is happening halfway through a month with 30 days. Of course, there are no three consecutive months with 30 days in them, but this setup keeps the arithmetic simple. Once we've verified that this tool is producing reasonable answers, we can add in the appropriate variables for FOMC meeting dates and the correct number of days in each month.

Massively wasteful, yes, but this approach is also incredibly powerful, since it allows us to leverage technology rather than plodding through an unrealistic closed-form solution by hand. The pendulum has clearly swung from computer time being the most expensive input to solve problems to human hours as the most expensive input, and not just by a little! The computer has determined a set of implied probabilities at the bottom of Table 2–6 that match the market price of

TABLE 2–6

Extending the Methodology to Three-Month Contracts

Month	FF1		FF2		FF3
x	1.00		0.00		1.00
1 - x	0.00		1.00		0.00
	4.50		4.75		4.75
4.25	4.25	4.50	4.50	4.50	4.50
Fed Funds	4.26		4.50		4.52
+9 bps	4.35		4.59		4.61
Theoretical 3m LIBOR	4.52				

the Eurodollar, given the structure of FOMC meetings and assumptions we discussed above. Problem solved? One of the limitations of this work is that there may be cases where the set of implied probabilities isn't unique. This means that there could be more than one set of probabilities to satisfy the equations, the logic for which is something along the lines of a 100% chance of a 25-basis-point move pricing the same as a 50% chance of a 50-basis-point move. Practically, the more realistically we specifys the system, the more limited is the set of possibilities that would solve the system and the less chance there can be for this uniqueness problem to crop up.

Table 2–6 illustrates that the process for determining implied probabilities for one Eurodollar contract but extending the work to multiple contracts is no more complicated in this case than it is with the Fed Funds valuation framework. Over and over again we use similar methodologies to solve problems, and the beauty of the approaches is evident when we push and pull at the concepts to extend the work in different ways. The reward for our detailed steps is a set of implied probabilities to let us make judgments about what the market expects the FOMC to do past what most traders are able to observe with the Fed Funds curve. This work is critically important for a few reasons. First it gives us a way of measuring value in the Eurodollar market that is distinct from other markets and a way of internally generating fair value levels for the market. The second, and probably most important aspect, is that we can now compare our own expectations about FOMC moves with what the market is expecting. How could anyone hope to implement a trading strategy without knowing what the market prices imply right now? For all the ignorant trader knows, the market could already be pricing in the phenomenon he is trying to capture. It's not until we determine a point of reference with the market price that we can set sail for our objective.

No matter how robust and realistic we make our analysis, there is one weakness that's inescapable. The whole probability tree is based on our assumptions regarding the spread between Fed Funds and LIBOR. The effective Fed Funds rate and the 1- and 3-month LIBOR move together, but the standard deviation of the difference is 22.3 basis points from 1990 through 2005. If we were to recalculate the probability tree using a spread between 3-month LIBOR and Fed Funds that is 1 standard deviation higher and lower than the average, the resulting probabilities would be different, but not by orders of magnitude. Rather than implying a 100% probability of a rate move, the value has fallen to just above 90% in the first month. As we expect, the differences cascade through the model from month to month and grow along with the expiration of the contracts. There's no real way to escape a judgment call regarding the appropriate spread between the two, but there's much to be learned from the analysis, regardless of this point.

Another problem with this analysis is that it hinged on the assumption that the Fed rate increments remained the same, whether 25 or 50 basis points. In reality, the Fed is free to choose whatever increments it likes, and some of the past cycles have mixed increments, either 25 or 50 basis points. In our closed-form work it was algebraically difficult to allow for this freedom, but our subsequent numerical solutions hinted at how it might be possible to incorporate such realism. Just as we put a logical switch into our equations to move the choice of future rate hike between 4% and 4.25% or 4.25% and 4.5% based on whether the probability of a hike was greater than 50%, we can also toggle between 25- and 50-basis-point changes depending on the implied probability. However, in order to do this, we have to use a two-stage estimation in which there are essentially two passes at the analysis.

The first pass is in the same manner as before, with a limit on the upper and lower probability bounds of 0 and 100%. If the implied probability necessary to match market prices is above 100%, then the set of possible rate moves for the next month are 25 basis points higher. If the implied probability is below 50%, then the set of possible rate moves is the same as it was for the previous month. The second pass on the analysis adds another logical rule to look at the implied probabilities. If the upper bound is equal to 100%, then it switches; the rate choices in the current month are 25 basis points higher. The motivation for the switch is that market participants are never in complete agreement about what a rate should be, and if an implied probability is at 100% when calculated using our 25-basis-point change assumptions, it means that the market is expecting some lower percentage chance of the larger move happening.

Two-stage estimation is essentially swapping one assumption for another. In order to make the model more realistic by relaxing our "constant speed" assumption about the Fed never changing gears once it's started a 25- or 50-basis-point cycle, the two-stage analysis allows for market expectations of changing rate moves. However, in order to get this desirable result, we have to give up the notion that every time the market is pricing in a 100% chance of a move with a smaller increment, the true expectation is of some lesser chance of a larger move. There will be times when the original assumption makes sense and times when the new two-stage analysis will produce more intuitively appealing results. The important conclusion is that implied Eurodollar rates can provide a great deal of information about future FOMC movements if interpreted within the appropriate structure.

TREASURY AND EURODOLLAR SPREADS

In the previous two chapters we detailed some fair value methodologies for futures that distinguished their behavior from the underlying risk, whether U.S. Treasuries or LIBOR are involved. This chapter details the behavior when the two are spread against one another. Spreads, rather than outright long or short positions, are perhaps the most popular trading strategies because they allow for a limited exposure to various risks. As the yield curve decomposition in the last chapter detailed, changes in the level of rates are by far the most volatile risk one can be exposed to in the fixed income markets, followed by changes in the slope of the curve as a distant second, and last by a change in the bow or curvature of the curve as the least volatile type of curve shift. Trades that are exposed to changes in the slope of the curve are spreads because they involve long and short legs at different maturity points. Trades with long and short legs of the same maturity are also spreads, and it's this type of trade that will highlight the unique risks of both Treasury and Eurodollar futures.

IDENTIFYING DRIVERS OF THE SPREAD

Spreads between Treasury and Eurodollar (TED) futures are normally correlated with the level of rates, except when things aren't normal. Many novices may find such a statement infuriating, but veterans can identify with the underlying truth. Just as with other products, TED spreads are usually quite well behaved, but there are periods when normally placid waters turn treacherous, as we'll detail later on. We have already done much to describe the performance of both Eurodollar and Treasury futures individually, but a maturity matched spread between the two highlights exactly the risks that are "left over" with credit products after removing the default risk-free Treasury rate. We have relied on econometric analysis in our earlier work but not to the extent that will be necessary to analyze spreads. Statistical work is apropos to this discussion since there are no hard-and-fast rules about what must or mustn't be true of a relationship, and the foundation upon which our analysis stands is based as much on judgment and interpretation as it is on the data.

Figure 3–1 is the most appropriate place to start with our analysis of TED spreads because it shows where the spreads have been since 1990, which is about as long as they've been actively traded. What's striking about this chart is what

F I G U R E   3–1

Historical TED spreads and 2-year yields

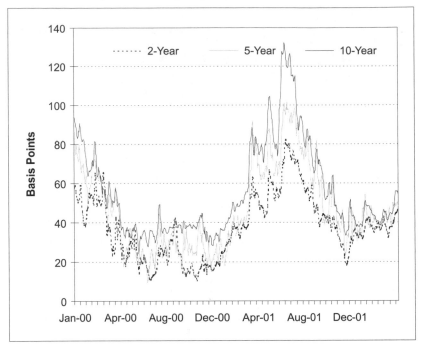

little information it really conveys. In contrast to our work with Treasury rates, interest rate swaps are in their infancy as a class of securities, with historical data rarely stretching back more than 10 years. On the surface a decade may seem to involve a mountain of information, but if we consider that the typical business cycle in the United States is 5 years and credit cycles may be roughly double that, then it becomes apparent how much of a newcomer LIBOR-based instruments are to the world stage.

This chart makes it apparent that most of the time TED spreads move with the level of rates. To say that there are exceptions, though, is an understatement because of the way that these exceptions crop up. As it turns out, the worst stress that fixed income markets ever endure are "flights" to quality. This type of trading is characterized by eroding confidence in private borrowers and a flight to higher-quality credits. Of course, the highest-quality credit in the world is the U.S. government, and there are times when Treasury notes and bonds are the only securities investors want to hold. In these periods prices for credit instruments gap lower and markets thin as dealers look to halt the bleeding that comes from the fact that they must hold some of these bonds themselves as part of the market-making process. While interest rate commodities like Treasuries and Eurodollars are just as easily sold short as they are bought, this is not true of credit markets in which individual firm names dot the landscape. The old Wall Street adage, "You can't make a market in someone else's inventory," comes into play here because dealers are usually long a fair amount of credit-risky bonds as part of the normal course of business.

Treasury and Eurodollar traders should take note of the phenomenon because of the way that prices slip in a flight to quality. Initially there is some piece of bad news that hits the corporate or emerging market; then selling begets more selling. As soon as individual traders in the dealer community begin to feel pain (remember that dealers are relatively thinly capitalized and operate on margin), trading halts and sellers are sometimes left with stark choices: catch a falling sword by trying to hold onto their bonds, or hit a bid and sell at prices low enough so that the new holder of the bond has sufficient insulation for conditions to worsen before the new holder is hurt. In these environments Treasury bonds ride a tidal wave to higher prices while corporate bonds are swamped. LIBOR represents an unsecured interbank rate, and if the financial condition of these banks has deteriorated in some way, possibly due to loan exposure to the sector in difficulty, then LIBOR rates should rise.

Normally TED spreads are correlated with the level of rates, falling in a rally and widening in a sell-off, but in a flight to quality the opposite happens. When there is a panic to get out of credit-risky bonds, the Treasury yields fall and Eurodollar rates do the opposite. Worse still, the correlation flips at exactly the time when a hedger needs the protection the most—when the market goes haywire. This is the inherent problem with using Treasuries to hedge credit-sensitive products, and it was highlighted dramatically during a credit meltdown in 1998, and more recently in terrorist warnings since 2001. Most of the time Treasury hedges are an inexpensive and efficient way to add or shed duration, but, as Figure 3–2 illustrates, during these two periods there have been hiccups that stood the typical relationships on their head.

Figure 3–2 is a rolling 90-day correlation between 2-year Treasury and Eurodollar rates and TED spreads. Correlation simply measures the strength of the relationship, and the change in sign that we've been discussing as characterizing a flight to quality is evident here. This chart begins to measure more precisely the behavior of TED spreads against Treasury and Eurodollar rates, and we perform the calculation against both in order to highlight that Treasuries are the more volatile of the two, although just barely. The average of the absolute value of the change in yields between the two series is 11 basis points for Treasuries and 10.6 basis points for Eurodollars, indicating TED spreads follow swap rates more closely than they do Treasuries. This also indicates that most of the time pricing information is hitting the Treasury market first and then filtering into the spread markets. Still, there must be a better way of explaining changes in spreads than to say that "they normally are correlated with rates, except when they're not," and, in fact, we can build a statistical model to attack the problem.

As we mentioned before, when officers of a bank participating in the pool for LIBOR rates face deteriorating credit conditions with their counterparties, their

FIGURE 3-2

Rolling correlations, TED spreads with rates

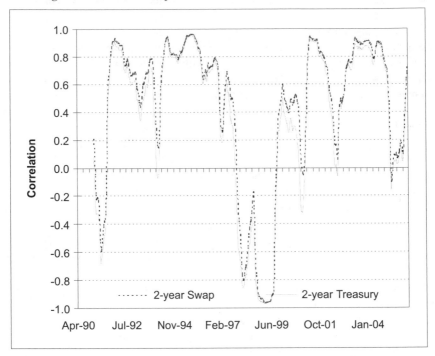

natural reaction is to raise rates. One might imagine that bank lending officers might not be the only people to notice this phenomenon, and equity investors in those banks might punish their stock prices for the same type of deteriorated credit. If the two markets were perfectly efficient, meaning that they had the same information at the same time, then equity prices would fall at the same time LIBOR rates rose. Of course, nothing is literally instantaneous, and it might take a trading session or two before the two markets linked up. Still it would make sense for stock prices to explain part of the change in LIBOR rates and TED spreads as well.

Many studies in financial economics capture the heart of a relationship but never dissect it to the fullest extent possible. Work that is "good enough" is often as deep as traders and their managers are willing to go, and it's hard to blame them! No one makes money at a brokerage by publishing research papers, and even in academia there are pressures that may keep the best work undone. Table 3-1 is an attempt to convey as complete a picture as possible of TED spreads and how different variables affect the value over time and in various combinations. The variables we choose to explain spreads are the S&P 500 Bank Index, the Mortgage Bankers Association Refinance (Refi) Index, and the level of rates at each maturity point. As we mentioned before, deteriorating credit conditions should show up in stock prices, and since banks that compose the Bank Index are

major swap counterparties, it would make sense for increases in their credit risk
to show up as a fall in the index. Similarly, signs of financial health would normally lead to higher index values, all else being equal.

That famous phrase, "all else equal" or *ceteris paribus* in Latin, is nothing
short of infamous. Arithmetically it's often translated into partial durations, where
all of the other variables in an equation are held constant to determine the sensitivity to changes in a single factor. The lunacy in translating these results to the
real world is that nothing ever happens this way. It would be convenient if bond
traders could trade just the level of rates on Monday, the slope of the curve on
Wednesday, and the curvature every other Friday, but the reality is that all three
elements are moving at the same time. The market doesn't conveniently pause to
let one thing happen at a time, and it's often the case that traders are trying to juggle changes in a dozen variables, all at the same time. This is why building a
model with the straight level of the Bank Index is doomed to fail, since it will rise
or fall with the general market for reasons having nothing to do with bank credit
specifically. One way to eliminate the problem is to measure the Bank Index in
terms of its relative performance against a broader index, like the S&P 500.

As Figure 3–3 illustrates, the normalized Bank Index volatility is far lower
than the outright series, which makes sense since we've removed any market

F I G U R E   3–3

S&P bank stocks deflated by general market performance

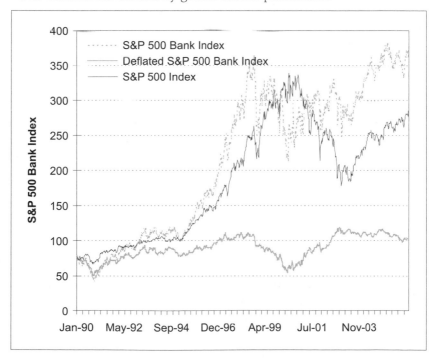

direction bias from the data. To construct the normalized series, we simply subtracted the return of the S&P 500 total return index from those of the Bank Index. Traditionally stocks have been analyzed in terms of their *beta,* which is the ratio of their volatility to the overall market. For example, a stock with a beta of 1.2 indicates that during the historical period measured, this security returned 1.2% for every 1% gain in the broader market. Including the Bank Index in Figure 3–3 in its outright level is equivalent to measuring the 1.2 beta in our example, but by normalizing the series, we are essentially measuring the 0.2. It's this smaller part, the 0.2% of the return that is unique to this security that is separate from the general market. By subtracting the returns of the S&P 500 from the Bank Index, we've identified returns that are unique to bank counterparty risk, rather than having this risk caught by the general tide of the market.

No such manipulations are necessary to get a better understanding of the Mortgage Bankers Association (MBA) Refi Index. This series covers around half of all U.S. retail residential mortgage originations, and the data is taken from mortgage bankers, commercial banks, and thrifts. An index of applications, rather than actual home loans, it is the broadest and best-tracked measure of activity in the housing market. As one might imagine, lower interest rates lead to more home loan applications because it makes homes more affordable to new buyers; there is also a point where interest rates are low enough that it makes sense for borrowers to pay the fees involved with refinancing their mortgage. Figures 3–4 and 3–5 graph the MBA Index and the 10-year Treasury yield, first as a time series and second as a scatter plot of one against the other. While not perfectly inversely correlated, there is an undeniable link between the two. Our interest in the series has to do with how refinancing activity spills over to mortgage hedging needs. When interest rates drop a little, the expected cash flows from that mortgage collateral accelerate, and more principal is prepaid as people refinance, shortening the duration of the mortgage.

New mortgages issued at prevailing rates add duration to the market, since their cash flows are expected to be more distant than the high interest rate loans they replace. The question about whether refinancing adds or subtracts duration from the market as a whole has to do with the path of interest rates, because lots of little moves are not the same as one big move. Put another way, mortgage prepayments are dependent on the path of interest rates, not just their level, which is why the MBA index deserves to be in our spread model, and why it's not just another way of measuring the 10-year Treasury rate. In a sudden and large shift down in interest rates, every loan originated at those higher levels will be eligible for prepayment, meaning that the incentive of a lower interest rate outweighs the cost of refinancing. This is not true in a gradual drift down in rates because loans are constantly being issued; in this situation there will be loans at the higher rate eligible for refinancing and loans that were issued at lower rates that are just slightly higher than current rates, but the incentive to refinance isn't sufficient to overcome the costs.

FIGURE 3–4

Mortgage Bankers Association refinance index

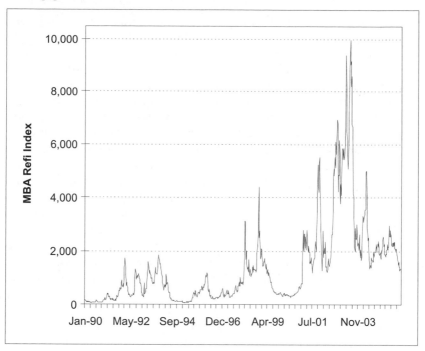

FIGURE 3–5

MBA index versus level of rates

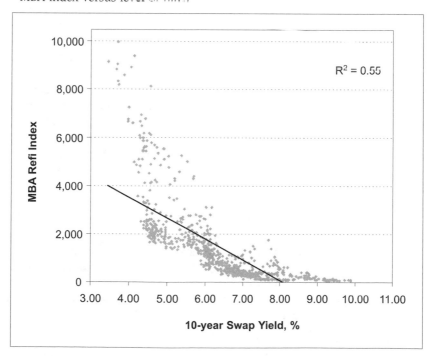

The story is different in the opposite direction because an increase in interest rates keeps everyone from refinancing. Of course, when the cost of a new loan is above one's existing cost, then there is no reason to get a new loan, and the expected cash flows from mortgage collateral become more distant as prepayments decrease. This is worth dwelling on for our spread model because an increase in interest rates leads to less refinancing activity, more duration in the mortgage market, and a greater need for firms that hold mortgages at high leverage to shed duration. Just how much duration depends on the path of interest rates and distribution of originations at each rate level, but as we mentioned before, interest rate swaps are the primary vehicle to capture that risk. The GSEs are a prime example of this activity, since they hold mortgages at high leverage—between 25 and 35 times levered—they will typically "pay" or sell the fixed leg of an interest rate swap. If end users are selling, this means that Wall Street is buying. Brokers are highly levered as well, and they need to hedge this risk by selling Eurodollar contracts at the CME. More "paying" or selling pressure by end users in interest rate swaps is transmitted to the Eurodollar market via Wall Street dealers. More selling in Eurodollars, the higher their rates and the wider TED spreads become. At least this is how it works in theory, but as we'll see, reality is messier.

The level of rates deserves to be in our spread model for a reason that's entirely distinct from any mortgage- or hedging-related activity and has to do with economics. More specifically, it has to do with an intuitively pleasing idea that TED spreads should be priced as a percentage of their underlying Eurodollar rate, so that when rates increase, so should spreads by the same proportion. It's not ridiculous to think that credit premiums should increase along with other premiums in the market like risk aversion and inflation. For this reason we would expect a spread curve that is upward sloping just like the yield curve is most of the time. Figure 3–6 illustrates that there is some basis for this belief in the historical data, since a theoretical swap spread series calculated as a fixed percentage of the underlying rate does track observed spreads relatively well. The standard deviation of the observed spread series is 3.6 basis points for 2-year spreads, but if we subtract the volatility of our theoretical spread series derived as a percentage of the underlying rate, then the standard deviation of the resulting series is just 3.0 basis points. Whenever we begin with a volatile series and can explain some of that volatility with another series, we've effectively highlighted and subtracted out a distinct risk. The more risks we can identify, the better our model is going to be, but there's a problem.

Why don't we just add more and more variables to our TED spread model, with the hope that there is something to be contributed by each of the new explanations? Even random noise might help explain a variable in statistical terms. This technique was in vogue in economics as computers became more capable during the latter part of the 1980s and analysts began enormous projects to attempt to model the U.S. economy. The process became known as *data mining,* and it showed remarkable results. Remarkably bad results, that is.

FIGURE   3–6

TED spreads as a percentage of rates

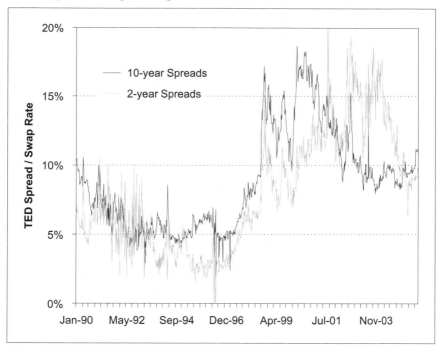

It turns out that if you hand the thinking over to a computer, what you end up with is exactly what you ask it for: a model with a near perfect fit for the historical data. The computers could search through hundreds or thousands of data series and choose the ones that would produce a model that nearly perfectly explained the historical data it had for the U.S. economy. The problem was that these models had no predictive power! They could explain what had happened in the past, but they had no theory behind them or judgment about what a reasonable driver of future events might be. If we just added more and more variables to our TED spread model, we would be in danger of doing exactly the same thing, building a model that perfectly explains the past but says nothing about the future.

There is another reason to stop at just a few variables in our TED spread model: the more variables we have, the more interactions there are and the more difficult it is to understand them all. Humans are able to understand one-dimensional information, like a one-column list. Two dimensions are normally not a problem either since most people have experience drawing on a piece of paper, keeping track of both the vertical and horizontal strokes. Thinking in three dimensions is more difficult, and there have been fabulous mistakes made even by experienced architects and builders because they couldn't judge information in three-dimensional reality. There's a famous story of a graduate student telling his professor that he could think in four dimensions, after which no one wanted to sit next to him in class. The point is that the more variables we have in our model, the more dimensions we add and the more difficult it is to keep track of them. If we can't understand what goes into our TED spread model, how can we hope to understand what's coming out? Economists would say that a model must be *parsimonious* and *interpretable,* meaning that it must be small enough to understand as well as have some basis in theory. Explaining crop yields with rainfall measurements makes sense. Explaining crop yields with the number of homicides in the nearest urban area does not. Additionally, the model has to be small enough to be digested by human intellect. From our perspective we are interested in explaining the past so that it teaches us some information that will be helpful to future trades. Simply listing statistically significant variables on a report doesn't go very far in the markets.

There is another subtler problem with any attempt we might make to build a statistical model for TED spreads having to do with time. More specifically, the problem is a lack of time, since we have to truncate our historical data at some point, and it's not as if there is an unlimited history available to be analyzed. Even if there were, computer power is significant, but still finite, and analyzing 10 years' worth of minute-by-minute changes in a bond price is still beyond the reach of personal computers. How far back in time do we have to go for our model to produce meaningful results? Traditionally, the rule of large numbers guides people to take no less than 30 data points for financial analysis. The whole question gets down to how many samples we have to draw from a large pool of observations before the samples look the same as the large pool. Technically speaking, one might say that in a repeated, independent trial the differences between the population and sample converges to zero as the number of observations goes toward infinity. Most of the time in finance these small sample issues don't crop up, since there are normally at least 30 observations for anything worth studying. Here is the problem: somewhere between 30 and infinity we have to truncate the historical data period used to determine our statistical analysis; so where do we cut it?

The answer is that we use a long enough sample so that it doesn't matter how long a sample it is. This is a long way to say that the horizon should extend back in time to a point where the results of the analysis wouldn't change if we included any further history. At some point the results of the TED spread analysis will be stable and won't change even if we add another year or 10 more years. There is another reason for using multiple sample lengths, besides searching for stability, which has to do with the "direction" of a data series. Stability in the results implies that there is no direction, but comparing the results using just the latest observations against a larger sample could shed light on how the series is evolving. While a financial series on spreads will certainly pass any kind of stability tests we throw at it, a self-conscious social scientist will know that no data based on human decisions are static. The whole theme of this book has been about how perceptions change along with the tools at our disposal to study the world and how over time all econometric relationships change. For this reason we present a number of tables in the following pages, so that we can judge not only the interplay of each variable on TED spreads but also how they've changed over time.

TED SPREAD EMPIRICAL MODELS

Table 3–1 gives us a two-dimensional view into weekly 2-year TED spreads, where we are long an appropriate amount of Eurodollar contracts in the white and

T A B L E   3–1

Two-Year TED Spread Models

	One-Variable Model		
	1990–2005	**2000–2005**	**Last 30 Weeks***
R²	7.18%	69.75%	50.87%
F	64.83	728.66	28.99
		Coefficient, *T Test*	
Rate	2.62, *8.031*	8.07, *26.99*	13.44, *5.38*
	Two-Variable Model		
	1990–2005	**2000–2005**	**Last 30 Weeks***
R²	12.06%	71.32%	53.82%
F	57.14	391.75	15.73
		Coefficient, *T Test*	
Rate	−0.34, *−6.80*	−0.27, *−4.16*	−0.42, *−1.31*
Stocks	0.38, *0.84*	5.52, *8.13*	11.83, *4.30*
	Three-Variable Model		
	1990–2005	**2000–2005**	**Last 30 Weeks***
R²	20.15%	71.39%	59.73%
F	69.98	261.16	12.86
		Coefficient, *T Test*	
Rate	0.005, *9.18*	0.0003, *0.84*	0.008, *1.95*
Stocks	−0.37, *−7.69*	−0.26, *−3.76*	−0.31, *−1.01*
MBA	3.61, *6.44*	5.94, *7.03*	22.33, *3.74*

* Last 30 weeks in 2005.

red packs and short a 2-year Treasury. The length of the historical period used in the analysis is longest with the left-hand column, a full 15 years from 1990 through 2005, and then shrinks as we move to the right. The middle column uses a 5-year history, and the right column uses only the final 30 weeks of 2005. The topmost row begins with the simplest model, and the number of variables grows moving down the table to end with all three variables we explored, the S&P Bank Index, the MBA Refi Index, and a history of the maturity-matched swap rate. The regression statistics are simple, and there are certainly more complex ways to analyze the data than linear regression; but all else being equal, we prefer the simplest method of analysis possible, and the results in the table are telling.

Before digging into the numbers, we review a few definitions. The R-squared (R^2) is the proportion of variation in the dependent variable explained by the independent variable. In this model the TED spread is the dependent variable, and the independent variables are the ones listed in the table. For example, the R-squared value in the top left is 7.18%, indicating that from 1990 through 2005 the 2-year swap rate explained just 7.18% of the movements in 2-year TED spreads. R-squared calculations are not infallible, and they tend to increase along with the number of variables included in the model, even if those variables are statistically insignificant. As a rule, in a multiple regression the R-squared increases when a variable is added with a T statistic that is above 1; but as we explore next, such a value may not indicate that a variable should remain in the model. Also, R-squared is a measure of goodness of fit for a linear relationship, but it is not a significance test and the interpretation of a "good" or "bad" value is subjective.

There is no threshold in R-squared at which we know that we have a good or bad model. Indeed, it's possible to have a model with high R-squared with each variable having low individual significance. If this happens, then it may be an indication of a uniqueness problem, in which each "independent" variable is not really independent of another and does not represent unique sources of information. This is the problem we mentioned before about including the MBA Refi Index and the level of rates. Because so much refinancing activity is driven by the level of rates, including both variables' risks is redundant. Conversely, it's possible to have a variable that is highly significant, but a low R-squared, indicating that although one significant driver has been identified, there are many more that are unknown. In this case even our "largest" model is relatively small with just three variables, and we can take the calculation on its face, as the percentage of TED spreads explained by our variables.

The *F test* is a measure of the significance of all of the variables jointly. In contrast the *T test* measures the significance of the variables individually. The difference is that each variable has a T-test value, but there is only one F test per model, since it tests for the significance of all of the variables together. With both measures, the higher the value the better, and the generally accepted threshold for significance of the T test is 1.96, but most people round up to 2. If the T-test value of any individual variable is above 2, there is evidence that it is an important driver of TED spreads. The threshold for an F test is a little different, since it depends on the number of variables used in the model. Since we don't suffer from any small sample problems (although our 30 observation model is getting pretty close), none of the threshold values are higher than 4.24. If the resulting F statistic is above this value, we can conclude that the variables in the model are statistically significant. In fact, all of the models in Table 3–1 have an F statistic that is higher than the threshold value, indicating that each is a reasonable way to explain TED spreads. If all of the models are reasonable, which is the best one?

Searching for the best model also affords insights into the behavior of TED spreads, which are essentially the set of risks left over in Eurodollars after Treasury returns are subtracted from them. The first thing that should be striking in the very first row of Table 3–1 is that the R-squared statistic jumps in each of the models when moving from left to right, peaking in the middle column, which measures the past 5 years of history from 2000 through 2005. In the one variable model, where we use just the level of rates to explain TED spreads, an approach that would work perfectly if spreads were a simple percentage of swap rates, the value goes from about 7% to 70% and then falls to just 51%. Results like these are exactly why we reran the regression using various historical time periods. The results from the middle and rightmost columns aren't all that different, at 70% and 51%, respectively. However, the 7% value for the full 15-year period is shockingly low. The results tell us that even with a relatively short horizon, just the last 30 weeks out of 2005, the results are similar to the past 5 years' worth of data. What happened during the 10 years from 1990 to 2000 to make the model perform so horribly?

Worse still, the results are comparable across the one-, two-, and three-variable models. The R-squared statistic is quite low using the entire data set, but much better using the most recent observations. Figure 3–7 illustrates the pattern with the 2000–2005 sample showing the best model fit, with the last 30 weeks' worth of observations a close second. There is another reason to graph the R-squared for the three models, which is to show how the results change as we add variables. In the one variable model, the rate factor is statistically significant, passing both the T and F tests. Rates remain a significant variable in the two-factor model, but just miss the 1.96 bar for significance with a T value of 1.31 (the sign doesn't matter for this statistic). On the other hand, stocks bounce out and then into significance with a T value of 0.84 during the 1990–2005 draw and then 8.13 and 4.30 for the 2000–2005 sample and last 30-week samples, respectively. It might not be surprising, then, that adding a variable that wavers in terms of significance and causes another variable to do the same only increases the R-squared in the middle column from 69.75% to 71.32%. Still, in two out of the three sample periods the stocks variable contributed meaningful information. Was it worth adding the second variable stocks and trying to explain TED spreads with more than just changes in the level of rates? The results of the three-variable model can help us answer that question.

Finally, the results of the full 15-year sample show that all three variables are significant, individually and jointly. The T values for rates, stocks, and the

F I G U R E   3–7

R-squared values across time and models

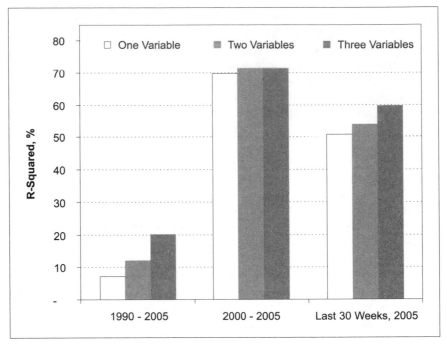

MBA index are all above 1.96 in absolute value, and the F statistic is at just about 70, indicating that the variables are jointly significant. Unfortunately, the R-squared value is still relatively low at just over 20%, which indicates that there may be more correlation between the variables than we had originally anticipated. The likely suspects for this are the rates and MBA index variables, and there is at least some truth to the idea that mortgage applications are less path dependent than some have argued in the past, since a long-term history indicates that there is so much correlation with just the level of rates. If the path of rates were any significant contributor to the MBA index, then this information would crowd out the level of rates, making it a less significant factor in the index. Looking at the results for the two other time periods in the three-variable model solidifies our conviction that including the MBA index may be a "bridge too far" in our model, and it could be excluded.

The T statistic for the rates variable moves in and out of significance depending on the historical time period used, indicating a problem. In the three-variable model the T statistic for the rates variable started at 9.18, then fell to 0.84, and rose back again to just about touch the critical threshold of 1.95 as the sample period shortened. This was not true of the results from the one-variable model, which indicate that rates are a significant driver of TED spreads, no matter the historical period. What changed to make the T statistics drop off between the first and third models? Of course, it was the introduction of the stocks and MBA variables. Even though the link between the relative performance of equity values for banks and interest rates is weak, there may still be one, since the shape of the yield curve does weigh on bank profits. As an aside, it's interesting to consider all of the interplays from the different variables. What may have seemed a simple exercise of slapping together a few variables in a regression model is actually quite a bit more complex if we carefully consider the results using various sample periods and numbers of variables.

Although there is reason to discount the problems we encounter when moving from the one- to two-variable model, it's not so easy to dismiss them in the final three-variable model. Correlation between the explanatory variables is the problem, and as we mentioned, there is some reason to believe that the stocks variable, normalized Bank Index values, has something to do with the level of rates. The only time this appears to be a problem is in the very small 30-week sample, where the T statistic falls to 1.31, which does not pass the significance test at the 95th percentile but still passes at around the 85th percentile. The fall in the statistic isn't cause for immediate alarm, but this is not the case with the three-variable model. Here the addition of the MBA index knocks out the rates variable in the middle column and knocks out both the rates and stocks variables in the far right column, though rates just miss the threshold with a value at 1.95. What's going on here?

Over very long periods of time, in this case 15 years, there is unique information in the MBA variable that separates it from just being a proxy for the level of rates. Remember that business cycles in the United States last around 5 years on average, which means that the changes in the slope of the curve take this long to play out on average. If the uniqueness in the MBA index comes from the fact that there are changes in the level of rates, slope of the curve, and the path of rates as well, it makes sense that a longer sample would be necessary to capture the frequency of this long-term cycle. Our motivation for studying this variable was that changes in mortgage applications would serve as a proxy for mortgage hedging. More applications would lead to higher prepayments in the short run and eventually more freshly minted longer-term loans, and it's at least theoretically pleasing to consider that this activity would spill over to the Eurodollar market and TED spreads. When the mortgage universe shortens duration, then mortgage hedgers tend to need to "receive" or go long the fixed-rate leg of interest rate swaps and buy Eurodollar futures via Wall Street dealers, who often serve as the transmission mechanism between the two markets. When mortgage applications fall, one might expect the duration of the mortgage universe to rise and for there to be more paying pressure in interest rate swaps and selling pressure in Eurodollars. This may in fact be happening, but what the analysis tells us is that it is far from the mysterious process that some might have us believe. In fact, this evidence suggests at least in terms of changes in TED spreads, mortgage refinancing activity is closely enough related to changes in the level of rates that we can ignore whatever small piece may be left over having to do with the uniqueness of the MBA index, whether it is the path dependence of mortgage prepayments or change in the slope of the curve.

The whole point of this analysis is to gain a deeper understanding of what drives TED spreads, and we've been able to rule in a number of factors as well as rule out one very commonly held belief. Mortgage activity is an important driver of the interest rate swap and Eurodollar market, but the evidence suggests that it spills over to the futures market in a very simple way that can be captured by including just the level of rates. This is why it makes sense to exclude the MBA index from our TED spread model and simply go with the level of rates and normalized Bank Index returns as predictors of fair value. As much touted as mortgage hedging and the uniqueness and importance of prepayment estimation is to the derivatives market, it appears that this is another instance of the kind of "good enough" management we detailed in the "perfection being the enemy of the good" discussion at the end of Chapter 2. Sometimes "close enough" is all anyone is interested in, and while it certainly shouldn't be the criterion for valuing mortgages directly, it is more than sufficient for judging the impact of mortgage hedging on the commodity interest rate market.

So far we have only analyzed Table 3–1, which deals with 2-year TED spreads, and made some sweeping generalizations for the rest of the market. Do these generalizations hold up if we conduct the same analysis for the rest of the curve? In the Eurodollar market so much of the open interest is concentrated in the front end of the curve that every maturity point we study from now on is slightly less relevant to the market, and we have already done much of the heavy lifting in terms of the factors that are relevant to TED spreads. The little voice that should have been nagging at us all during our prior analysis should have been saying that all of this analysis is on the 2-year point, but there is an enormous amount of hedging that happens farther out on the yield curve. The 10-year Treasury is the most actively traded single instrument in the fixed-income market. What does this analysis have to say about this point? Also, subprime mortgages and 228 ARMs (where the fixed-rate period is 2 years and the floating-rate period is 28 years) are about the only structures short enough where the hedging needs can be satisfied with just the 2-year point. The fact that only a handful of mortgage structures would be appropriately hedged with a 2-year strip of Eurodollars keeps hope alive that we might see a more significant impact from some of the variables in the model, including the MBA index when we look at 5-, 7-, and 10-year TEDs.

Tables 3–2 and 3–3 illustrate the results of the same analysis as Table 3–1 did, except that these latter tables focus on 3- and 5-year TED spreads. Keep in mind that contracts used are not simply an equally weighted bundle of contracts. Broadly speaking we see the same pattern of increasing R-squared values as the sample period shortens. In the 3-year TED, the R-squared is as low as 2.52% in the one-variable model from 1990 to 2005, which means we have some wood to chop in terms of explaining spreads farther out on the curve. While all of the models have passing F-test statistics, there are two instances in which the individual

T A B L E   3–2

Three-Year TED Spread Models

	One-Variable Model		
	1990–2005	**2000–2005**	**Last 30 Weeks***
R^2	2.52%	55.57%	32.59%
F	21.56	395.19	13.54
		Coefficient, *T Test*	
Rate	1.85, *4.64*	8.63, *19.88*	12.37, *3.68*
	Two-Variable Model		
	1990–2005	**2000–2005**	**Last 30 weeks***
R^2	15.78%	61.90%	34.54%
F	78.05	255.86	7.12
		Coefficient, *T Test*	
Rate	−0.67, *−11.45*	−0.66, *−7.23*	−0.36, *−0.90*
Stocks	−2.99, *−5.32*	1.65, *1.58*	10.94, *2.92*
	Three-Variable Model		
	1990–2005	**2000–2005**	**Last 30 Weeks***
R^2	26.12%	63.29%	43.48%
F	98.06	180.46	6.67
		Coefficient, *T Test*	
Rate	0.006, *10.79*	0.002, *3.45*	0.009, *2.02*
Stocks	−0.66, *−12.11*	−0.52, *−5.27*	−0.29, *0.75*
MBA	1.76, *2.56*	4.82, *3.50*	23.22, *3.31*

* Last 30 weeks in 2005.

variable statistics differ in the 3-year analysis compared to the 2-year analysis. The first instance is in the 2000–2005 period for the two-variable model, where the stocks variable is knocked out in terms of having a T value that falls from 8.13 in the previous analysis to just 1.58 this time around. The second case where we pick up significance is in the 2000–2005 period in the three-variable model, where the rates variable once again passes the par in terms of statistical significance. It's interesting to note at this point that if we had accidentally stumbled onto these results and were not a careful consumer of statistical analysis, we might have accepted them and moved on without understanding whether the results were robust or not.

T A B L E   3–3

Five-Year TED Spread Models

	One-Variable Model		
	1990–2005	**2000–2005**	**Last 30 Weeks***
R²	5.13%	69.73%	36.87%
F	45.11	727.96	16.35
		Coefficient, *T Test*	
Rate	3.27, *6.72*	13.99, *26.98*	14.64, *4.04*
	Two-Variable Model		
	1990–2005	**2000–2005**	**Last 30 Weeks***
R²	18.87%	71.55%	37.66%
F	96.87	396.07	8.16
		Coefficient, *T Test*	
Rate	−0.82, *−11.88*	−0.49, *−4.49*	−0.24, *−0.58*
Stocks	−3.58 *−4.89*	7.68, *5.14*	13.70, *3.42*
	Three-Variable Model		
	1990–2005	**2000–2005**	**Last 30 Weeks***
R²	25.05%	74.58%	43.37%
F	92.68	307.01	6.64
		Coefficient, *T Test*	
Rate	0.005, *8.28*	0.003, *6.11*	0.007, *1.62*
Stocks	−0.79, *−11.73*	−0.11, *−0.93*	−0.22, *−0.57*
MBA	1.18, *1.29*	16.31, *8.16*	23.37, *3.28*

* Last 30 weeks in 2005.

We should sound a note of caution about the analysis at the 3-year point because the program was suspended in May 1998 until May 2003 and there was no active 3-year note during this time. While the Treasury data that help make up the TED spread analysis come from the Federal Reserve H15 statement, widely regarded as one of the cleanest and more accurate historical series in the market, it was necessary for the Fed to interpolate a 3-year yield to approximate where the note would have been. Building a trading book based on someone's interpolation is a risky business, which is why we can look to the 5-year point for more reliable results. Before abandoning the 3-year analysis, it's important to step back and judge what we have so far. Both 2- and 3-year TED spreads can be explained, for approximately two-thirds of their total behavior, by the handful of variables we've identified. If there ever was an indication that we were on the right track in terms of explaining the essence of the market, it should be the fact that we've covered two parts of the most actively traded part of the Eurodollar curve and received similar results, indicating that we've identified something of value.

Just as with the 2-year TED analysis, the results of the 5-year analysis in Table 3–3 illustrate that both rates and stocks deserve to be in the model, but things get rocky when the MBA index is added. In the two-variable model for both the 1990–2005 and 2000–2005 results, both variables are statistically significant with high T values. However, the results in the three-variable model are not at all what we would expect. In the 2-year spreads adding the MBA index knocked out the rates variable in terms of its T value, but this time around it didn't in either the 15- or 5-year histories. Surprisingly, the MBA variable knocked out the stocks variable, indicating a correlation between these two explanatory variables. After all of our concern over the similarities between the MBA index and rates, it's odd to find an interaction with the stocks variable. While one might make a case that the credit curve has to be upward sloping because the chances of any default increase with time and that the stocks variable should be increasingly important in the analysis, unfortunately it's unclear why there should be less significance this time around.

While it's increasingly clear that the MBA index shouldn't be included in our model, it is encouraging that we can account for more than two-thirds of the variability of 5-year TED spreads with just two simple variables over the past 5 years. We've now identified three points on the yield curve, spanning the most actively traded Eurodollar contracts that can be well explained by just two variables, although we have shown that they represent a multitude of risk factors. What we haven't done yet is explain why there is such a poor fit for all of the models with the analysis based on the full 15 years of data. The fit for the last 30 weeks of data is passable, and so is the 5-year history, but what happened between 5 and 15 years ago that threw off all of our statistics? Embarrassingly enough, we could have picked up on the problem right away if we had used another important diagnostic tool: our eyes.

Graphing the series we're interested in studying would have been a prudent first step to let us visually detect any strange periods. Figure 3–8 illustrates TED spreads along the yield curve, and it's clear that there was a jump in all of the series in late 1998. A "jump" is a mild way to put it, given how spreads blew out to never-before-seen levels in the wake of a crisis of confidence in the fixed income markets. As it turns out, this was the period when Long Term Capital Management was building up and subsequently unwinding its bets, before imminent failure caused the Federal Reserve Bank of New York to step in with a bailout. It will always serve a trader well to remember that LIBOR is a credit product, and although Eurodollars have only the extremely limited counterparty credit risk of the CME Clearing Corporation, interest rate swaps are subject to the

F I G U R E   3–8

Swap spreads spiked in 1998

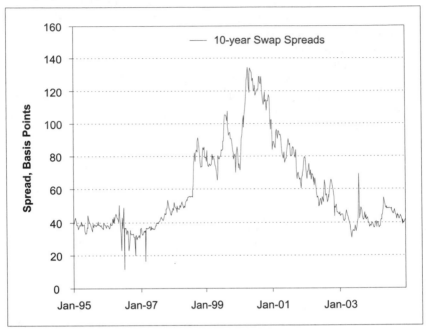

credit conditions of those who use them. Although swaps are normally collateralized, no market could withstand the collapse of one of the dominant players since the risks of interest rate swap counterparties are so interconnected.

At the time there was no precedent for a bailout of this magnitude, and no one in the market guessed that it was going to happen. If a large hedge fund failed, it would cause losses to its largest trading partners, one or more of whom might fail to perform on their interest rate swap obligations, which are essentially just corporate bonds at the end of the day; and this would spill over to the Eurodollar market in terms of higher yields and lower prices, especially in the front end of the curve. It's fascinating to see that although the market perceives no counterparty credit risk in futures contracts, their pricing certainly responds to general credit conditions through the chain of events we list here. Like an impulse response function, similar to an EKG reading of a heartbeat, the effect hit its zenith in late 1998 and then slowly subsided as it became clear that the Fed would lead a consortium of banks to provide credit to the hedge fund until it could unwind all of its bets in an orderly fashion.

While Long Term was a heavy futures user, even its collapse would have had a limited effect on the futures markets, and it could only affect other users who used the same clearing firm. Losses in a default of one customer are limited to the clearing firm and are insured against spilling over from one clearing firm to another. Also consider that the size of the entire Long Term bailout was only moderately bigger than the funds at the disposal of the futures clearing corporation to insure the integrity of its markets. The vast majority of the funds that went to Long Term from the Fed bailout didn't go to cover losses, but rather to meet margin calls; although it never reached that loss point, there would have been ample liquidity in the Chicago Board of Trade Clearing Corporation and CME Clearing Corporation to cover even these severe losses. Additionally, there was also some volatility in the early 1990s that is uncharacteristic of the rest of the series, and this period is best explained by the relatively thin markets in these instruments that existed at the time. Even though 1990 is generally considered the birth of modern interest rate swaps, the market didn't really heat up (and neither did Eurodollar volume) until years later.

The following two tables are a contradiction. While the model we built does a better job explaining 7- and 10-year spreads, they are less actively traded than the others we've looked at. Here again is a chicken-and-egg problem. Are they not actively traded because people don't understand them, or haven't people spent the time to understand them because they aren't actively traded? Whatever the reason, there is normally just a small fraction of the total open interest in Eurodollars past 5 years, which makes the work in Tables 3–4 and 3–5 largely academic. Still, there is value in studying how TED spreads perform farther out the curve because it sheds light on performance of the contracts in general. As before, the two-variable model offers the best results since all of the variables are individually and jointly significant and the R-squared values are quite high. Even though they are relatively thinly traded right now, the back-month contracts weren't even listed 10 years ago, and it's inevitable at this point that a full spectrum of maturities will be available out to 10 years. This work also high lights that the market uses back-month contracts slightly differently from the first few contracts.

The first thing to note is the continued trend higher in R-squared values. The model we specified does better with every historical sample period and number of variables in the models as we move from the 2-year to the 10-year TED spreads. Another trend continues the farther out the curve we go, and that is that the bulk of the variability is explained by the rates variable in the one-factor model. While the additional two variables do contribute some unique information, as indicated by their significant T values, the marginal gain from their addition is quite small. For instance, moving from a one-variable model to a three-variable model in 10-year spreads only increases the R-squared by 3.9% on top of an already respectable 81.6%. In fact, it's not until we view the results for the whole curve that we could consider doing the conceptual opposite of what we've done so far.

To date, we began with individual variables and added more one by one to determine if the new variables were significant. The same analysis could have been conducted in reverse using the F test to determine how much was being lost by eliminating variables from the model. Take the middle column in Table 3–4,

T A B L E   3–4

Seven-Year TED Spread Models

	One-Variable Model		
	1990–2005	**2000–2005**	**Last 30 Weeks***
R²	7.40%	74.52%	49.12%
F	66.66	924.10	27.03
		Coefficient, *T Test*	
Rate	3.81, *8.16*	16.03, *30.40*	18.20, *5.20*
	Two-Variable Model		
	1990–2005	**2000–2005**	**Last 30 Weeks***
R²	23.61%	75.52%	49.21%
F	128.70	485.99	13.08
		Coefficient, *T Test*	
Rate	−0.85, *−13.29*	−0.37, *−3.60*	−0.08, *−0.22*
Stocks	−3.74, *−5.28*	10.69, *6.80*	17.87, *4.61*
	Three-Variable Model		
	199–2005	**2000–2005**	**Last 30 Weeks***
R²	27.94%	77.20%	51.35%
F	107.55	354.37	9.15
		Coefficient, *T Test*	
Rate	0.004, *7.08*	0.002, *4.80*	0.004, *1.07*
Stocks	−0.82, *−13.21*	−0.13, *−1.20*	−0.08, *−0.22*
MBA	−0.09, *−0.11*	16.92, *8.47*	23.75, *3.53*

* Last 30 weeks in 2005.

illustrating the results for the 2000–2005 period in 7-year spreads. Starting at the bottom the F value is 354.37, which certainly is above the threshold value for all of the variables jointly passing significance, which is 2.60. What happens when we lop off variables one by one? Does the model as a whole remain statistically significant? The middle row for the two-variable model has an F value that is 485.99, which is actually higher than the previous model. Of course, the threshold value is slightly higher, at 3.00 rather than 2.60, but the model easily clears that hurdle. If we can move from a three-variable model to a two-variable model and still produce statistically significant results, why don't we?

T A B L E   3–5

Ten-Year TED Spread Models

	One-Variable Model		
	1990–2005	**2000–2005**	**Last 30 Weeks***
R^2	5.77%	81.60%	62.68%
F	51.03	1401.31	47.03
		Coefficient, *T Test*	
Rate	4.27 *7.14*	24.93 *37.44*	24.39 *6.86*
	Two-Variable Model		
	1990–2005	**2000–2005**	**Last 30 Weeks***
R^2	28.62%	83.29%	34.82%
F	167.06	785.22	22.72
		Coefficient, *T Test*	
Rate	−1.22, *−16.33*	−0.59, *−5.65*	−0.07, *−0.19*
Stocks	−7.31, *−8.31*	15.22, *8.31*	24.67, *6.29*
	Three-Variable Model		
	1990–2005	**2000–2005**	**Last 30 Weeks***
R^2	29.73%	85.50%	63.60%
F	117.32	617.15	15.14
		Coefficient, *T Test*	
Rate	0.002, *3.61*	0.003, *3.81*	0.0003, *0.79*
Stocks	−1.21, *−16.34*	−0.39, *−0.93*	−0.05, *−0.16*
MBA	5.18, *4.92*	22.69, *11.22*	28.73, *4.43*

* Last 30 weeks in 2005.

Even more dramatic, we can move from the middle row to the top row, further restricting the number of variables to just one, to see that here too we find passable F statistics. Why not move to a model where we use just one variable? Dispassionate analysis would say that we could. However, judgment and observations have taught us that there is more going on in TED spreads than simply following the level of rates as a percentage. While that may be the most efficient guess of future movements from a statistical perspective, traders have to walk a fine line. As we mentioned before with the example of the computers searching for models of the economy by going through hundreds of possible specifications, essentially mining the data with no theory behind the choices—only analytical results—these models never held up when used in the real world. While technically brilliant, there was something missing that would have caused anyone who relied on the predictions for profitable guidance to lose money. This time around, we have to balance the valid conclusions produced by the TED spread analysis with a trader's instinct to include as much information as possible. Like infantry soldiers who always err on the side of bringing too much ammunition into the fight, traders are always wary of cutting the explanatory variables in order to produce "elegant" econometric results.

In this case, we can take something from each mindset. While the computer would tell us to pare the model back to just one variable from three, we can use our judgment to include the second variable stocks to pick out information that makes intuitive sense but doesn't always come to the forefront in the data. Just as with the case of the flipping correlations for Treasury and credit rates, the time when we need models to work most is during financial panics. Unfortunately, this is the time when everything tends to break down. Including the stocks variable is one way to give ourselves a safety net, since we're allowing the equity market to do some of the research into current events that would ultimately affect credit spreads. Like a canary in a coal mine, stocks tend to be the first to be hit on a rumor or innuendo of problems. Of course, rumor and innuendo aren't terrific to have in our model, but over the long term the stock market is quite a good judge of value, and our two-variable model draws from both fixed income and equity disciplines.

Now that a complete picture of the TED spread curve has helped us decide upon what variables to include in our model—rates and stocks—it's time to put them to the test as predictors of actual market values. We are further along in our prediction than it may at first have appeared because we already have everything we need to start making predictions of TED spreads from our model. Taking the values from the middle row of the middle column of Table 3–5, we can predict what the "fair value" of 10-year spreads should be:

$$TED_{10} = -7.68 \bullet Rate - 1.24 \bullet Stocks + Const$$

The only variable that should look new here is the constant (Const) which was omitted from all of the tables. In our linear regressions this variable simply kept track of where the line intersected with the y axis, and a statistically significant or insignificant y intercept has only an ambiguous meaning at best. Now that we're armed with the coefficients for each variable, we can predict what TED spreads should be for December 30, 2005:

$$TED_{10} = -7.68 \bullet Rate - 1.24 \bullet Stocks + Const$$

$$TED_{10} = -7.68 \bullet 4.89 - 1.29 \bullet 101.9 + 215.2 = 51.3$$

Here the values corresponding to the variables *Rate*, *Stocks*, and *Const* are the observations on that Friday of the 10-year Eurodollar strip rate and the S&P

500 Bank Stock Index, plus the constant (which doesn't change no matter what the current values of the rate or stocks variables). It's gratifying to see that our prediction is reasonably close to an actual settlement value on that day of 51.7 basis points, but this isn't the end of the story.

Rather than simply observing the predicted and actual data for a single day, we can look at how the model performed during the whole period. Graphing the work in the preceding tables brings it to life and sharpens our focus down to a single value, which is what would be driving our profits or losses if we used this work for trading! The errors in Figure 3–9 are just differences between the actual and predicted values in a statistical model, but they would show up as dollar values of around $800 per million dollar face of our 10-year spread if we were long a strip of Eurodollars, short a 10-year Treasury, and earning the repo rate in a financed position. Every basis point now has a dollar figure attached to it, and it behooves the trader to review the careful decisions we made about including and excluding variables in the modeling work above. Far from the rosy picture that the latest observation gave us, to the far right of the graph, there have been periods when the predicted values drifted away from the actual values for substantial periods of time. Perhaps it would be more accurate to say that the opposite happened.

The steadier of the two series is our prediction, while the actual value has bounced around the prediction. For traders comfortable with mean reversion trades, where they identify a "natural" value for a particular series and trade against any deviation from that level, Figure 3–9 should make them right at home. The reality is that everyone in the market assumes mean reversion to some extent. There are values of the stock index and of yields that people just come to expect, and they are reinforced by historical patterns. The S&P 500 might appreciate by 7% in a year that people think is average, because this has been the approximate long-run return of the market, but they are disappointed in a 1% year and thrilled to receive 15%. A return of 50% would shock and amaze investors. Similarly, Figure 3–9 establishes a fair value for the 2-year TED spread that has been accurate over the long run, but the market hands out shorter-term deviations from the fundamental value. In fact, if we summed up all of the errors, both positive and negative, they would sum to zero. This isn't an accident, but rather the by-product of the regression analysis we used.

What is even more startling is that the predicted level for the 2-year spread, what we're terming the "fair" difference between Eurodollar and Treasury yields, is remarkably stable across the last decade and a half. While the actual market has bounced around, the predicted value has merely drifted from a high just under 60 basis points to a low just over 20 basis points. Two-thirds of the time this spread has been between 30 and 44 basis points, with 37.6 as the average value. When viewed in light of the volatility of the inputs, graphed in Tables 3–3 and 3–4, it's a remarkable result to find series that offset one another to some extent and also draw a "center line" around where TED spreads may eventually revert.

FIGURE   3–9

(a) Actual versus predicted 2-year TED spreads; (b) residuals, basis points

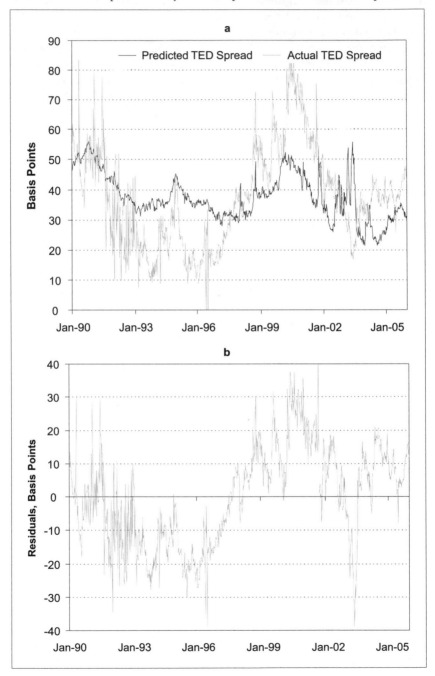

Amazing though it might be from an intellectual perspective, a trader may look at the residuals shown in the bottom (b) portion of Figure 3–9 and declare them too high to take advantage of. After all, when you get paid annual bonuses and "long-term trades" last between Thanksgiving and Christmas, then it would be almost impossible to stomach differences in the predicted and actual results of 12.5 basis points, which is what they are in terms of the average absolute values (of course, the average value is zero by definition, but this doesn't mean there won't be swings in profit or loss). Is there a next step to be taken that can wring some extra performance from the modeling work that we've already done? There is, and it uses a statistical trick common in time-series modeling. While we may not know what the value of the TED spread will be by the end of this week, we certainly know what it was at the end of last week. Why not use the previous value to help predict next week's value? There is no need to torture ourselves for months on end with residuals that are consistently above or below the long-term average.

This type of regression work is *autoregressive,* since the model relies on past values of the series it attempts to predict. One might imagine that this type of model might dramatically increase the predictive capability of our efforts, since we would have a direct handle on the series we're trying to predict, and regarded strictly according to the numbers it does. However, as with some of our other work, the results are not quite as black and white as the numbers make them out to be. While it certainly helps to know where TED spreads have been in order to predict where they may go in the future, the past is not a perfect indicator of future results, which is a platitude that should be well known to anyone who's ever heard or read a securities advertisement. If we are able to determine a long-term fair value for a series, how does it help us to know how irrational or not the market is? The answer has to do with a time horizon. While we might understand what the long-term fair value should be, there might be shorter-term fluctuations that can't even be explained by a past "irrationality" of the market. The danger of getting used to a world turned on its head is that things go back to normal! If the market is pricing TED spreads differently from our model and we're convinced that the model should predict the appropriate value in the long term, then shouldn't the market revert to the true value right away? It's interesting that the deeper we delve into the statistical work, the more abstract the choices become.

Philosophical questions aside, it's clear from Figure 3–10 that we've dramatically reduced the error in our model. The only difference between the two models is the addition of a lagged value for the spread:

$$TED_{10} = 0.013 \bullet \text{Rate} + 1 - 0.037 \bullet Stocks + 0.951 \bullet TED_{t-1} + Const$$

$$TED_{10} = 0.013 \bullet 4.89 - 0.037 \bullet 101.9 + 0.951 \bullet 55.3 + 6.0 = 54.9$$

Here the new term TED_{t-1} is the same as the series we are trying to explain, except that it is lagged by 1 week. The average absolute value for the errors in our original model was 16.2 basis points, but this is substantially reduced in the autoregressive model to just 3.4 basis points. However, consider the change in

(a) Actual versus predicted 2-year TED spreads, autoregressive model; (b) residuals, basis points

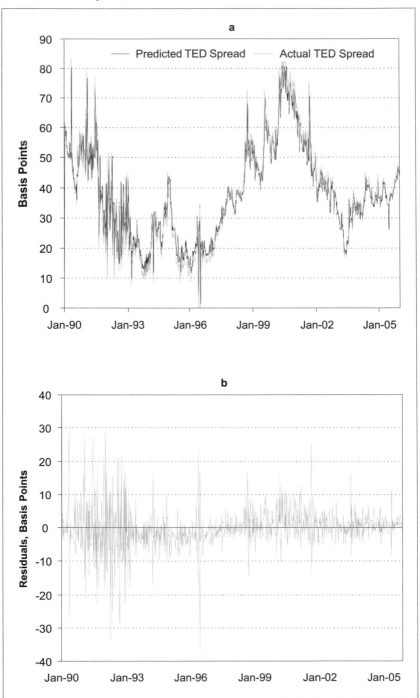

maximum absolute error. In our first effort it was 59.7 basis points, but the second time around it's still 37.8 basis points, which is relatively close. How can the average be so different while the maximum or minimum values are so close? This gets back to our earlier point questioning how much value there really is in putting in an autoregressive term. When the market does something unexpected, both models are caught unaware and produce roughly the same error. However, the difference between the first and second approach is that the second will then compensate for the mistake in subsequent forecasts.

Theory could only tell us so much before empirical study is warranted. In the earlier chapters, we could only cut broad strokes between pure interest rate or credit risks, but the distinctions were unwieldy and so broad that they afforded little direction regarding how trades to take advantage of discrepancies in the market could be structured. This regression work, based on slightly more than 15 years of data, which is probably longer than the TED spread market was actively traded, provides insights into the role that the level of rates has on the market as well as on stock prices and on that highly mercurial variable, mortgage refinancing applications. Methodically testing the predictive capability of each variable and how variables interact with each other is the best way to understand the risks that are left over in Eurodollar contracts when the Treasury yield is subtracted. Rather than just listing the risks involved, the regressions in this chapter provide a concrete framework to determine where spreads may be heading and how factors in the broader market drive them.

BUILDING AN EVENT MODEL
TO PRICE OPTIONS

Just as futures contracts offer traders a source of liquidity that's not available anywhere else, the same is true of exchange-traded options. Earlier chapters have focused on the behavior of Treasury and Eurodollar futures, but not on the options that are available on these contracts. The same give and take between listed and over-the-counter markets happens with options on futures, and there is a unique and unifying aspect to these markets that we can exploit to value them. Rather than deal with options on Eurodollars or Treasury futures separately, it makes sense to use the same fair value approach with both since their common characteristic is that they have relatively short expirations, all within 1 year. A single conceptual approach can be used to value all short-term options, no matter the underlying security, because the key in these types of options is how they respond to the handful of economic news that will be released during their relatively short life. While long-term options encompass so much news that it generally fades into a broad market expectation, fair value in short-term options on futures can be estimated with an event model. Before building such a model, we will briefly review the basics of arbitrage in options.

WHY VOLATILITY DRIVES OPTION PRICES

The worst misconception about options is that their value depends solely on contract prices at their expiration, but this is not true. Of course, the intrinsic value of the option is the difference between the strike price and the underlying price. People should be willing to pay $2 today for a call option that allowed them to buy a bond at $100 in a certain month that is now priced at $102, because if prices don't change, they could exercise the option paying $100 to sell the note for $102 and make $2. The important question is how to price the option prior to expiration, and this question doesn't solely depend on where prices end up. Prior to expiration it's unknown whether this option will expire worthless or not, and so it's necessary to rely on a probabilistic approach to translate expected volatility into the chance of an option expiring with intrinsic value. The most widely known and most commonly used of these models is Black-Scholes (BS). Rather than replace BS, an event model will determine the most important input to the model, will assess the expected volatility, and will help overcome some of the ambiguity in implementing the BS approach.

The chances of future price movements have to be boiled down to a distribution. Black-Scholes begins with a normal distribution, and while prices in futures can only change by the same minimum increment, the probability of moving a tick in price is different depending on whether that 1-tick change comes at a price that's near or far from the current price. If the current price is $100, then the next cent in price change is more likely to be to $100.01 than it is to be from $95.01 to $95. The BS model determines the probability for each of these price changes occurring, and just as with normal distributions for other phenomena, they fall along a bell-shaped curve like the one depicted in Figure 4–1. Every cent price change can be assigned a probability, with the center of the distribution resting at the current market price. We know what the intrinsic value of an option is by subtracting the strike price from the market price, but now that difference has a probability assigned to it.

If a trader had to arm himself with only one piece of information about options before marching into a trading pit, it should be an understanding of an option's *delta,* which involvess two things at once. First, there is the price sensitivity of the option along the same lines as the duration for a bond. Rather than calculating the change in price for a change in yield, delta measures the change in price of the option for a change in the underlying commodity. If a 5-year Treasury

FIGURE 4–1

Normal distribution, one standard deviation, 68% of the area

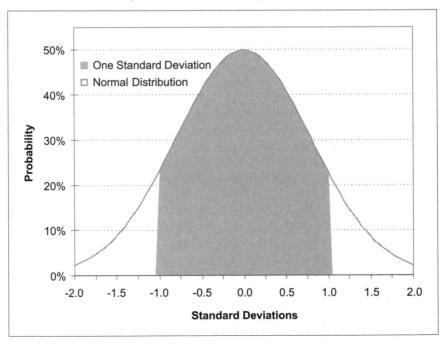

futures contract changes price by 1 point, then delta would calculate how much the price will change for the option on 5-year Treasury futures. Simultaneously, delta also implies a probability that an option expires in-the-money because of Figure 4–1, which links prices to probabilities. In Figure 4–1 this is the sum of the probabilities from the strike price, all of the way out to the extreme end of the tail. Just as with duration, we can determine the dollar value of the option for a given price change of the underlying commodity by multiplying the market price of the option by its delta to produce a *dollar delta.*

In fact, this isn't the only similarity option risk metrics have with those common in the rest of the fixed income and broader finance world. Just as delta is the price change of the security we're interested in, given a price change in the underlying commodity, *gamma* is another statistic measuring the rate of change of delta. Figure 4–1 is useful to determine probabilities, but it needs to be transformed into a cumulative distribution in order to be of use going forward. If delta is the probability of an option expiring in-the-money, it's easy in Figure 4–2 to see the nonlinear S shape the cumulative normal distribution takes. Clearly, the slope of the curve is changing, and gamma measures the rate at which it does so. It's useful to keep Figure 4–2 in mind when considering baskets of options. Given the same amount of delta dollar risk, do we want a basket of options with a high

F I G U R E   4–2

Cumulative normal distribution, option delta

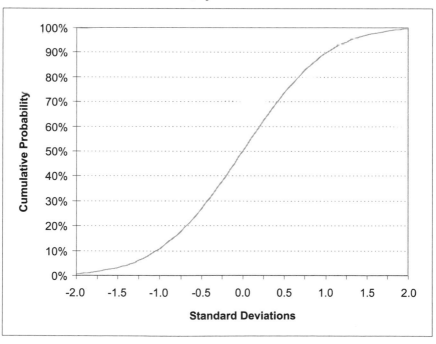

or low gamma? The question is equivalent to asking if we want the dollar risk of our position to be volatile or not, and, as with all things, the answer depends on whether we're long or short the option.

All things being equal, the holder of an option prefers to have as much gamma as possible, which makes it clear where on this chart she would prefer to be. Delta changes the most in the very middle of the S shape, where the option is on the edge of going from in-the-money to out-of-the-money. Just as convexity is at a premium in the bond market, so too is gamma in options. If the prices and duration dollars are equal, the holder of long options should prefer to own the basket of options with as much gamma as possible, and the reason has to do with how an option "pays its way" over time, which we'll explain in a moment. Before diving into the mechanics, let's consider the parallels between the risk measurements we're already used to with those for options, as shown in Table 4–1.

Far from mysterious, much of the terminology for options is parallel to that in the fixed income market. Long ago option traders developed a unique jargon that used to set them apart from the rest of the fixed income universe, but over the years much of the uniqueness of the terminology has been lost or bastardized because of the sheer number of other types of securities with embedded option risk. The term *delta* always means price sensitivity no matter the context, but traders also use it to talk about the risk of outright bonds, as if it were the duration dollar of that bond, and traders generally substitute terminology horizontally as shown in Table 4–1.

Volatility is the one concept that may seem slightly different from what traders encounter in the rest of the fixed income market, but as we'll see, it is very closely tied to carry, which is a topic most bond traders know by heart. Just as futures differ from the spot price of the underlying commodity and are always converging to that price, options are a wasting asset and are always trying to converge to their intrinsic value. Since the intrinsic value of an out-of-the-money

TABLE 4–1

Parallel Concepts

Bonds	Options	Description	Math
Duration	Delta	Price change	First derivative price/underlying
Convexity	Gamma	Rate of change	Second derivative price/underlying
Carry	Theta	Price decay/day	Square root of time
	Vega	Price/volatility	Price from change in volatility
	Rho	Price/financing	Price from change in risk-free rate

option is zero, these options are constantly falling in price. Seeing a negative net basis in Treasury futures confuses people for this reason because it looks like a negative option price. Of course, we have already detailed the special circumstances surrounding squeezes in Chapter 1. The normal relationship is simple:

Intrinsic value + time value = option premium

Why buy something that is rapidly becoming worthless? There is always a chance that the option ends up with intrinsic value, and most of the trading in options is done in out-of-the-money strikes. When an option goes far in-the-money or out-of-the-money, its delta converges to 1 or zero, respectively, and loses its conditional nature. Additionally, buying an option that is in-the-money costs more than one that is not because the buyer has to pay up for the intrinsic value but receives a less sensitive instrument than either a position in the underlying or an option closer to being in-the-money. Traders are trying to judge the premium they have to spend on an option against its ultimate value at expiration. As we mentioned earlier, it's not simply a bet on where prices are going to go, because there is a clear no-arbitrage relationship that dictates where option prices should be at any day prior to expiration. Although the BS equation produces quite accurate fair values for option prices, no one can do the calculation in his head, and it has little intuitive appeal to most people who actually are tasked with trading. Alternatively, most traders consider the no-arbitrage relationship and the price of maintaining a market-neutral position as the true measure of value in the market.

Two key pieces of information are necessary to understand the relationship. The first is that when we sell an option, whether it is a put or a call, we collect the premium up front. The second is that a delta hedge involves buying or selling some number of the underlying commodity so that the overall delta of the position is zero. Suppose that one calculated from Figure 4–2 that the delta of each of her 5-year note put options was −0.50 and she had 100 option contracts. In this case the delta of her position would be −50, and in order to make that position "delta neutral," she would have to buy 50 of the 5-year note contracts, which means her position has no exposure to changes in the price of the 5-year note contract. The delta for puts is negative, and is the mirror image of Figure 4–2. There are two things about delta hedging that are worth remembering. The first is that the delta of an option is always changing with the market, which means that the position has to be constantly adjusted, and 5-year note contracts have to be bought or sold, to keep the position market neutral. The second is that this activity has a cost, since the mandate of a delta hedger means that he will be buying contracts when the price increases and selling contracts when the price falls. Buying high and selling low isn't a strategy for success in the markets! Delta hedging entails some cost, and the cost depends on how prices change.

Armed with this information, we can now determine the no-arbitrage relationship in options. If one were to sell a straddle, a combination of puts and calls with the same strike price, and delta-hedge that position, one could create a market neutral portfolio. In an efficient market with perfect foresight there should be no premium left over when the options expire, and the cost of the delta hedge should equal the initial premium collected from the sale of the straddle. If we sell a straddle and collect the premium and delta-hedge the position every day and there is money left over after the options expire, then something unexpected would happen. In this case the person who bought the options from you paid too much. Either the price of the options was too high given the expected cost of the delta hedge or the cost of the delta hedge fell below the levels expected when the option was sold. Either way, the seller of the options got a deal that we wouldn't expect to persist. Conversely, what if the cost of the delta hedge were greater than the premium collected from the sale of the option? Option sellers should have collectively waited until prices were high enough to at least compensate for the delta-hedging costs.

For example, suppose that for whatever reason we have a hunch that empirical yield volatility is going to fall on 10-year note futures options to just around 12% going into the holidays at the end of 2005. The first step is to see if the market has already priced in our belief, by checking to see what the implied yield volatility is in the market. On October 3, 2005, the 10-year contract was at 109-18 and the implied yield volatility of the December 109 call and put were 16.89% and 16.79%, respectively. Since it's clear that the market doesn't share our view on future volatility, we can sell the 109 straddle for an average implied yield volatility of 16.69% and delta-hedge the position so that there is no market exposure and no resulting profit or loss from a move in 10-year yields. The only change in profit or loss depends on whether realized volatility is above or below 16.69%. Since we are short the straddle, we have collected the premium from the options; our bet is that realized volatility is lower than this value and that the cost of the delta hedge is less than the initial premium we collected. The cost of delta-hedging depends on realized volatility, and every day that rates move, our delta hedge is going to bleed some money from the premium we collected, but our bet is that realized volatility will be below the volatility implied by the options.

Table 4–2 works through the daily profit and loss of the position, and we can see that the initial premium collected is $1,718,750 for selling 1,000 contracts each of the Dec 109 put and call. In an option sale the maximum profit is known, and this $1.7 million is the most that we could possibly hope to make on the trade if realized volatility were zero and there were no cost to the delta hedge. To determine how many contracts are needed to make the position delta neutral, we have to calculate the delta for each option; initial delta for the call and put is 0.6068 and −0.3887 respectively. We know from Figure 4–2 that if the delta were 0.50, that would imply a 50% chance of the option expiring in-the-money, whether it was a call or a put (the negative sign is dropped in this case). A delta greater than 0.50 means that the option is in-the-money, which is true of our 109 call since the market was at 109-18 when we initiated the trade, and of course, if the 109 call is in-the-money, the 109 put must be out-of-the-money and have a delta that is less than 0.50. In this case the put delta of −0.3887, implies that there is a 38.87% chance of this put expiring in-the-money. It's interesting to see day by day how the delta of

TABLE 4-2

A Delta Hedging Example

| | | 109 Straddle Price in Points | | Delta | | | | | Delta Hedge | |
	Days	TYZ5 Price .32	Call	Put	Call	Put	Sum	Net Delta	Trades	Price Change '32s	Total Ticks G/(L)
3-Oct	50	109.180	1.14	0.58	0.61	-0.39	0.22	-218	218	-9.0	-1963
4-Oct	49	109.195	1.16	055	0.61	-0.38	0.24	-237	19	-10.5	-202
5-Oct	48	109.215	1.17	0.50	0.63	-0.36	0.27	-269	32	-12.5	-397
6-Oct	47	109.215	1.16	0.48	0.64	-0.36	0.27	-274	5	-12.5	-66
7-Oct	46	109.235	1.17	0.44	0.65	-0.34	0.31	-308	33	-14.5	-48
11-Oct	42	109.200	1.09	0.47	0.63	-0.36	0.27	-268	-40	-11.0	440
12-Oct	41	109.075	0.84	0.61	0.55	-0.44	0.11	-109	-159	1.5	-238
13-Oct	40	109.000	0.75	0.75	0.50	-0.49	0.01	-7	-102	9.0	-917
14-Oct	39	108.295	0.69	0.77	0.48	-0.51	-0.03	27	-34	11.5	-392
17-Oct	36	108.285	0.64	0.75	0.48	-0.52	-0.04	43	-16	12.5	-201
18-Oct	35	108.315	0.66	0.67	0.50	-0.50	0.00	1	42	9.5	399
19-Oct	34	109.035	0.70	0.59	0.53	-0.47	0.06	-59	61	5.5	333
20-Oct	33	109.040	0.69	0.56	0.53	-0.46	0.07	-69	10	5.0	49
21-Oct	32	109.180	0.94	0.38	0.64	-0.35	0.29	-287	218	-9.0	-1965
24-Oct	29	109.055	0.67	0.50	0.55	-0.45	0.10	-98	-189	3.5	-661
25-Oct	28	108.235	0.45	0.70	0.43	-0.57	-0.14	142	-240	17.5	-4199
26-Oct	27	108.075	0.28	1.05	0.30	-0.69	-0.39	390	-248	33.5	-8313
27-Oct	26	108.150	0.34	0.88	0.36	-0.64	-0.28	283	107	26.0	2786
28-Oct	25	108.135	0.31	0.89	0.34	-0.66	-0.32	316	-33	27.5	-905
31-Oct	22	108.145	0.31	0.86	0.35	-0.65	-0.31	306	10	26.5	266
1-Nov	21	108.115	0.25	0.89	0.31	-0.69	-0.38	379	-73	29.5	-2163

TABLE 4–2

(Continued)

	Days	TYZ5 Price .32	109 Straddle Price in Points		Delta			Net Delta	Trades	Delta Hedge Price Change '32s	Total Ticks G/(L)
			Call	Put	Call	Put	Sum				
2-Nov	20	108.040	0.17	1.05	0.23	-0.76	-0.53	528	-149	37.0	-5514
3-Nov	19	107.240	0.09	1.34	0.15	-0.85	-0.69	693	-165	49.0	-8091
4-Nov	18	107.225	0.06	1.36	0.12	-0.88	-0.76	759	-66	50.5	-3349
7-Nov	15	107.270	0.06	1.22	0.13	-0.87	-0.74	744	16	46.0	714
8-Nov	14	108.100	0.14	0.83	0.24	-0.75	-0.51	510	234	31.0	7250
9-Nov	13	107.285	0.06	1.17	0.13	-0.87	-0.74	738	-228	44.5	-10156
10-Nov	12	108.110	0.13	0.78	0.24	-0.76	-0.52	525	214	30.0	6410
14-Nov	8	108.005	0.06	1.05	0.14	-0.86	-0.72	721	-197	40.5	-7966
15-Nov	7	108.110	0.09	0.75	0.21	-0.79	-0.58	581	140	30.0	4196
16-Nov	6	108.265	0.17	0.33	0.39	-0.61	-0.22	222	360	14.5	5214
17-Nov	5	109.010	0.23	0.20	0.52	-0.48	0.05	-47	269	8.0	2152
18-Nov	4	108.235	0.05	0.31	0.23	-0.77	-0.54	542	-589	17.5	-10310
21-Nov	1	109.005	0.09	0.08	0.53	-0.47	0.06	-59	600	8.5	5103
22-Nov	0	109.090	0.28	0.02						0.0	

				Gain / (Loss)
Premium from sale	$1,718,750			
Cost to cover shorts	$296,875			
Premium before hedge	$1,421,875			
Cost of delta hedge	-$1,035,609		Ticks	-33,139
Bid/ask, 1/2 tick	-$79,941		Dollars	-$1,035,609
Premium after costs	$306,325			

the two options changes depending on the price of the 10-year contract. Veteran traders will find this trivial, but there can be no better education for people new to the market than watching a daily profit and loss statement, especially if it's theirs.

The next two charts illustrate the flip side of the same coin. Figure 4–3 tracks the trades that are necessary to keep the option position delta neutral. It is apparent that the more the market moves, the more contracts are necessary to stay market neutral. Moreover, it's necessary to buy after the market goes up and sell after the market goes down, which entails a certain cost. Figure 4–4 tracks the cumulative cost of all these trades, and it's obvious that the option premium is falling roughly in proportion to the rate at which the delta-hedge cost is increasing. This makes sense because in a market where volatility could be perfectly anticipated, the two would move by exactly the same amount, only with opposite signs. In this example our directional bet on volatility worked out, and the cost of the delta hedge was a little lower than the premium we collected from the option, but nonetheless the chart does illustrate the link between option pricing and daily rate moves. If there were no link, then it would be possible to consistently buy conditional protection from the option market for less than it's worth.

As the contract price falls, delta of the call falls as well; since we know that deltas are probabilities that must sum to 100%, we can guess that the delta on the

FIGURE   4–3

Rate moves and the trades needed to stay delta neutral

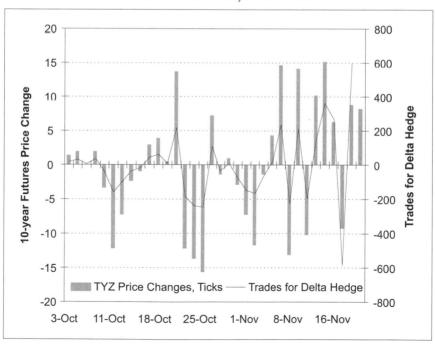

FIGURE 4–4

As the number of trades rises, so does the cost of the delta hedge

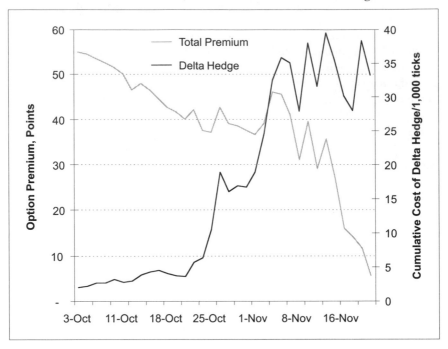

put is rising, and this is the case. On October 3 when we initiate the trade, the call has a higher delta than the put since it's in-the-money slightly and the total delta of the position is −0.2181; remember that the sign is flipped since we are short the options. This means that we have to buy 218 contracts so that the delta of the position is zero. The next day, October 4, the market rallied by 1+ ticks, which gave the position even more positive delta. Since we are only interested in exposure to volatility but not changes in the underlying contract, we again delta-hedge by selling 19 more contracts; after the first day we have a gain on those first 218 contracts we bought, but over the life of the hedge we lost 9 ticks on them since the price fell from 109–18 on October 3 to 109–9 at expiration of the option on November 22. Every day we have to buy or sell more contracts depending on how the delta changes, and the cost of the delta hedge is evident—since we have to buy high and sell low, we can see what each day's worth of trading costs. The P&L is the difference between that day's closing price and the final settlement of the contract multiplied by the number of contracts we needed to buy or sell that day to keep the position delta neutral.

The profit and loss of the whole position turns out to be positive, although it was by no means a home run. The initial premium collected was $1,718,750, but the call and put expired with some intrinsic value and we suppose we bought the contracts back an instant before they expired, at 9 and 1/2 ticks, respectively. Since we were short the options, suppose that we bought them back on this last day of trading right before they settled. The cost of buying back both options was $296,875, which leaves $1,421,875 in premium from the initial sale. We aren't done tallying up the costs, since the delta hedge rings in at just over a million dollars, at $1,035,609. Now there's just $386,266 left from the original $1.7 million, but we're still not done counting up the costs. The numbers in Table 4–2 assume frictionless purchase and sale of the contracts at their settlement price, but although the futures market is efficient, there is a bid/ask spread. Assuming that each trade just paid the minimum increment of 1/2 tick in 10-year contracts, the delta hedge necessitated trading an astounding total of 5,116 contracts back and forth every day, which adds up to $79,941 in bid/ask spread, leaving just $306,325. The costs aren't through yet, because the exchange charges a fee as well as broker's commissions, which vary depending on the activity of the trader; the total value could end up costing the equivalent of another 1/2 tick per contract. Even though we're left with just $226,384, which is a mere 13% of the original premium we collected, many traders would do this in a heartbeat since it could be scaled up thousands of times.

There is also the important matter of volatility actually falling over the period to consider. The price of the 10-year contracts changed because there was yield volatility, and of course we know how to measure that. The standard deviation of the log changes in rates from Table 4–2 is calculated in Table 4–3, and it amounts to 16.20% when annualized. We sold the position implying a volatility of 16.84%, but there was slightly less realized volatility, and that's why there was some money left over. If the implied and realized volatilities had been equal, the cost of the delta hedge would have been approximately the same as the premium we initially collected, but we would have incurred bid/ask spreads on over 5,000 contracts traded as well as commissions and exchange fees, which likely would have put the position in the red. The trade worked out in this instance because the trader took a view on volatility that turned out to be correct, but we haven't yet determined what yield volatility to expect during any future period. We still need help determining whether volatility should be higher or lower.

This no-arbitrage relationship hints at the interesting concepts involved in option pricing. Just as with any other security, prices have to be set today for a future that is uncertain, and we can only know after the fact whether the prices were fair or not. Most importantly, we've established an intuitive link between daily price changes in the market, the cost of a delta hedge, and option prices. While this framework is enough to understand the basic interactions, it's not specific enough to be useful in a trading setting. To do that, we have to rely on the BS equation, but the conventions for quotation in exchange-traded options is sometimes slightly different from the BS formula as specified; so we have to make a few transformations for the information from the futures markets to be of any use. The biggest difference between options at the CBOT and the CME is that options on Treasury futures have their volatilities quoted in price volatility, while those on Eurodollars are quoted on yield volatility. Not surprisingly, the over-the-counter

T A B L E   4–3

Calculating Empirical Yield Volatility

	Stdev	Ln (Chg)	Stdev	Ln (Chg)
3-Oct	4.31	15.44%	4.390	16.00%
4-Oct	4.30	−0.0023	4.380	−0.0023
5-Oct	4.28	−0.0047	4.360	−0.0046
6-Oct	4.28	0.0000	4.370	0.0023
7-Oct	4.28	0.0000	4.350	−0.0046
11-Oct	4.32	0.0093	4.390	0.0092
12-Oct	4.37	0.0115	4.450	0.0136
13-Oct	4.38	0.0023	4.480	0.0067
14-Oct	4.40	0.0046	4.480	0.0000
17-Oct	4.41	0.0023	4.500	0.0045
18-Oct	4.40	−0.0023	4.490	−0.0022
19-Oct	4.38	−0.0046	4.470	−0.0045
20-Oct	4.38	0.0000	4.460	−0.0022
21-Oct	4.31	−0.0161	4.390	−0.0158
24-Oct	4.37	0.0138	4.450	0.0136
25-Oct	4.46	0.0204	4.540	0.0200
26-Oct	4.52	0.0134	4.600	0.0131
27-Oct	4.49	−0.0067	4.570	−0.0065
28-Oct	4.51	0.0044	4.580	0.0022
31-Oct	4.49	−0.0044	4.570	−0.0022
1-Nov	4.51	0.0044	4.580	0.0022
2-Nov	4.54	0.0066	4.610	0.0065
3-Nov	4.59	0.0110	4.650	0.0086
4-Nov	4.60	0.0022	4.660	0.0021
7-Nov	4.59	−0.0022	4.650	−0.0021
8-Nov	4.52	−0.0154	4.570	−0.0174
9-Nov	4.58	0.0132	4.640	0.0152
10-Nov	4.51	−0.0154	4.550	−0.0196
14-Nov	4.57	0.0132	4.610	0.0131
15-Nov	4.52	−0.0110	4.560	−0.0109
16-Nov	4.45	−0.0156	4.490	−0.0155
17-Nov	4.42	−0.0068	4.460	−0.0067
18-Nov	4.45	0.0068	4.500	0.0089
21-Nov	4.42	−0.0068	4.460	−0.0089
22-Nov	4.37	−0.0114	4.430	−0.0067

interest rate swap market quotes options in yield volatility, borrowing from the market where they most often shed their risk. The transformation from price to yield volatility is a simple one:

$$\sigma_y = \frac{\sigma_p}{\text{Yield} \bullet \text{Duration}}$$

Here σ_y is yield volatility, σ_p is price volatility, and the yield and duration are for the bond that is cheapest-to-deliver into the Treasury futures contract. While the denominator is always yield and duration, not everyone chooses to use the yield and duration for the cheapest-to-deliver issue, since the underlying of the option is the Treasury contract, not the CTD issue (at least, not directly). While using the statistics for the CTD issue simplifies calculations, it's somewhat imprecise.

As an aside, this equation can help illustrate a point made in the Introduction regarding yield volatility in butterfly trades. One of the reasons that traders sometimes choose not to use duration dollar weights for their butterfly trades is that the trade may use maturity points that are spread far enough out along the curve that duration's assumption of equal yield volatility no longer holds. When yield volatility is different along the curve, and it most often is falling as maturity rises, then a 1-basis-point move in 10-year yields will lead to more than a 1-basis-point move in 2-year yields. Calculating the yield volatility from the implied price volatility of some CBOT options makes the point:

Yield Volatility	Yield Beta

$$\sigma_{y,2-\text{year}} = \frac{1.26}{4.33 \bullet 2.30} = 12.65\% \qquad 0.82$$

$$\sigma_{y,5-\text{year}} = \frac{5.72}{4.30 \bullet 4.19} = 31.75\% \qquad 2.1$$

$$\sigma_{y,10-\text{year}} = \frac{4.19}{4.32 \bullet 6.32} = 15.35\% \qquad 1.0$$

These calculations illustrate that the market is expecting lower yield volatility as maturity of the Treasury futures contracts increases. The column to the right of the equations shows the yield beta compared to 10-year yields, which is the ratio of yield volatility of each point in relation to the reference maturity.

Although we calculated the yield volatility for Treasury futures, we can use the BS formula to determine a fair price for each option based on price volatility, as the equation was originally specified. This equation has been reproduced in countless texts, and we include it here merely as a reference in order to contrast against a rule of thumb to compute the option prices. Suppose that the price of a 10-year note futures contracts were 108-18 and the call option we were interested in pricing had a strike price of 109, with 118 days left until expiration (remember that with Treasury futures options the expiration of the contract is usually about 6 weeks after that of the option). Given the implied volatility we calculated above, the BS formula would be calculated:

$$c = P(0,T)[f_0 N(d_1) - XN(d_2)]$$
$$c = 108.56 \cdot 0.4462 - 109 \cdot 0.4359 = 0.9275$$

$$d_1 = \frac{\ln(f_0 / X) - \sigma^2 T / 2}{\sigma\sqrt{T}}$$

$$d_1 = -0.1352$$
$$N(d_1) = 0.4462$$

$$d_2 = \frac{\ln(f) - \sigma^2 T / 2}{\sigma\sqrt{T}} = d_1 - \sigma\sqrt{T}$$

$$d_2 = -0.1615$$
$$N(d_2) = 0.4359$$

Where:

c = price of the call option

$P(t,T)$ = the price at time t of a zero coupon bond maturity at T

f = the forward price of the underlying asset with maturity T

f_t = the forward price at time T

X = the strike price of the option

N = normal distribution

The 0.9275, or 59.4 sixty-fourths is a theoretical price, but of course we're able to observe how the market prices the structure, and in this case the market price is 59.4 sixty-fourths, which is identical to the theoretical price to the first decimal. It's one thing for a model to be accurate and quite another to perfectly reproduce the market price. What's going on here?

We pulled a fast one because the price volatilities calculated above come from implied price volatilities. The *implied* term is necessary because volatilities are implied from market prices using the BS model. If we use the market price to imply a volatility and then use that same volatility to reverse the calculation, of course we match the price. We come up with the same price since we're using the same BS equation, but merely solving for different variables. Strike price, market price of the underlying put or call, and days to expiration are all observable, but what if we're interested in verifying whether the market is pricing an option appropriately? The one variable we didn't mention was volatility, and it's this variable that is the crux of why we are interested in building an event model. If the BS formula makes it somewhat difficult to follow the importance of volatility in option pricing, then the rule of thumb of "basis points per day" should make the link perfectly clear. Rather than use the BS formula, traders often make an approximation using this calculation:

$$\frac{\sigma_y \bullet \text{Yield}}{\sqrt{252}}$$

Again σ_y is the yield volatility, Yield is the yield of the CTD bond, and the denominator is the square root of the number of trading days in a year. Often this value is approximated as the square root of 256, which equals 16. This value calculates the daily change in price necessary in the underlying commodity in order to break even on 1 day's worth of time decay on the option, and for this reason it's sometimes called *break-even basis points per day,* but most often the name is truncated to *basis points per day.* Holding all other variables equal, if we know the daily price drop of the option, then why not sum up all of the daily price drops to find the total price? That's exactly what many traders do, but here again we need to layer rule of thumb on rule of thumb, because options do not decay linearly. Consider Figure 4–5, which illustrates the price decay for an option using the BS formula.

We also graphed the simple function $\sqrt{\text{time}}$ to illustrate that if there is no change in volatility or the broader market, then BS collapses to this simple equation. The problem with simply summing up the daily price decays or multiplying the basis points per day by the number of days until expiration is that there is a sharp decay when the option is close to expiring, yet the basis points per day is a linear measure when used this way and will miss the sharp downturn.

While the basis points per day calculation implies that the time decay of an option is the same every day, it's more realistic to estimate that an option will decay at a rate equal to the square root of time. If we take the basis points per day calculation and multiply it by the number of days left before the expiration of an option, the result is likely to overestimate the true value of the option. For this reason traders sometimes multiply the basis points per day by the number of days and take 80% of that value to predict the total premium for the option. Where did the 80% come from? It is a rule of thumb that often works, but Figure 4–5 illustrates that, like all rules of thumb, the result may be passable, but not perfect. Given that technology has progressed to the point of being able to run the BS formula on handheld computers, these rules of thumb may pass into memory and the next generation of traders will marvel at why anyone needed to simplify calculations or take shortcuts, given how easy they are to perform with the technology at hand. Every exchange in the world, if it even has a trading floor left and hasn't gone fully electronic, mandates that its brokers use handheld computers to aid in their job. No matter how ubiquitous computer power becomes, these rules of thumb strike some simple chords that underpin the important elements of the options markets.

No matter how easy it is to run the BS equation, a computer will never be able to judge what inputs should be fed into the equation, and we keep returning to the volatility input as the wild card in the equation. One way to estimate the

FIGURE   4–5

Options prices are expected to decay at the square root of time

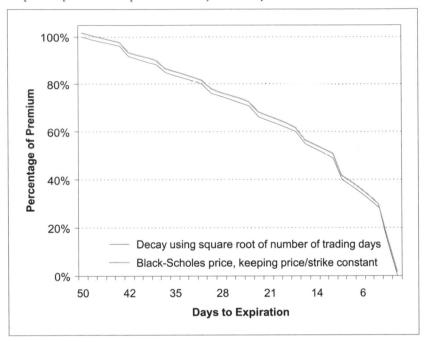

volatility factor is with an event model that attempts to measure the impact of upcoming economic news on the security we're interested in. How much should the 5-year futures contract change in price if its life spans one nonfarm payroll release? What about a consumer price index release? Of course these economic releases are regular and can be scheduled on a calendar. Rather than trying to predict what the number will be, so that one might make a directional bet on the market, why not measure the value of the event itself in terms of how it has changed prices in the past? If we can link volatility to price changes and ultimately option prices, an event model will allow us to add one more link to the chain that determines fair value for option contracts.

CREATING A VOLATILITY MAP TO PROJECT FUTURE VOLATILITY

It should be evident at this point why such a model is apropos of pricing options on futures. While economic releases are scheduled regularly, it's difficult to keep track of more than a few months' worth of releases, given how schedules change. FOMC meetings, for example, aren't even announced farther into the future than the current year, although most releases are regular enough that we can guess where they should be on the calendar. Consider what we're attempting: to keep track of a range of economic variables on the calendar and, without trying to predict the values of the variables themselves, judge how they will impact market movements. In essence we're creating a volatility map and if we can predict the volatility landscape during any period, then we can translate this into an option price. The key to this approach will be to know how each economic news release has impacted the curve in the past. Before beginning these measurements, we have to spend time on one more definition.

While we've examined how the yield volatility factor is used in option pricing, both in BS and basis points per day as a rule of thumb, we haven't described how to measure it empirically. Yield volatility is defined as the standard deviation of log changes in yields. For example, the rightmost column of Table 4–3 takes the daily yield history that corresponds to the futures prices used in the delta hedge and calculates the actual yield volatility during the period. The factor for annualizing returns depends on the frequency of the observations, not the length of the sample. For example, if we had monthly data, we would annualize it by multiplying by the square root of 12; if we had weekly data, then by the square root of 52. However, these factors don't change depending on whether we have 10 observations of monthly data or 100.

It is important to make the distinction between annualizing standard deviations of yields or prices and annualizing the standard deviation of returns. While using the square root of the frequency of the observations is perfectly acceptable for annualizing a series that doesn't compound, it is inaccurate if we are measuring a series of returns. In options theory, much of the work depends on continuously compounded rates of return, and using the square root rule will be somewhat inaccurate. A more precise calculation for a series that compounds is:

$$(1 + R_{ann}) \cdot \sqrt{[\exp(\sigma_{ann}{}^2) - 1]}$$

Here σ_{ann} is the annualized volatility using the square root of the frequency of the observations rule. Under normal interest rate scenarios, where σ_{ann} isn't massive, a reasonable approximation for this equation is:

$$(1 + R_{ann}) \cdot \sqrt{frequency \cdot \sigma_{frequency}}$$

Here the term frequency refers to the frequency of the observations per year, that is, the square root of 12 if the observations are monthly.

This is a powerful calculation that we can leverage in our event model. While Table 4–3 measured volatility of a historical series, the same process could also measure the volatility of a theoretical series that we construct from a calendar of upcoming economic news releases. If we know that the GDP report is being released in 10 days and in the past this release has moved the 5-year point by 10 basis points in yield, then we can place a 10-basis-point change on that future date in our timeline. If the nonfarm payrolls report is coming in 5 days and it normally moves the market by 15 basis points, then we can put a 15-basis-point change on that date. On days when no economic news is released, we can assign a zero yield change to that day. Everyone knows that there is volatility that comes from unexpected news, like terrorist attack warnings or surprises from policymakers, but how can you measure the unexpected? The next best thing is to measure all of the volatility that does come from regularly scheduled events and compare that with what the market is expecting. In this way we may even measure the "unexpected" premium put into prices. There could always be more or less volatility than a map of economic releases might suggest because of surprise news. As we'll see, even though we know that the market is going to have to absorb certain amounts of new information, it's possible that the market shrugs off the news. Psychology certainly impacts how traders absorb news, but since we can't measure psychology, we must rely on past actions and suppose that in the future traders may behave in similar ways.

Now that we know how to measure volatility, we have to decide what to measure. Already we've used nonfarm payrolls as an example of an important indicator for the market, but why? As we discussed in the Introduction, the fixed income market is designed to deliver positive real returns, although we know that it doesn't always do so. Just knowing this one piece of information can help us choose which economic releases to measure: those that influence real returns through price stability. Similar to the dual mandate of the Federal Reserve to keep prices stable and promote full employment, fixed income traders are concerned with signs of inflation and how the Fed may respond to such news. Employment is a major consideration, because in the short run there is a trade-off between employment costs and inflation, which is the Phillips Curve. Wages are an important contributor to demand for goods and to price increases; therefore, when unemployment is low, there are a great many people making money and bidding up the prices of goods and services. Conversely, when workers are laid off, there is less upward pressure on prices in the short run.

One of the basic tenets of modern economic theory is that there are differences between short- and long-run effects. In the long run one might imagine that the productive capacity of an economy is fixed, since there are only so many people, machines, and money. No matter what you pay people, they can't work 24 hours a day because people are not like machines. We get tired! An interesting illustration of this was in China during Mao's Great Leap Forward, where the leaders attempted to increase the size of its economy and modernize at the same time. Small iron works were installed in communities and after working a full day in a factory, workers were expected to go home and spend their evenings forging iron. Although production did increase for a few years, it eventually dipped back down again close to the previous level as workers simply exhausted themselves. While short-term factors like higher wages or political mandates may change behavior in the short run, there is little that can be done about the fundamental productive capability of an economy in the long run. If economic development were as easy as adopting a few enlightened policies, there would be no poverty, but evidently there are deeper issues at work.

The Federal Reserve knows this all too well, and consequently it watches employment figures like nonfarm payrolls closely as a cue for future policy decisions. While employment may be a leading indicator of what's happening to changes in prices, the market is also concerned with price level indices themselves, even though they measure past price changes. For this reason the consumer price index and producer price index are also important to the market. Over the years the U.S. Treasury has pushed TIPs issuance and tried to develop an inflation-linked note market, with modest success. In contrast, almost half of the outstanding government bonds in the United Kingdom are linked to inflation, and one might imagine that inflation indices capture quite a bit more attention in those markets than they do in the United States Treasury market, where just about 7% of the market is linked to the consumer price index. Still, high inflation does eat away at bond returns, and they remain a focus of fixed income traders. In between employment and inflation indices lie manufacturing and confidence surveys. Changes in manufacturing payrolls is of decreasing importance to the U.S. economy as it becomes more service-based, but this industry is also the most dependent on advantageous financing and Fed decisions. Similarly, low consumer confidence normally leads to restrained spending and less upward pressure on prices. Without delving too deeply into what each of these statistics mean, it's enough for the purposes of building our event model to simply say that they are important! Table 4–4 lists a dozen types of economic releases that are among the most important to the market.

TABLE   4–4

Economic Releases That Drive Volatility

Release	Frequency
Payrolls	monthly
Humphrey-Hawkins Testimony	twice yearly
FOMC meeting	eight times per year
Durable Goods	monthly
Consumer Price Index	monthly
Chicago Purchasing Managers Index	monthly
University of Michigan Survey	monthly
Retail Sales	monthly
GDP	quarterly
Empire State Manufacturing	monthly
Producer Price Index	monthly
Institute of Supply Managers (ISM)	monthly

Now that we have a dozen variables to watch, it's necessary to measure how the market has reacted to each in the past. In order to do this, we measure the closing yield on the day before the release and the day of the release to look for differences. Of course, there are other factors that will move yields on these days, but if we have enough measurements, the extraneous noise will hopefully be canceled out and we will be left with as clear an indication as possible of how each piece of news moves the market. Take Figure 4–6, for example, which lists past values of nonfarm payrolls. No doubt missed expectations and surprises in the data have differing effects on the market. Even an unpredictable series will have varying impact on the market because people can't be permanently surprised. While an extremely high payroll report might shock the market the first time it's released, some will come to expect a higher number the next time around, and as this iterative process continues, more precise expectations are developed.

The importance of payrolls has changed over the months, and this implies an interesting question: do we take the average change or use the trend to predict where the next observation will be? The problem with using the trend is that although it may be more accurate for the next observation if we carry the projection out far enough, it will either end up at zero or some value that's astronomically high in terms of the normal daily market moves. This is a facet of the

F I G U R E   4–6

Historical impact of economic news by Eurodollar pack

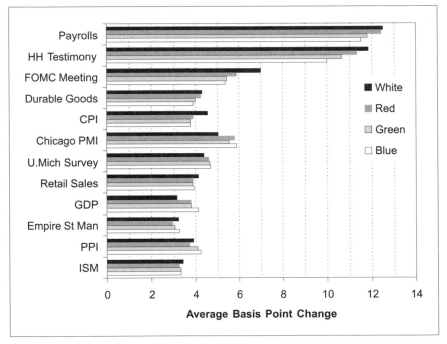

analysis that might be mined for more intricate models, perhaps blending a projection along with some sort of mean reversion, but for the purposes of this model we simply take the average value and plot it according to the next release date. Figure 4–6 illustrates the average historical impact each release has had on each Eurodollar pack. While the examples so far have been discussing Treasuries, the event model could project the volatility of any instrument so long as there is a history of yields to measure.

As we have mentioned at several points in the book, the yield volatility of short-maturity bonds tends to be higher than that for long-maturity bonds, and Figure 4–6 is another illustration of this. Clearly nonfarm payrolls have been the most important economic news day in the market, and as we would expect, it moves yields the most in the White and Red packs. Interestingly enough, this chart does indicate that the Red packs often lead the way in terms of yield changes, either to higher or lower rate regimes, and the White pack is a close second. There is also a slight difference between the impacts of each economic release along the curve, with news that is most relevant to Fed decisions, like payrolls, impacting the front end more than the back end, but the opposite pattern prevails on days when the producer price index is released. While the strength of these differing curve impacts isn't likely to be strong enough to quantify or project, it is interesting to note some intuitively pleasing characteristics of the results.

We are making progress in terms of building the event model because we've now identified our dozen important economic releases and their historical impact on the yield curve, and now we need to put them in chronological order. As Table 4–4 details, each release comes with differing frequencies, but all are predictable. Every trader should be generally familiar with the typical calendar for a month in the fixed income markets. Payrolls are released on the first Friday of the month, PPI around halfway through the month, and then CPI about a week later. If we are interested in valuing an option that expires on the 25th of the month, then it will cover most of the releases but, of course, miss everything that happens afterwards. In order to measure the volatility, we have to put events on the timeline in the order they appear, and Figure 4–7 does just that. As we map the volatility to a timeline, it will be important to consider the direction of our shocks to market prices.

Remembering that the standard deviation of a series measures the differences from the mean, we can build our timeline in different ways, attempting to identify the extreme cases, and can then choose something in between. What if every shock moved yields in the same direction? Then we would have a stair-step pattern where yields moved up on every release date. Alternatively, yields could all move in the same direction initially but then immediately revert back to their original values the next day. Finally, yield movements could alternate so that in the worst-case scenario each release moves yields in the opposite sign, and then the market ignores the release the next day, and then returns to the original value. Not all of these scenarios are realistic, but they are illustrative. The stair-step scenario produces the highest standard deviation, since the beginning and ending values are the farthest away from the average. Next in back of that is the alternating scenario,

F I G U R E   4–7

Alternative future yields scenario using volatility map

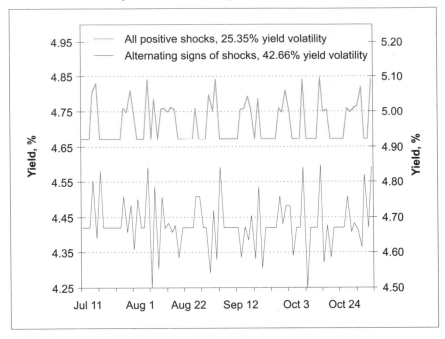

and although it may seem unlikely, there have clearly been periods where the data are inconclusive, and it certainly seems like real life is emulating this scenario. Finally, the tamest standard deviation value is where the series returns to its starting point. The standard deviation of this series is 25.25%.

Again there is an opportunity to build more detail into the projection by adding an impulse response model. Rather than a series drifting away from the original value, as our stair-step model would, or returning perfectly to the original value, like the other two models, we can make the series more realistic with a small change. Impulse response and mean reversion models produce similar results, but differ in their implementation. An impulse response series will jump with new economic news, but then that effect will slowly fade according to some formula, usually exponentially with time. Alternatively a mean-reversion model will always be pulling deviations back toward the mean, so that the longer a time-line goes on, the more likely it is that future values will fall along the mean. Either one of these approaches results in a series that would be more digestible than the "all or nothing" choices presented in Figure 4–7. For the purposes of illustration, we use the third model from this figure, where the yield changes are all positive but then immediately revert back to the original value.

Most of the hard work has already been done, and all that's left is to translate the volatility of our theoretical series into an option price by measuring the standard deviation of log changes yields for Figure 4–7, and there are a number of points worth noting. The shorter the measurement horizon, the more volatile the result. Also the longer the measurement horizon, the less each individual release matters and the values seem to be converging. This series has a daily standard deviation of 24.45% as an annualized standard deviation. Given that there are 118 days left to expiration and we can observe the strike of the 109 call with the underlying at 108-18 from the market, we have everything needed to run through the BS equation and calculate a theoretical option price. In this instance we reproduced an option that is actually trading in the market, and the theoretical fair value is 59.0 sixty-fourths, which is quite close to the market price of 59.4 sixty-fourths. In order to perfectly match the market price, the annual standard deviation would have to be slightly higher than what we constructed with our event model, but not by very much. Calculating an absolute value of volatility that mirrors the market price is encouraging, but the real power of this approach comes when we compare options with different expirations to value what a basket of economic releases should be worth in terms of options prices.

What are the trade-offs that one has to make as an option seller? In a sense he is giving away news that could potentially impact the market enough for an option to "pay its way," meaning that the actual market move is above the implied breakeven basis point per day move, indicating that an option gained in value more than its time decay. Of course an option seller doesn't want this to happen, but how does she know the value of the information she is giving up? It's precisely this event model and corresponding volatility map combined with the BS equation that can help to answer that question. There are serial futures options, expiring every month between quarterly expirations, which afford some measure of granularity to the work. Rather than accounting for news 3 months at a time, the quarterly options allow for the kinds of trade-offs we've been talking about. Additionally, an even finer precision in expiration can be gained by using weekly options available on Eurodollar futures at the CME.

The CME has deepened its market for the already successful midcurve options by listing weekly expirations on the fifth quarterly Eurodollar future, the first Red contract. At any one time there are at least five expirations on this contract, including the existing serial and quarterly midcurve options. Sometimes a few notes are all that separate a discordant rumpus from an immaculate symphony, and these new expirations represent individual economic news in a way that hasn't been possible before in the futures markets. In fact, these weekly options are the perfect complement to our work on mapping volatility and allow us to take the next step to discern how traders are positioned for each week's economic releases.

Midcurve options are short expiration options on longer-dated contracts, which are unique to the rest of the options listed on Eurodollar contracts or Treasury futures at the CBOT whose option expiration mirrors that of the underlying contract. The June '07 midcurve option, for example, will expire on June '06, 1 year before the underlying futures contract. The advantage of midcurve options is that they have less time value than if they expired at the same time as the under-lying contract, which allows them to represent more distant maturity points without the accompanying hefty premiums. Prior to weekly expirations, the gold midcurves were the most recent addition to the lineup, and these options allow for a reasonably complete means of conditionally trading the Eurodollar curve. Though their introduction initially seemed like an incremental step, weekly expi-rations filled out the CME options offerings in a way that allowed for something unique: measuring the volatility that traders expect on any given week.

As we detailed earlier, volatility expectations are important because they are the one subjective input in pricing options and no one knows what this value should be ahead of time. Weekly expirations are important to determine expecta-tions for individual releases because the existing option expirations potentially cover many months worth of releases, making it difficult to determine pricing for any individual event. A 3-month option, for example, might cover Humphrey-Hawkins testimony from the Fed Chairman, three nonfarm payroll releases, GDP, and three CPI reports. There's no way of knowing from the aggregate volatility over the entire period what the market is assigning to each event since the option spans the entire group. The only way to tease out the answer is to watch how the implied volatility changes after each release to see how the market is pricing the remaining news, but an ex ante measure doesn't do us very much good for trading.

What if we worked the process in reverse? In this case we would begin with a short expiration that would cover the news only through that date. Next we would add another expiration that covered the first time period plus 1 more week, and 1 more week's worth of news. The difference between the implied volatilities of the first 2 weeks is unique to each week's worth of news. A third weekly option would cover the first 2 weeks' worth of news plus be influenced by an additional week's worth of news, and the difference in implied volatility between the 2-week and 3-week option lets us measure the expectations for that third week alone. The important realization is that the economic calendar is fixed, and each option cap-tures a unique list of economic news.

When building our volatility map it's important to contrast the work with event options, which are also auctioned at the CME. Event options were origi-nally auctioned over-the-counter and the "strikes" of the options would cover a range for each economic number. For example, one might buy an option that paid off if nonfarm payrolls were between 100,000 and 105,000 but pay nothing if the release was outside those values. The dealers that conducted these auctions were quickly overwhelmed by the process and trading was moved to the CME, which has the infrastructure and institutional experience to handle the work. An event option is digital, it is either in-the-money if a trader picks the right value or it is worthless. Instead of gaining value with accurate predictions, an option on a bond gains in value if the market is surprised and volatility increases because and traders predict the wrong number. Conceptually these instruments are flip sides of the same coin—one depends on accurate prediction while the other depends on inaccuracy and the market badly predicting the actual economic release.

Veteran options traders may realize that the volatility map implies the same volatility no matter what strike is used, and out-of-the-money strikes tend to have higher volatilities than at-the-money strikes. An event model will be mute on such a topic, and it's for this reason that it's most appropriate when used to price options that are either at-the-money or very close to being so. Adjustments for skew in implied volatilities can be made through other means, but even skew adjustments depend heavily on getting the at-the-money volatility right, and our work can help to do just that. Aside from the finer points of implementation, there is a deeper question here that needs to be addressed, and possibly exploited for futures traders. Does volatility in the market happen because of a calendar event or because the new information is surprising in some way?

The distinction is a subtle one, but economic news moves the market when the number is in some way shocking, as shown in Table 4–5. Anyone who has ever waited all month for an unemployment report to generate some volatility, only to see the release fall exactly at the market consensus and the market trade sideways, will appreciate the point. Switching from a model that relies on the average volatility caused by a release to one where that volatility is attached to some error in forecasting doesn't change the event model predictions. But it will help in scenario analysis to answer questions such as, "If the nonfarm payroll release is above or below expectations by a hundred thousand jobs, what will the market volatility be?" Before, we were just counting on past volatility occurring on a date based on a history of market moves, but now we can link those market moves to a missed expectation very precisely. Missed expectations are a strange currency to deal in, but if we want to dial up or back the expected "misses," then we need to know what value is implied for each economic statistic.

Twisting and turning ideas to understand all of the implications is the hallmark of intuitive understanding, and with the work we've developed so far we can

T A B L E   4–5

Average Historical "Error" by Release, 2004 and 2005

Payrolls	64,390 jobs
Humphrey-Hawkins Testimony	NA
FOMC meeting	32 basis points
Durable Goods	2.19 index points
Consumer Price Index	22 basis points
Chicago Purchasing Managers Index	4.78 index points
University of Michigan Survey	1.44 index points
GDP	0.19% YOY change
Empire State Manufacturing	7.30 index points
Producer Price Index	1.12%
Institute of Supply Managers (ISM)	1.77 index points

turn the event model on its head. Rather than looking at past market moves and mapping them to upcoming economic releases, we can work in reverse to look at market expectations of future surprises. We have said repeatedly that there is no use in attempting to model surprises because they are, by definition, unexpected. However, this is the one exception. It's not an intuitive idea, but in a very real way the market prices have embedded in them some sort of surprise attached to each group of economic data; otherwise the standard deviation of the upcoming rate series would be zero. The market is trying to "expect the unexpected" to use an often abused phase. Traders are getting their hands on the upcoming news in some way, although no one knows whether the surprises will be positive or negative.

Returning to our earlier example, where the implied volatility from the market was 16.89 but the predicted volatility from the event model was 17.00, we can now calculate what the market expects in terms of surprises. For example, we measured that in the past the average surprise, the difference between expected and actual values for nonfarm payrolls, was 64,390 jobs. If the implied volatility from the market price of the option is 0.11 above what the model would project, then we can scale up the projection so that it matches the market. In doing so, we are also scaling up the expected surprise in terms of the number of jobs the payroll reports. If the typical move on unemployment Friday were 5 basis points for the 5-year note future and the average difference between consensus forecast and actual value is 64,390 jobs, then a surprise of 100,000 jobs higher than expectations should lead to a basis point change that is 1.6 times higher than the typical 5-basis-point move: 7.8 basis points. This new value would be fed into the theoretical yield series in Figure 4–7, and a new standard deviation would be calculated for input into the BS model. All of the pieces are linked in this way. The first step a trader must take before touching a "buy" or "sell" ticket is to understand what the market is expecting, because it's quite possible that the market is expecting exactly the same thing that the trader is, in which case there would be no change in price if the future unfolded according to plan. Contrasting market expectations to one's personal beliefs is the necessary first step to a successful trade, and an event model is one way to back out this information from the market.

APPENDICES

COMMITMENT OF TRADERS REPORT

From time to time there are headlines regarding the Commitment of Traders (COT) report from the Commodity Futures Trading Commission (CFTC) alleging that a change in the composition of traders is behind a move in the market. There could be no better illustration of the underlying theme of this book than the misguided notion that the COT has any bearing on the market. In order to prove that the COT is irrelevant, we have to understand it first. The CFTC is the regulator for the futures market, and it compiles weekly statistics about the holders of futures contracts. Of course, for every long contract holder there is also someone who is short of that contract. While the number of long and short contract holders must be equal, the same contracts are not always held by the same types of traders.

The broadest distinction between groups of traders is that of hedgers and speculators. In agricultural commodity markets, these distinctions make perfect sense because a hedger normally intends to do something with the underlying commodity: grow it, grind it, or eat it. Someone whose business doesn't naturally include the risk of crop prices changing but is involved in trades futures contracts is considered a speculator.

Many aspects of the futures markets betray their origins in agriculture, although today trading in financial futures far outweighs that in agricultural products. The CFTC labels for hedgers and speculators are one of these examples, and the two groups are called "commercial" for hedgers and "noncommercial" for speculators, which makes sense in the context of farmers or mills, whose "commercial" business it is to traffic in commodities. Unfortunately, the distinctions aren't so clear in financial products because no one is producing or consuming the underlying commodity. CFTC Rule 1.3(z) defines a hedge as "economically appropriate to reduce the risk of a commercial enterprise and [it] must arise from a change in the value of hedger's assets or liabilities." The definition continues: ". . . no transactions or position will be classified as bona fide hedging unless their purpose is to offset price risks incidental to commercial cash or spot operations and [unless] such positions are established and liquidated in an orderly manner in accordance with sound commercial practices." This is an interesting definition, since it only refers to risk reduction coming from "cash or spot operations." A basis trader, for example, certainly is reducing the risk of his cash holdings with futures, although we know that the trade is in fact speculative.

FIGURE A–1

Diminishing importance of the COT report

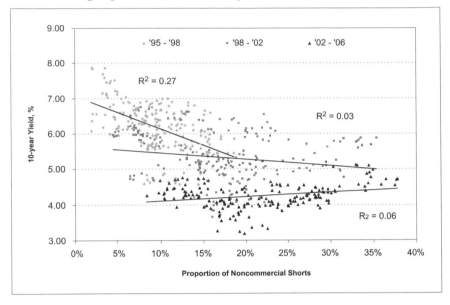

It is possible that a firm that is clearly engaged in hedging, such as a mortgage servicer, which is underwriting loans and using futures to offset that interest rate risk, could also use futures as a speculative tool. It is virtually impossible to simultaneously execute a hedge at the same instant a loan is underwritten, and most firms match their risk on a daily basis. Isn't the fact that there is a gap between assuming the price risk of a loan and offsetting that risk with a derivative itself a form of speculation? Firms tolerate the gap because in most instances the risk is small, but even the timing of execution can be influenced by a managers intuition about market moves, and hence the traditional definitions of hedgers or speculators is blurred. Floor brokers will sometimes jokingly refer to hedgers who make small speculative bets with the timing of their hedges as "hedge-ulators," but the underlying truth is that it's sometimes hard to distinguish one type of trade from another. For this reason, it's quite difficult to understand who belongs in what category reported by the CFTC, and, not surprisingly, there is evidence that the distinction between the two categories has been blurred over time.

Figure A–1 compares the percentage of noncommercial short users of 10-year futures with changes in 10-year yields. Traditionally one would think of noncommercial users of contracts as speculators and would expect their trades to push the market one way or another. Even if their trades didn't move the market, one might expect a savvy trader to realize that there is a trend in yields and to hop on board. Either way, if you believe the traditional interpretation of noncommercial users of the contracts as speculators, then the two series should be related in some way and a regression line would have some slope to it. If there were no relationship between the two series, then the regression line would be either vertical or horizontal.

The data in the chart is segregated by time, with the first of the three periods lasting from 1995 to 1998, the second until 2002, and the third until 2006. It is clear that the landscape has been dramatically altered during that 11-year span. In the earliest period there is some slope to the regression line, and the R-squared statistic—which measures the proportion of variation of 10-year yields explained by changes in the proportion of speculators in the market—is 27%. This is a relatively high value and indicates that a little better than half the time speculators got it right.

Unfortunately, this 1995–1998 period may have been the heyday for both speculators and the value of the COT report. As time went on, the relationship deteriorated, and in the middle period, from 1998 to 2002, the R-squared statistic dropped from 27% to just 3%. What happened? Exactly the sort of muddling of categories that we described earlier. As the difference in behavior between hedgers and speculators became less distinct, the value of knowing the proportion of noncommercial shorts (or longs for that matter) fell dramatically.

Although firms cannot hold separate classifications between commodities, a single trading entity cannot hold different classifications in the same commodity. What could also be happening is that as firms grow and add more strategies there is no longer a single overriding position in the contracts. Anecdotally, it seems as if the days of "the one smart guy model" trading the entire book are giving way to many smaller strategies, as hedge funds and money managers look to diversify not just their product offerings but their strategies as well.

Hopefully the 2002–2006 series is the final nail in the coffin of the idea that the COT report is of any value in predicting market swings or of determining who is the "weak hand" in a particular position. Just as with the earlier 1998–2002 data, the R-squared level is insignificant, at just about 6%. More significant than a low R-squared level is the slope of the regression line, which is indistinguishable from zero in the final two periods. The evidence is clear: the COT report has had no explanatory capability in the second two periods we measured, although it appears that at one time in the past there was some value to understanding the composition of players in the market. There is a broader point to be made, and this is especially true in commodity markets, as open interest grows and the users of derivatives become ever more diverse; it's next to impossible to determine the impact an individual participant or group of traders will have on the market. Regression analysis using multiple variables relies on the assumption that other factors in the market are held constant, just manipulating the factor we're interested in studying. This manner of analysis has become so ingrained in the way of thinking of many analysts and traders that they forget that the practical value of this work is next to nothing because *no* variables ever remain constant.

In 2005 the story of "Asian central bank buying" has been the knee-jerk reaction to every move in the market, and it's true that this is a source of demand for duration, either through cash notes or derivatives. This demand didn't exist before, but who's to say that a buyer of duration didn't exit the market at the same time? Did the Enron bankruptcy remove a large user of derivatives from the market? Many traders think that oil prices have something to do with economic activity, inflation, and (therefore) interest rates, but there certainly are few stories about players exiting markets. although the CFTC certainly isn't trying to mislead anyone and is clearly interested in promoting transparency, in this case one can't take their reports at face value.

DELIVERY AT THE CBOT

In this book we have covered a number of aspects about futures fair value but haven't detailed the specifics of delivery. This is one topic that everyone has a vague idea about what happens, but few know the actual rules. This review borrows from the CBOT literature on the topic, and the fact that there have only been a handful of revisions during the last two and a half decades is an indication that the current rules may remain in effect for many years to come. Futures contracts are called "contracts" because they are legally binding obligations to either make or take delivery of underlying notes or bonds if held on a certain date. Two ironies in the market are that few traders actually want to go through delivery, but the threat of delivery is normally enough to force contracts to behave predictably. Also, from the perspective of the holder of long contracts, delivery is often the least economical way to obtain the underlying notes, and why would anyone participate in a process that, under normal circumstances, is guaranteed to unfold to his or her detriment? While the Treasury futures complex at the CBOT was not primarily designed as a vehicle to transfer cash notes, it is certainly possible using these procedures.

One thing to keep in mind when looking at the securities that are deliverable into contracts is that eventually even a 30-year Treasury bond will age to the point that it fits the delivery standards for 2-year notes. Once a bond, always a bond—and the CBOT distinguishes between "bonds" as being original 30-year instruments and "notes" as everything else (with original maturities of either 10, 5, 3, or 2 years).

TWO-YEAR NOTES

With a $200,000 face value, these U.S. Treasury notes, from original term to maturity, must be held no more than five years, three months from the first day of the contract expiration month. The remaining term to maturity must be no less than one year, nine months from the first day of the contract expiration month and no more than two years from the last day of the contract expiration month.

FIVE-YEAR NOTES

With a $100,000 face value, these U.S. Treasury notes, from remaining term to maturity, must be held no less than four years, two months, and no more than five years from the first day of the contract expiration month.

10-YEAR NOTES

With a $100,000 face value, these U.S. Treasury notes, from remaining term to maturity must be held no less than six years, six months, and no greater than 10 years from the first day of the contract expiration month.

30-YEAR BONDS

With a $100,000 face value, these U.S. Treasury bonds, both the maturity date and, if callable, the first call date, must be no less than 15 years from the first day of the contract expiration month.

THREE-DAY DELIVERY PROCESS

As we have discussed, the timing of deliveries is critical because, unlike the cash Treasury market, the CBOT does not allow for failures-to-deliver. Incidentally, it's this rule that may force a holder of short contracts to choose an issue that is not the cheapest to deliver if this note is too scarce. Any failure to make or take delivery on CBOT Treasury futures in complete satisfaction of contract specifications can result in economic and regulatory penalties to the failing party and the failing parties clearing firm. From a practical perspective no one ever has to worry about the specific penalty because no reputable clearing firm will allow a client to fail to the CBOT. From the clearing firm's perspective, they would rather deal with the legal risk of an individual client than an industry regulator that could, at least in theory, shut down their entire operations. It is this asymmetry that will often compel a clearing firm to involuntarily unwind a futures trade that is in trouble rather than deal with inquiries from the CFTC.

Unlike over-the-counter markets, where trading occurs directly between counterparties, trading in futures is handled between clearing firms on behalf of the customer. In this way, clearing firms are the agent of the customer, and deliveries are handled between clearing firms, not directly between customers. This establishes another layer of guarantees in the process, since the clearing firm vouches for the performance of its account holders and is on the line if the account holder refuses to honor any part of the contract.

A clearing firm receiving notes or bonds from a long position that is going through delivery must allocate the securities it receives to the appropriate accounts and collect the appropriate proceeds to pay for the securities. A firm making delivery has a slightly higher burden because it must guarantee that it has possession of the securities before they can be transferred, and they must be "in the box," meaning they must be held by the firm's custodian. A firm making delivery for a customer with a short futures position must find deliverable notes or bonds in sufficient quantity to meet the contract requirements and distribute the money it receives to the appropriate accounts.

It is worth bearing in mind that the clearing firm itself is financially responsible to the CBOT, and how seriously firms take this obligation is indicated by the fact that there has never been a delivery failure since the contracts were introduced. It is possible, although it has never happened, that a clearing firm could fail to guarantee the performance of a customer. In such a case, the CBOT Clearing Services Provider would step in as the ultimate guarantor of the integrity of the delivery process. The guarantee of the CBOT Clearing Services Provider is not explicitly meant to prevent any financial loss, but is in fact more limited to the need to "pay reasonable damages proximately caused by the default."

The Clearing Services Provider is not obligated to pay damages greater than the difference between the delivery price of the specific commodity and the reasonable market price of the commodity at the time of delivery, nor is it obligated to make or take delivery of the cash security. The Clearing Services Provider is not obligated to pay any punitive damages that relate to the completeness, accuracy or subsequent failure or insolvency of banks or entities involved in deliveries. Interestingly, there is only a sixty-minute window provided for the performance of a clearing firm; if delivery obligations are not met within that time, the Clearing Services Provider deems a default to have occurred. Rule 771 of Chapter 7 of the Chicago Mercantile Exchange Rulebook and CBOT Regulation 1050.01 provide the legal language of the Clearing Services Provider's guarantee.

Short holders of contracts face the following timeline for delivery:

- **First Position Day.** This occurs two business days prior to the named delivery month. The short holder of contracts has no obligation.

- **Day 1: Intention Day.** By 8 p.m. the short clearing firm notifies the Clearing Services Provider that it intends to make delivery on an expiring contract. Once the Clearing Services Provider has matched the short clearing firm with the clearing firm for the oldest long contract, this declaration cannot be reversed.

- **Day 2: Notice Day.** By 2 p.m. prior to the last notice day and by 3 p.m. on the notice day the short clearing firm invoices the long clearing firm through the Clearing Services Provider, passing to them the appropriate dollar and face values.

- **Day 3: Delivery Day.** Short and long clearing firms have until 9:30 a.m. to resolve invoice differences. By 10 a.m. the short clearing firm deposits Treasury securities for delivery into its bank account and instructs its bank to transfer securities via Fed wire, to the long clearing firm's account versus payment no later than 1 p.m.

The operation timeline for long holders of contracts is similar:

- **First Position Day.** This occurs two days prior to the named delivery month. By 8 p.m. two days prior to the first day allowed for deliveries, the clearing firm reports to the Clearing Services Provider all open long positions by origin (customer or house accounts) and trade date (which is used to match deliveries from the short to the oldest long contract).

- **Day 1: Intention Day.** By 8 p.m. all clearing firms report to the Clearing Services Provider all open long positions in expiring futures, according to house or customer accounts, by trade date.

- **Day 2: Notice Day.** By 4 p.m. the long clearing firm provides the short clearing firm with the name and location of its bank.

- **Day 3: Delivery Day.** By 7:30 a.m. the long clearing firm makes funds available and notifies its bank to remit the funds and accept Treasury securities. By 1 p.m. the long clearing firm's bank has accepted and paid for the Treasury securities via Fed wire to the short's clearing account.

The only obligation of the Clearing Services Provider, barring a default, is on Day 1: Intention Day. By 10 p.m. the Clearing Services Provider matches the delivering short's clearing firm to the clearing firm with long positions having the oldest trade date. The long is then informed of the short's desire to make delivery. Delivery must be made with one security only for each contract, meaning that the minimum face value of a bond or note of any value for delivery is $100,000 or $200,000 in the case of 2-year futures. It is not possible to delivery $75,000 of note A and $25,000 of note B to satisfy a contract with $100,000 face value. The short holder of contracts is allowed to deliver different securities into different contracts, as long as all of the securities delivered are eligible according the maturity constraints mentioned earlier.

The beauty of the whole process is that it is transparent and public: the CBOT posts the vintage of long contracts being delivered and the clearing firm (although not the customer name) taking delivery. However, the short holder of contracts is not required to notify the long what issues will be delivered, although this is a minor point since the cheapest issue is most likely to be delivered and the long hopes for an issue other than the cheapest. In this way ambiguity can only help the holder of long contracts. The one exception to this is when firms cannot be short securities and try to eliminate their price risk by selling the delivered note before it has been received. In this case there is only a narrow window to determine which issue is coming in so it can subsequently be sold. Although it's clear that the oldest long will be delivered first the allocation is made randomly within the contracts going through delivery on that particular day. Vintage of long contracts do not matter for making the random selection with short contracts.

While delivery is made with equal face values, the invoice price of different securities is different, which is what allows for the embedded option in the contract for the short to choose the issue with the lowest cost in the market. The dollar amount of each issue going through delivery can be broken into principal and interest. The principal amount is:

Principal amount = futures settlement price × contract size × conversion factor

For example, if the final settlement price were 115-16 and the conversion factor were 0.9010 for 5-year notes with a face value of $100,000 then the principal invoice amount would be:

$$1.1550 \times \$100,000 \times 0.9010 = \$104,0655.00$$

In this example there was no need to round, but dollar values are rounded up to the nearest half-penny. Accrued interest is based on the standard convention in the Treasury market and does not involve the conversion factor. The semiannual coupon payment divided by two is multiplied by the appropriate number of days between the last coupon payment and the delivery day. Delivery on CBOT futures is made by book entry and is handled by any commercial bank that is a member of the Federal Reserve System and has capital in excess of $100 million.

EMPIRICAL DURATION

With all of the work on various ways of modeling fair value for embedded options, one might ask, what is the empirical duration of Treasury futures? We can only answer a slightly different question, what *has* it been in the past, since measurements of a historical series are necessary. The necessary framework is to compare changes in a reference yield to prices in Treasury futures. It makes sense to use the on-the-run Treasury note value for each basket for simplicity, although any security within the basket is justifiable. Using a simple linear regression in Figure C–1, we compare the price change in 10- and 5-year futures to the corresponding yield changes in the on-the-run note from June 2005 to June 2006. The regression statistics are listed for each, and to get a handle on the scale, a result of −0.0634 indicates a dollar value per one basis point change in yield of $634 per million. Direct measurement of the risk in each futures contract is useless unless we can put the numbers into context.

Suppose there were no delivery option. In such a case, the DV01 of the futures contract would be the DV01 of the CTD note divided by the futures contract. In the case of 10- and 5-year futures, this value is:

CTD Note DV01/C. Factor = Futures DV01

10-year futures: 54.41/0.8870 = 61.34

5-year futures: 36.88/0.9317 = 39.58

Compared to the empirical measurements of 63.40 and 37.90 for the 10- and 5-year contracts, these "quick and dirty" estimates of 61.34 and 39.58 about the risk of the contracts are quite close. Of course, traders ignore the optionality of the contracts at their own peril, but this approach at least affords a rule of thumb to get the magnitude right. There is a reason why we expect the measured risk of the futures contract to be slightly higher than the risk calculated by our rule of thumb. Consider that during the year we measured, the shortest issue was CTD into both contracts, which means that delivery option could be hedged with puts. Since the duration of the contract can be decomposed into the duration of the note plus the risk of the embedded options, then it would make sense that a short put position would extend the duration of the contract slightly, since puts have negative duration but a short position adds duration to the contract.

FIGURE C–1

Empirical duration of 5- and 10-year Treasury futures

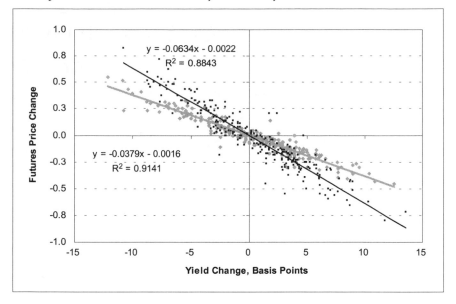

CARRY AND OPTION STRIKES

There are a number of ancillary considerations when trading options on forward contracts, not the least of which is the role that carry plays. Few people take into consideration where the futures price will be at expiration of the option. It goes without saying that no one knows what direction prices will move to, but with forward contracts we do know that at least some of the change in value of the contract will depend on the net carry rate and the passage of time. While most of the value of the note or Eurodollar future will depend on the randomness of the market, at least a portion is quite predictable. Suppose that the spot price for a note is $100, and the forward price is $99 even. This price difference implies that there is $1 in carry between now and the expiration of the contract, and the price will rise by $1 when the forward converges to the spot price.

Carry can mean that an option that is in-the-money today may be out of the money at expiration, even if yields don't change. Options on forward instruments face the dual decay of time value and an underlying price that is always trying to converge to the spot price. Most often in fixed income derivatives markets there is positive carry and forward prices are below the spot price, which means that call options that are slightly out-of-the-money have a better chance of expiring with some intrinsic value than put options that are slightly out-of-the-money. While futures options are relatively short-lived, they are on some of the instruments with the highest carry in the fixed income world, and as we detailed at the end of Chapter 1, the financing rates for bonds that are cheapest-to-deliver into Treasury futures can be negative in extreme cases. Carry is a consideration when a trade is held for more than a few days, and one would suspect that calls that are close to going in-the-money would be priced as if such an event were imminent because of carry, but this is often not the case. The market prices options based on where the market is today, often ignoring this potentially important factor.

DEFINITIONS

There are a handful of definitions that are used commonly in the book and the market.

Car: Shorthand for one futures contract. This term has its origins in the early days of the futures markets for agricultural contracts where the specifications for one contract required delivery of approximately one rail car's worth of the commodity. In grains, for example, one rail car can hold approximately 5,000 bushels.

DV01: The dollar value of a 1-basis-point change in yields. It is the DV01 of various instruments that would be matched in a "duration-neutral" trade. It does not indicate that the position is literally duration neutral, rather that it is duration-dollar neutral. The DV01 is calculated by multiplying the face by the duration by the price.

Factor: This is sometimes used as shorthand for "conversion factor," for use with U.S. Treasury futures at the CBOT. Conversion factors are two things at once: the price of the note if its maturity were rounded and its yield were 6% and also the number of contracts that would be used for a conversion factor–weighted basis trade. For example, a factor of 0.9363 would imply 936 futures contracts per $100 million face of the Treasury note.

Notional: A notional characteristic in a derivative, used only for reference and to calculate some other final statistic, like the price or DV01. Relying on notional characteristics as if they represented the same thing as they do in the cash market can be treacherous. For example, the notional coupon of a Treasury futures contract is currently 6%, and it is this coupon that is used to calculate the price of the contract. Does this mean that we can use the notional coupon and price to calculate a yield? It is certainly possible, but it is unclear what this yield represents in a security with no cash flows and only price changes.

Stub: Eurodollar futures are forward obligations that cover a period *beginning* with the expiration of the contracts at some future date. The "stub" is the period from today to the expiration of the shortest-dated contract. For example, if a Eurodollar contract covers a 3-month period beginning in December, and it is currently November, then the contract does not hedge against the risk that one-month money market rates may change for the period from November to December. The stub is usually not a major consideration for hedging notes or bonds, but it is significant in money market hedges with short maturities.

Tick: This is sometimes referred to as the minimum increment a contract can move, but most often it refers to either one thirty-second in price for Treasury futures or one basis point in price for Eurodollar futures. The term "half ticks" is either one sixty-fourth in price on a note or a half of a basis point in price of a Eurodollar contract. One thirty-second in price on a Treasury futures contract with a $100,000 face is worth $31.25, and one basis point in price is worth $25 on a Eurodollar contract.

INDEX

ABOUT THE AUTHOR

David Boberski is Head of Interest Rate Strategy at Bear, Stearns & Co. and has been named to the All American Fixed Income Research Team by Institutional Investor for his work in federal agency debt and interest rate derivatives.